THE MILLION EURO DECISION

*'Those who get lost on the way to school will
never find their way through life'*
– German Proverb

THE MILLION EURO DECISION

How Education Changes Lives

Waterford City and County
Libraries

Paul Mooney

The Liffey Press

Published by
The Liffey Press Ltd
Raheny Shopping Centre, Second Floor
Raheny, Dublin 5, Ireland
www.theliffeypress.com

A catalogue record of this book is
available from the British Library.

ISBN 978-1-908308-88-7

Printed in Spain by GraphyCems.

Contents

Contents

Acknowledgements[1]

It's standard fare to offer a thank you to people who've helped construct a book. In this case, the thanks go well beyond the normal courtesy. This book could not have been completed without insight from a range of people who gave generously of their time and expertise. A sincere apology if I've given anyone an incorrect title; hopefully you've been promoted and not relegated!

Expert Contributors: Michael Armstrong (Associate Faculty, NCI), Julie Bernard (Manager of Access and Civic Engagement, DIT), Patricia Byrne (Access Officer, IADT), Dr. Josephine Bleach (Director of Early Learning Initiative, NCI), Sean Campbell (CEO, Foroige), Professor Pat Clancy (UCD), Tom Costello (Former Executive, Atlantic Philanthropies), Tom Crean (School Liaison Officer), Dr. Paul Downes (Director of Education Disadvantage Studies, St Patrick's), Fergus Finlay (CEO, Barnardos), Grainne Foley (Publishing Designer, NCI), Deirdre Giblin (Industry Liaison, NCI), Dr. Aine Gray (Psychologist, Public Jobs), Dr. Sara Gwiazda (Medical Doctor), Dr. Cliona Hannon (Director of Access Programmes, Trinity College), Norman Hart (HR Department, Irish Rail), Professor Áine Hyland (UCC), Nicky Kehoe (political activist), Naomi Lester (Nurse), Beverley Maughan (Women's Rights Activist), Dr. Tom McCabe (former Multi-national Executive), Larry McGivern (St Vincent de Paul), Ann Miller (Dublin inner-city Community Worker), Brian Mooney (Educational Correspondent, *The Irish Times*), Anthony Moyles (Manager, Canal Communities

---

[1] In a very small number of cases, people wanted to make off-the-record comments and this has been respected.

Training Programme), Professor Mark Morgan (Trinity College), Alex McDonnell (Senior Consultant, Tandem Consulting), Paula O'Brien (Principal, Colaiste Eoin), Aine O'Keefe (Programme Manager, Foroige), Marie O'Neill (former Primary Teacher), Rory O'Sullivan (Principal, Killester College of Further Education), Dr. Kevin O'Higgins SJ (Director of JUST in Ballymun), Dr. Aideen Quilty (Outreach Director, UCD), Ger Robinson (Teacher/Motivational Speaker), Ellen Roche (Search Consultant, PwC), Lynn Ruane (Senator), Fiona Sweeney (Manager, UCD Access Centre), Ita Tobin (Head of Access, DCU), Dr. Bill Toner SJ (Treasurer, Jesuit Community), Dr. Mary-Liz Trant (Solas), Professor Ferdinand Von Prondzynski (Principal and Vice-Chancellor, Robert Gordon University), John Walshe (former Education Editor Irish Independent).

Financial/Modelling: Dr. Brian O'Kelly (Adjunct Professor DCU) completed the heavy lifting on the numbers in the business case chapter. The graphics (Education Roadmap) were designed by Sean Mitchell. Brian O'Sullivan (Bank of Ireland) helped make some of the statistics more accessible.

Additional Expertise: Tom Boland (Chief Executive, Higher Education Authority) was supportive from the outset and Orla Christle and the HEA Access team were enormously helpful at every step along the way. David Givens and the expert team at The Liffey Press team steered the publication through to completion. Mary Buckley (Librarian, NCI) was great, as always. Niamh McAuley (NCI Student Services) helped to source student stories. I'm deeply indebted to Robert Ward (Marketing Director, NCI) for his technical marketing expertise.

Sponsorship: Grateful thanks are acknowledged to Bobbie Bergin and AIB for the generous support in the publication of this book. Cecilia Ronan and CITI, along with the National College of Ireland, supported the launch event.

All royalties from the sale of this book go to the
Peter McVerry Trust for the homeless

Education Changes Lives:

Michael Armstrong

Mature Student, National College of Ireland

I started school in St Paul's CBS (Brunswick Street). It's often referred to as the 'School Around the Corner,' following the RTÉ programme fronted by Paddy Crosbie who taught in Brunner for years. I sailed through the early years unscathed. But secondary school was a different story. It took me a long time to come to terms with multiple tutors/subjects and I ended up with a very average Leaving Certificate. At the time, college seemed financially impossible. Among my peers there was zero conversation about it; a few lads went, but not many.

My Dad wasn't the domineering type, but he always suggested that the best way to eek out a decent living was through education. 'Youth being wasted on the young' and all that, I ended up in a succession of manual jobs. Eventually, full of entrepreneurial spirit, I became a taxi driver. Long hours, split shifts and everything rented meant that it was hard to make any money. In the meantime I'd gotten married. Sharon and I opted for Australia to find the pot of gold. Whilst enjoyable, after 18 months we were homesick and decided to return.

In 2005 I was looking for a job in a progressive organisation, eventually securing a role in a pharmaceutical company. It looked like a decent opportunity to progress. Then our world turned upside down with a phone call telling me that my brother, Stephen, had died in his sleep. He was 36 years old and left a wife and a young son. Cruelly taken in an instant by Sudden Adult Death Syndrome. More than ten years on, we still struggle with the enormity of his loss. Medical screenings followed for the whole family.

It was established that I had a degenerative heart defect (Dilated Cardio Myopathy) combined with an extremely fast abnormal rhythm called Atrial Fibrillation. I'd never heard of either, but the bottom line was that I couldn't get past the medical for the new job. I struggled to come to terms with my new life. An implantable defibrillator was placed in my chest. For a period of three years, I was taking 48 tablets daily. It was a brutal period. Unemployed, I felt like an invalid, depressed and lost.

Around that time, my uncle suggested the possibility of returning to full-time education. It shook me up in a positive way. Instead of feeling sorry for myself, I began to think that, unlike my brother, I now had a second chance. I enrolled at the National College of Ireland for a Bachelor of Arts. As the start date edged closer, I was gripped by fear. Who was I kidding? Would I have the brains for this? The staying power? Surely everyone would understand if I pulled out with all the medical stuff going on? The first few days were certainly challenging. For one thing, everyone in the class was about 10 years younger. I eventually plucked up the courage to mention this and was given reassurance by my classmates: 'Look Granddad, don't sweat it, you'll be fine.'

Those years went quickly, but not without incident. One day, just before an end of term exam, I had to have a Cardio-version (under medical supervision, your heart is stopped and re-started, using defibrillator paddles; it's not pleasant). To date, I'm on number 13 of these, so it's lucky I'm not a cat! On the morning of that first hospital discharge, I headed straight into NCI to do the exams, determined to complete the process. A member of the Disability Team, Stephen Kennedy, had gotten wind of this. While somewhat annoyed at me for not formally registering with the service, he then put a number of supports in place and I'm hugely grateful to him. Other faculty, including Dr. Eugene O'Loughlin, Dr. Keith Maycock and Ron Elliott, were incredibly supportive. I continued my studies and picked up a BA in Technology Management. Being a complete sucker for punishment, I subsequently completed a Masters (MSc.) in Web Technologies. I'm not saying it was easy, but I made it.

In 2012 I became a Teaching Assistant at NCI and now tutor across multiple courses. I suppose I've a soft spot for students who lack a bit of confidence. I try to inspire them to take that leap of faith, a belief that they can complete the journey. Like life itself, there are bumps along the educational road, but it definitely opens up new possibilities. Education has really changed my life and it's never too late to change for the better. That's my new motto!

Chapter 1

UNDERSTANDING EDUCATIONAL DISADVANTAGE[1]

Q: *Is this a real problem that needs to be addressed?*

A: *Yes, it is. Educational disadvantage is alive and well in Ireland.*

The Proclamation of the Republic, issued by the Provisional Government during the Easter Rising in 1916, put forward a range of rights for Irish citizens. Specifically, it contained a promise to 'cherish all the children of the nation equally.' 100 years later, while that aspiration endures, it hasn't been attained. Across Ireland, there are glaring anomalies in educational achievement. While the number of people completing third level has dramatically increased in recent years, this positive trend sits alongside pockets of disadvantage where participation rates are on par with developing countries. The global research evidence is unequivocal on one point. An early exit from education carries a huge personal cost. People who don't attend college have reduced employment opportunities, lower earnings, decreased self-esteem and a shorter life expectancy.[2] In what's sometimes referred to as 'the lottery of the womb'[3] some people begin life with the odds stacked against them from birth. Education is potentially the great leveller, a mechanism for individuals, families and communities to improve their social and financial circumstances. In a sense, education is the machine that converts the philosophy of 'all children being cherished equally' into a working reality. Education is the space where talent can surface and be nurtured as it touches the lives of every single citizen. More than this, Senator Lynn Ruane argues: 'Education can serve as a catalyst for social change.'[4]

Target Audience

While that's the *potential*, the evidence presented here is that progress in Ireland on Access to Education has been less than stellar.[5] Students from socially disadvantaged areas, people with disabilities, older learners, Travellers and students from ethnic minority backgrounds[6] fall out of the education system too soon, leave with poor results and are heavily underrepresented in further and higher education. In some colleges, the numbers of students in these categories are miniscule. While educational disadvantage has been on the political radar for many years, the problem has proven stubbornly difficult to shift. Despite gains made in specific areas, declaring victory in this war is massively premature. The data uncovered shows that swathes of students are being left behind in the qualifications race. As a single example, almost 10 per cent of schoolchildren don't complete second level education and leave before attaining the Leaving Certificate. In parallel, the changing nature of employment means that well-paid jobs are now almost impossible to secure without significant education. It follows that we are witnessing the rapid development of a two-tier economy, where Ireland is actually becoming more unequal. Overall, there's zero room for complacency here.[7]

Lost Potential

Educational disadvantage is negative – both for the individual and for the economy.[8] However, outside of a small group of specialists in the education and welfare sectors, the full impact of poor educational achievement on individuals and communities is neither widely understood nor debated. Further, the downside impact on the economy goes almost completely unmeasured.[9] The central purpose of this book is to take a deep dive into the question of educational disadvantage, to understand what it is, who it damages, to diagnose root causes and suggest clear solutions. What's clearly emerged is a strong business case to invest in educational equality. The positive economic impact of investing in education sits comfortably alongside the broader social justice arguments made. Given the central importance of education, both socially and economically, we need to cheerlead for the lost potential. Thomas Gray has expressed this eloquently:

> Full many a gem of purest ray serene
> The dark unfathom'd caves of ocean bear
> Full many a flower is born to blush unseen
> And waste its sweetness on the desert air.[10]

Whole System Perspective[11]

The approach taken follows a *systems perspective*. We will consider the Access jigsaw as a whole, rather than scrutinize the individual pieces or drill down into the education system on a stand-alone basis. This broader lens allows us to better understand root causes. As a society, the challenge is making tomorrow better than today; helping people to complete their educational journey is a key strand in this. We will see later that the elimination of educational underperformance requires interventions – real actions – delivered to individuals, families, communities, within each layer of the education system and across the political spectrum. In simple terms our task is to understand the problems and figure out what's causing them. We then need to envisage a better tomorrow with clear aim points. Finally, we need the courage to put the required fixes in place and measure the outcomes.

Target Audience

Not everything is fixable. In educational terms, some groups are extremely difficult to reach or are perhaps unreachable – students from seriously dysfunctional family backgrounds, learners who present with significant mental health problems, people engaged in criminality who have deliberately chosen an alternative path. In dissecting the topic of educational disadvantage, this book targets the 'hard but not impossible to reach' cohorts, the normally bright students who exist across all social classes. But in commencing this quest, we have to recognise that 100 per cent market share is not attainable.

Soccer Players

Late one evening I was returning to the National College of Ireland having attended an external meeting. Two kids were playing with a football, hitting the ball full force into one of the office windows. I stopped to talk to them along the following lines. 'It's good to see you improving your soccer skills. But, please don't hit the windows. Hit the ball against the wall. This is your college and we want this place to still be here when you get a bit older.' The older of the two lads replied: 'Why don't you fuck off and mind your own business.' At a guess he was 8 or 9 years old. Perhaps already lost to the educational system. I walked away, saddened. Later, Dr. Josephine Bleach suggested that, in walking away, I had essentially mirrored society's response to these children and should have said who I was and tried to better explain my concern. 'Nothing changes when people walk away.' She was exactly right.

Future State

So, what would 'not walking away' look like? Imagine a future point in time when the Access to Education question is resolved. What would we see?

◊ Students from disadvantaged areas and ethnic minority groups will aspire to degree and post-graduate qualifications at the same rate as people from middle class areas.[12]

◊ Disabled students will reach their full potential by being offered the requisite supports.

◊ 'Second chance' education pathways will be simpler, allowing mature students in the workforce to return to education and upgrade their skills.

From the outset I want to clarify one centrally important point. Going to college means staying on the education path *beyond* secondary school. For example, securing an apprenticeship is a major learning opportunity, which has offered fulfilling careers for many thousands of Irish people. So, the focus here is on post-secondary education and not exclusively third level. As a way into this topic, it's worthwhile to reflect on the existing elements that are working really well.

Good News: The 'Participation' Rate is Improving

Key elements of the education system are currently working well. For example, at policy level, every Irish citizen has the opportunity to complete a free[13] education, a stepping-stone on the way to maximising his or her potential. At the time of writing, circa 65 per cent of school completers attend college,[14] successfully completing their education journey. In the academic year 2011-2012, 220,531 students were enrolled in third level.[15] Like indoor plumbing, a college education has moved from the preserve of an elite to becoming almost universally available. Securing this high level of participation represents a tremendous achievement; Ireland currently ranks in the top third of developed countries in terms of third level attendance.[16] With the younger age cohort (25-34) only Korea, Japan and Canada report a higher level of people attending higher education.[17] While it might be difficult to argue that Ireland is an island of saints, based on these numbers we are slowly becoming an island of scholars. Statistically, there have been improvements across the board. For example, enrolments on flexible/part-time courses increased from 7 per cent in 2006 to 16 per cent in 2012, while the number of full-time and part-time mature student entrants increased from 18 per cent to 21 per cent in the same period.

In relation to students presenting with a disability at college, the numbers have also improved dramatically in a relatively short space of time. The 2011 Census reported that 13 per cent of the Irish population have a disability. Equal access data (2012 figures) indicates that circa 6 per cent of new entrants to higher education present with a disability, a figure which has risen from less than 3 per cent in 2008.[18] Without doubt, students with a disability face a difficult educational journey. They have higher drop out rates after primary level and lower completion rates at all stages of the system: '... of the total with a disability almost 37 per cent had ceased education after primary education level, compared to 15 per cent of their peers.'[19] While it's still a struggle, the trend is positive.

There's more good news. In recent times, the numbers participating at primary and secondary level have both shown significant growth versus historical data. In 1960, 20 per cent of secondary school students completed the Leaving Certificate Examination. This figure increased to 75 per cent in 1995 and has now levelled off at circa 90 per cent.[20] While harder to 'detect', there's also good news at a policy level. In Ireland, there's an accepted view that educational disadvantage won't go away on its own, that is, Access needs to be heavily supported. This isn't just a throwaway point. In other countries where the funding of local schools is driven by local tax revenue, disadvantage becomes hardwired into the system and is perpetuated.[21] Here Access, originally seen as a means to 'fill empty seats at the back of auditoriums', has become an accepted part of the educational landscape.

Education History

There have always been 'failures' in the educational system, or to put it another way, the educational system has always 'failed' up to a quarter of the student population. According to Áine Hyland, at the end of the nineteenth century, when completion of the Fourth Book in National School was regarded as a minimum educational requirement, at least 25 per cent of pupils failed to reach that level. Fifty years later, when the benchmark for minimum achievement was the Primary Certificate, at least 25 per cent of pupils failed to pass the exam. Following the introduction of 'free' second level education in 1968, when completion of the Junior Cycle was the target minimum achievement, about 25 per cent of pupils didn't pass either the Intermediate Certificate or the Group Certificate examination. In more recent years, when the Leaving Certificate is now regarded as the benchmark, almost 25 per cent of 18-year-olds fail to reach a sufficient standard in the Leaving Cert to enable them to progress to further or higher education.

We can see from the above that the education threshold has moved upwards several times. Indeed, there's reasonable evidence to suggest that it's moving upwards again, with an ever-higher percentage of students now completing undergraduate degrees. There's good and bad news in this. The fact that we are keeping most students in school until they are 18 is certainly positive. But all along this educational journey we can see that there has been a consistent hard to reach group who've consistently fallen out of the system, underperforming educationally vis a vis their peers. And, who are this stubborn, hard to shift group? To put it prosaically, 'it's the poor who have always suffered.' Over the past decade, between 2006 and 2016, the percentage of non-completions of the Leaving Certificate is static. In other words, the needle is stuck[22] and we can't seem to make progress on what John Walshe refers to as 'the forgotten 10 per cent.'[23]

Higher Education

Over the past 20 years, four national plans (spanning different time periods) have been developed to tackle educational disadvantage. According to Professor Patrick Clancy, Ireland was one of the first countries (following the lead taken by Australia and the UK) to embed the issue of educational disadvantage into third Level planning, led by the Higher Education Authority (HEA). And, it wasn't just a case of inserting a statement of philosophy as a platitude into the national plans; the idea was given traction in the funding model – the means by which exchequer monies are allocated to third level colleges.

Funding Model

The first element required in any funding model is solid data. Colleges had to be able to identify where students were coming from. While there are always methodology debates, according to Professor Patrick Clancy, the existing data collection mechanism was deemed to be robust and fit for purpose. Once this was agreed, the HEA allocated funding to third level colleges based on student headcount – with a premium being paid to colleges for 'Access Students' who met one of the five criteria identified earlier.[24] Where the fund for a traditional intake student was 100 per cent, an Access Student qualified for 133 per cent – a formal recognition that these students required more support. This additional funding was not subsequently tracked, that is, it was up to each college to decide locally how to use this. Whether the extra funding was ringfenced to be spent on access initiatives or found its way into general expenditure is somewhat unclear, and practices may have differed across the sector.[25] With the decline in overall funding in recent years, colleges have inevitably come under pressure to balance the books and there may have been some leakage of access funding into general expenditure. Professor Clancy makes the point that altering the funding formula to 'reallocate a diminishing budget' is hardly a solution. Colleges have to be funded at a level to provide Access services that can really impact the problem of educational disadvantage – more on this specific point later.

Education System Redesign[26]

It would be churlish to deny that these trends represent solid gains, ground that's been hard won over many years. We now have a strong foundation to build on. For example, one re-design of particular note was the development of the Leaving Certificate Applied (LCA) and Post-Leaving Certificate (PLC) options. In Ireland, historically, the education system was twin-track. Those students who made it all the way to the Leaving Certificate *passed* their exams, achieved high points and went to college. Or they *failed* (unable to reach the high academic standard) and went to work. The Leaving Certificate Applied (LCA) and the Post-Leaving Certificate (PLC) programmes were both designed to provide academically weaker students (and those who simply underperformed in the final exams) with alternative routes to educational success.[27] The rationale is as follows: if you climb Everest, the path taken doesn't matter. Today, more and more people are using these options, navigating their way into college by what the late Christina Murphy of *The Irish Times* described as 'the scenic route.'[28]

> ### *Key Point*
>
> The structural changes to the design of the education-al system highlight the fact that 'access' is philosophically supported within the Irish education system. There's a recognition of the importance of the topic and a willingness to make big, structural changes to progress this. Yet, while the continuous development of the education system is admirable, sometimes *movement* can be mistaken for *progress*. Despite *some* structural changes, the progress made under the 'access to education' banner is far too slow. We still have pockets of educational disadvantage that have proven stubbornly difficult to shift.

Educational Poverty Is a Feature of Irish Society

Given the structural changes noted and the overall high participation rates, you'd be forgiven for thinking that third level education is no longer the preserve of a wealthy elite but an avenue now open to all Irish citizens. While it's an easy assumption to make, you'd be mistaken. Educational inequality 'hasn't gone away you know.' The growing numbers that attend third level mask the fact that the overwhelming majority of these students are middle class.[29] Despite gains made in recent years, children from disadvantaged areas, along with people with disabilities, immigrants, older learners and members of the Traveller community are massively under-represented. Indeed, while the participation rate is as high as 95 per cent in some communities, in other areas that figure drops off the side of a cliff with participation rates declining to less than 10 per cent,[30] a figure comparable with countries in the developing world. These educational blackspots are hidden from view by statistics reporting the overall trend, that is, that more people are attending college. While the expansion of Irish higher education has been impressive – over six-fold in the last 40 years – the increasing numbers are disproportionately drawn from managerial and professional groups.[31] This finding around intergenerational causes of educational disadvantage is reflected internationally. Across the EU, people aged between 25-64 whose father or mother had attended third level are three times more likely to go to college themselves than if their parents only received basic schooling.[32] Further, the headline numbers reported in Ireland mask a *qualitative inequality*, where access to particular institutions (the universities) and particular fields of study (for example, Law and Medicine) are closed to certain cohorts of students.[33] In short, the rising educational tide hasn't raised all boats; in terms of educational equality, some people are *drowning*.

Unintended Consequence

This picture gets worse. The rising proportion of middle class students who attend college may have had a negative 'unintended consequence' for people who don't attend. It has deepened the belief that the reason some people don't go to college is due to a lack of personal commitment (laziness) or an intellectual deficit. It has also set the bar higher for jobs as many employers now seek third level qualifications for jobs historically completed by people holding a Leaving Certificate. An unspoken bias has built up based on the following (mistaken) assumption:

◊ The education system in Ireland is free right up to third level with few monetary barriers to entry

◊ Any student/learner who has the brains and the motivation to do well can do so – there are so many pathways and second chance opportunities that education is now open to all

◊ When individuals don't succeed in navigating the system, it's a reflection on their lack of ability, poor commitment or both.

In short, the structural disadvantages across society and within the educational system itself (which we will outline in some detail later) are ignored and the blame is placed squarely at the door of individuals.[34] We will see later how individuals and entire communities are invisibly steered into educational under-performance, with brutally negative social consequences for the next generation. While we congratulate ourselves on the high participation rates achieved, the educational disadvantage problem is slowly becoming worse for particular groups.

Who's Up in Arms?

Given the fundamental importance of education in shaping people's lives, you might expect a strong *social justice* campaign targeted at rectifying educational disadvantage. Mass public protests and demonstrations to right this societal wrong? Roadblocks outside Dáil Éireann, stopping the traffic to highlight this discrimination and the fact that it's being allowed to continue? That campaign doesn't exist for four reasons:

1. Educational disadvantage is largely invisible

2. In terms of immediacy, educational disadvantage is pushed off centre stage by more pressing issues

3. The route forward is both complex and uncertain

4. The educational cycle doesn't fit with the political cycle.

Let's consider each of these points in turn.

Reason #1: Educational Disadvantage Is Largely Invisible

Access to education has largely become invisible because people believe that the 'problem' has gone away. Like the eradication of Smallpox, educational poverty is seen as a thing of the past, something to read about in history books or enjoy during an evening's entertainment watching a Seán O'Casey play ('God, things were tough in those days'). We congratulate ourselves that we've surmounted this problem and decry those too lazy or unmotivated to take up the range of opportunities that now exist. When educational disadvantage is raised as a topic, personal responsibility is often trotted out as a defense: 'You can lead a horse to water, but you can't make him drink.'[35] Certainly, personal responsibility is a red-thread running through this debate which cannot, and should not, be ignored. And, we have to accept that Access to Education will never be fully resolved. Like poverty or perfect health, completion rates will always be less than perfect; 100 per cent market share is simply not attainable. However, a recognition that a problem cannot be completely eradicated is a very different mindset to complacency about the progress made to date. Perhaps we should bask in the glory of our current rankings – feeling superior to other countries that have done an even worse job in this area? No, I don't think so either.

What Do We Call This Thing?

Part of the poor visibility issue is driven by the fact that we don't have a label to frame this debate. In some academic circles there's the continuing use of the term *access* (shorthand for Access to Education). Others argue that *widening participation* offers a more accurate description and suggest substituting this term. In constructing this book, I've also struggled with naming the problem, flipping between *educational disadvantage, educational poverty, access* and *widening participation*. Paul Downes and Ann Louise Gilligan called educational disadvantage a 'jaded metaphor.'[36] Dr. Cliona Hannon, arguing that the label is important, said, 'We need to move beyond a deficit concept'. Trinity College is currently working on a concept called 'The 21st Century School of Distinction', to give a sense of pride to schools making strides under this heading. On an individual basis, perhaps the most apt title is *educational discrimination* – for that's exactly what it is. Those who toil in Access Departments might be the only people on campus who work under an alias! But they dust themselves off and continue, knowing that they're not just in the education business; they are in the business of changing people's lives. The overall point is that it's hard to get people excited about a social problem when we can't even decide what to call it! Meanwhile, back in the real world, children in disadvantaged areas, those struggling with a disability, older learners, Travellers[37] and the 'new Irish' are blocked from reaching their full potential. While we debate *labels*, they underachieve, are disconnected from high earnings and become marginalised, sometimes for life.

Reason #2: Social Immediacy: The Urgent Replaces the Important

Access to Education gets pushed off the radar by higher profile, more immediate concerns. Perhaps Fáilte Ireland should offer the following instruction to tourists:

> If you want to see Irish people exercising the 'gift of eloquence' don't bother visiting the Blarney Stone. Just start a conversation about water charges. To add fuel to the debate, ask whether charges should be levelled on a 'flat tax basis' or 'pay by usage'? Then stand back a safe distance and watch the conversation explode.

A high intensity anti-water charges campaign provides clear evidence of the depth of feeling on that particular subject. Some argue that this was the proverbial straw that broke the camel's back. There was also anger at the banks who've needed a massive capital injection to stay solvent, anger at individuals in business for ethical lapses, anger at the Financial Regulator for falling asleep at the switch, anger at politicians for not reigning in bloated expenses, anger (and fear) in the private sector about the level of job losses, and anger in the public sector that staff were scapegoated for Ireland's economic ills and that pay sacrifices have not been acknowledged.[38] Arguably, a lot of this anger found an outlet in the water charges campaign. It has some competition. At the time of writing vigorous campaigns around the lack of social housing and homelessness are occupying the national spotlight. Indeed, there's always competition for headline social issues. In November 2015, following a referendum to amend the Constitution, same-sex marriage became legal in Ireland and all couples that wish to get married can now do so.

The central point is as follows: social issues occupy a *hierarchy of importance* in the public mind at any moment in time. While educational disadvantage has a profound impact on people over their lifetime (certainly, a much deeper financial impact than whether or not someone pays a few hundred euro a year for water), it's simply not *on the radar*. Stated more forcefully, being denied access to third level education is an enormous, but hidden, discrimination. This fundamentally important issue has been relegated in social discourse. Invisibility (partly) explains why this topic has disappeared. But, there's another reason. Educational disadvantage is a topic that no one seems to know how to 'fix'.

Reason #3: The Absence of a 'Going Forward' Roadmap[39]

Let's assume that we could convince the 'powers that be' that Access to Education for all Irish citizens is a burning topic and needs to be addressed as a matter of urgency. Great stuff. We now immediately encounter a third major obstacle in the Access debate. There's no agreement on exactly what needs to be done, no 'roadmap' to show the best way forward.

Imaginary Scenario

You've secured an additional €1 billion of government funding to spend on education. You are passionate on the Access question and want to target it. How would you spend the money? Would you spread the money equally across a wide range of potential solutions or focus on 'high impact' initiatives? What exactly would those initiatives be? Perhaps you'd target specific geographic areas? Or direct all the money towards improving physical infrastructure – tearing down every temporary Portakabin and housing all students in 'triple-glazed' cosy classrooms. Would the college participation rate increase? Perhaps if we invested heavily in information technology and built high-spec classrooms with lightning fast broadband, that would do the trick? Maybe if we made a huge effort to reduce class sizes, hiring double the normal quotient of teachers. Would that strategy pay off in 10 years when those kids reached college-going age? It all sounds good. The problem is there's no consensus around what would work.

While there's no shortage of ideas around tackling educational disadvantage, there's little agreement on the best way forward, no definitive answer. Indeed, even if the government pumped millions of euro into the system, it is often the better-off children who benefit.[40] Even those who acknowledge the importance of educational disadvantage often lack a clear understanding of how to push this agenda forward. There's no one clamoring for the adoption of a particular solution, declaring 'Eureka', they've discovered the magic oil. The topic of educational disadvantage becomes mired in endless policy and technical debates[41] around 'evidence-based' initiatives ('can you prove that particular initiatives work?'), causality (in the social science arena, it's difficult to determine exact cause and effect)[42] and pet projects, for example, philanthropic support for particular topics. Where people become passionate that maths or languages or computer programming or music or sports or something else is the answer, they tend to get busy on the arguments to support their specific idea rather than the proof that it works.

Ideological Contradictions

In trying to understand educational disadvantage, we bump up against two ideological contradictions. Social commentators on the left tend to blame 'the system', in other words, capitalism has destroyed opportunity in Ireland by moving tranches of jobs to high profit locations. For example, Dell in Limerick relocated manufacturing to Poland with the loss of 1,900 jobs. Additional elements of 'the system' that attract blame are the Government (insufficient services), Local Authorities (building urban ghettoes), the Church (failing to speak out and supporting elitism in education), the Judiciary (punishing public crimes committed by the working class while ignoring the private/white-collar crimes of the middle classes) and so on. Under this rubric, the tendency is to absolve the individual or the family from any meaningful part of educational underperformance, reinforcing the idea of *learned helplessness*.[43]

Those to the right of the political spectrum take a different tack. The 'root causes' are clear: a lack of family and individual ambition and the hard slog that accompanies it; the real enemy in educational underperformance is the parent. It's reminiscent of the

Conservative MP Norman Tebbit advising people to 'get on your bike' – mirroring the behaviour of his then out of work father who needed to secure employment. Before you get busy on the 'lack of personal responsibility' blame-game, consider the following: One study reported that 18 per cent of children in four disadvantaged communities in Blanchardstown (West Dublin) were 'often, very often or every day too hungry to do their work in school.'[44] One writer described this as the process of 'victim-blaming': 'A brilliant ideology for justifying a perverse form of social action designed to change, not society, as one might expect, but rather society's victim.'[45]

Certainly, the lack of ambition perspective doesn't gel with my experience. I've met countless parents in working class areas who have high educational ambitions for their children.[46] While they definitely understand its importance,[47] somehow that ambition doesn't get realised. C.D. Jackson said: 'Great ideas need landing gear as well as wings.'[48] Yet, there has to be some element of personal responsibility in the mix. So, how do we square these contradictory ideas?

Personal Responsibility

The opposing political philosophies outlined above find an equivalent expression in the economics arena. Those who favour the Keynesian model believe that it's okay for a government to 'run a deficit', spending money on capital and infrastructural polices to create employment. Under this broad heading, the responsibility for unemployment rests with the government. Those who lean towards a Monetarist approach (the term we most often associate with the former Prime Minister Margaret Thatcher in the UK) believe that the job of the Government is to 'balance the books'. The people who have responsibility for securing employment are the unemployed themselves who should essentially study their way out of unemployment. It's another illustration of victim blaming where the problem of unemployment has shifted from the government to one of individual capacity to learn.

Diagnostic Dilemma

The contradictory ideas sketched above pose a diagnostic dilemma. If a tranche of people are not making it through the education system, should we get busy on fixing the system? Alternatively, should we locate the blame squarely at the door of individuals, under-ambitious families and communities? Even if we decided which particular side of this argument to support, how would we fix the system, that is, what specific issues would we address? Likewise, if we accepted that the central task was to convince individuals to stay in education for longer, how would we go about it? We've seen already that the Access question is somewhat invisible and gets pushed off the public stage by more topical issues. When we add in the fact that it often appears *un-diagnosable* (and is therefore seen as *un-solvable*), it's hardly surprising that educational disadvantage sinks to the bottom of the in-tray on both sides of the political divide. People think of Access in the same way that they think of the poor, that is, 'it will always be with us.' And, it is complex. Educational deprivation is part of a wider debate about general social deprivation. Dr Paul Downes argues:

> Some kids are coming from bad places. Is this spoken about? No. But, there's a media obsession with obesity and healthy eating. If you are living in a household where people are struggling with mental health issues, drug-taking or violence, having a packet of Tayto is pretty far down your worry list.

This lack of will to even debate Access means that educational disadvantage becomes an *orphan issue* that few really understand and no one seems able to fix. It's hardly surprising therefore that people go back to focusing on flood alleviation or hospital overcrowding – issues that at least seem open to resolution.

A Complex, Multi-Faceted Issue

When both the problem itself and the potential solutions are multi-faceted, most of us intellectually want to 'run away'. Many times during the construction of this book – perplexed by the complexity of the topic and my feeble attempts to make sense of it – I was sorry I'd started. The questions which emerged don't lend themselves to easy answers:

◊ At the level of individual families, why do some parents in the same community value education more than others and what impact does this have?

◊ Are mothers more attuned to the benefits of education than fathers?

◊ Or have many community interventions actually led to the exclusion of fathers?

◊ How can we explain the fact that some children overcome almost insuperable odds and become high educational achievers?

◊ In terms of communities, how does support for education within peer groups impact individuals?

◊ Could we get entire communities – those that lack a tradition of educational success – to place more value on this?

◊ If we ran powerful marketing campaigns around the benefits of 'going to college', would this shift their thinking?

◊ On the question of timing, is 'later too late'? Do we need to begin to implant this idea really early? If so, by what age?

◊ What role does each *level* within the education system play in this, for example, pre-schools, primary schools and secondary schools?

◊ At third level, should we reward colleges who perform best in the Access space and/or take sanctions against those who ignore this agenda?

And so on. What's abundantly clear is that organising a campaign on a single, identifiable issue is much easier. 'Stop Water Charges' is easy to understand – a combined statement of the problem and the solution captured in a three-word sentence! Complex social issues like educational disadvantage are much more difficult to unravel. Dr. Mary Liz Trant describes it as follows:[49]

> The Access issue is enmeshed across society. It doesn't lend itself to a simple diagnosis nor a magic bullet solution. Even when the 'needle can be moved', it seldom moves dramatically. What's required is a range of integrated activities. We have to think about resolving this in the medium-term, by making multiple changes.

There's certainly no instant fix. And, precisely because of this, educational disadvantage bumps up against a final barrier – the lack of political airtime.

Reason #4: Educational Disadvantage Gets (Almost) Zero Political Airtime

While I was writing this introductory chapter (early 2016), Ireland had just experienced heavy flooding as a result of Storm *Desmond*. Storm *Frank* followed closely on its heels. In a huge public outcry, there were calls for active government intervention to install flood-prevention infrastructure, make immediate welfare payments to people affected and to put pressure on the insurance companies to provide cover in high-risk areas. The flooding problem is easy to understand. Living close to the Shannon might be idyllic in good weather, but no one wants a river running through their living room. Arguably, the flooding issue is also 'easy-ish' to fix. A smart 12-year-old can grasp the mechanics of an engineering solution and there are locations where this seems to have worked really well, for example in Clonmel. In stark contrast, the issue of educational disadvantage is much more obscure and the timescales are elongated, sometimes, multi-generational. Because it doesn't lend itself to an easy analysis and requires a multi-year *fix*, educational disadvantage simply doesn't fit with the political cycle.

Politicians in Ireland are elected to serve for a period of five years – assuming that the government of the day runs its full term – and it follows that priority is given to issues that meet the criteria of *immediacy*.[50] When budgets are limited (as they always are), issues that don't bring immediate political benefit tend to be ignored. Educational disadvantage has to compete against every other social issue and normally comes off a poor second. Indeed, in purely electoral terms, 'kicking this can down the road' makes perfect sense. Charles Handy said: 'Most politicians know what to do. They just don't know how to get re-elected if they do it.'[51] Issues that require long-term planning fight for oxygen at the political table. In my experience, the topic of educational disadvantage is starved, that is largely ignored, across the political system. According to Professor Patrick Clancy it has always been so:

> Educational Disadvantage has never been a 'hot political topic'. Go back and look at the last number of elections. It's never even been on the agenda.

It's hard to become exercised about a problem that no one sees.

Importance of 'The Debs'

As a simple illustration of a class issue at play, consider the following vignette. One community activist I met lives in a socially disadvantaged area in West Dublin. He made the point that symbols are incredibly important within some communities.[52] For example, girls in the local area often complete second level schooling because they want to go to 'the Debs' – experiencing a night when they are the centre-stage princess (stretch limousine, beautiful dress and so on). In communities where marriage is not centrally important, 'the Debs' ranks disproportionately as a key life event. For some people, this might be the biggest night out they ever experience. I can almost hear a 'tut tut' from middle class readers. Yet consider the following list of *upsides* of working class culture suggested by Bill Toner:[53]

> Working class people are generally warmer, more spontaneous, less given to posturing than their middle class counterparts. They are also likely to be less concerned with material success, and less likely to sacrifice their personal happiness to the need to get ahead. They live in the present rather than the future, and have a great capacity for celebration. They support their neighbours and are tolerant of personal failings.

23

The central point here is not that middle class people are *better* or *worse* – they are just *different*, two tribes inhabiting the same island. Those two tribes sometimes make uncomfortable bedfellows, with an awkwardness when they meet.

The Spanish Trip

A couple of years back, my wife Linda booked a last-minute deal to a hotel in Benalmadena in southern Spain. The break was just what we needed after a particularly busy period. We had three kids with us, the youngest, Nicole, being about five at that time. While swimming with Nicole in the pool, a young lad from Dublin (he was about eight) came over to us. He looked at my daughter and then at me asking: 'Are you her Grandad?' I was mildly offended (Linda thought it was hilarious) until I realised that in his community people have children early. Then the cycle gets repeated. In my late forties (at the time), I was indeed Grandad age. Each afternoon the hotel ran a Happy Hour with reduced priced drinks between 16:00 and 17:00. The consumption of alcohol was huge. This was accompanied by shouting across the pool, full-on conversations about 'last night,' where people were going 'tonight' and so on. I was busy reading my book at the pool, talking to no one, sipping orange juice and being judgmental. There can be an unease when middle class and working class values clash, which often makes both tribes feel uncomfortable. Putting the issue of class under the microscope allows a perspective on Access to Education that's much broader than 'tweaking' internal practices in third level colleges. As this research unfolded, it became abundantly clear that solving the 'Access question' requires interventions at several different levels. While the educational system itself is an obvious target, solutions that ignore individuals, families and communities will not be successful. We need an authentic understanding about what's important in particular settings and how to appeal to local values.

> ### _Key Point_
>
> We can't solve a problem that we don't understand. Pushing the benefits of education while avoiding discussing class is like trying to sell beef burgers to a vegetarian audience.

Political Correctness Rules OK

There's another political factor at play that isn't always easy to discuss which is _political correctness._ In Ireland, unlike some other developed countries, there isn't much historical class consciousness to borrow a Marxist term. Over many years, the dominant political parties, Fianna Fáil and Fine Gael, have a broad centre or centre-right political philosophy. Their separation in policy terms is one of degree, rather than diametrically opposed platforms. This centre view of politics rests on the underlying assumption that 'we are all in it together.'[54] There's very little acknowledgement that different classes of Irish citizens have very different experiences of education and views about life in general. Perhaps because of our particular history, it's not deemed 'politically correct' to speak about class in this way, with the implications of Upstairs/Downstairs groups and the uncomfortable idea that some people might be classified as better or worse than others. It's safer to stick with the myth that we are all equal. Opportunities to progress are open to all and Ireland offers a mini-version of the American Dream, that is, anyone from any strata in society can attain any position. As Vladimir Lenin said, 'A lie told often enough becomes the truth.' In Ireland that lie is that educational equality has been attained.[55]

Family History

My own interest in education took a long time to develop. As the youngest of a family of 10 children, I grew up in Cabra West, a Local Authority housing estate on Dublin's Northside, known at that time as 'the Wild West'. A standing joke was that if someone had less than six kids they were Protestant! Cabra was more famous for producing entertainers (Dickie Rock) and footballers (Liam Whelan[56]) than scholars. Arguably, Cabra's academic claim to fame is a stone inscription on Broom Bridge which spans the Royal Canal, where a mathematician had a breakthrough. The text on the plaque reads: 'Here as he walked by on the 16th of October 1843, Sir William Rowan Hamilton in a flash of genius discovered the fundamental formula for quaternion multiplication: $i^2 = j^2 = k^2 = ijk = -1$' (I didn't understand it then and nothing has changed since).

My father was a road sweeper and a binman with Dublin Corporation. Later he worked as a janitor in the men's public toilets on O'Connell Street (since closed). This led to what was probably my first lie, told repeatedly over many years. When anyone asked, 'What does your Da do?' I said he was a carpenter! My father never learned to read or write and had little understanding or experience of the education system, having left school at 11 or 12. Sadly, I didn't know that he couldn't read until many years after he'd died. He carried the shame of that all his life and it was kept secret. My mother, who also left school early, moved from Wexford to work as a cleaner in Dublin when she was 12 or 13. She was self-educated, became an avid reader and we often reflect on how smart she was, albeit we didn't fully recognise nor acknowledge it at that time. In the 1950s, having done well at secondary school, my eldest brother John was awarded a scholarship to study at Trinity College where he completed an undergraduate degree in business and then a Master's in literature. While my mother and father must have been proud, I have no memory of it ever being spoken about at home. In the strong Catholic ethos that prevailed, blessings were offered up as were hardships. The 'hand of God' was seen as the strongest influence in life – captured in the saying – 'Man plans, God laughs.'[57]

Gifted Kids

For a student from Cabra West to go to college in the 1950s was certainly exotic. Of the 2,000+ houses in the local area, it's estimated that circa 0.1 per cent (one tenth of one per cent) of children attended third level at that time.[58] The wags often commented that the only way someone from Cabra could get into Trinity College was in a uniform (as a security guard, a cook or a cleaner). Indeed, there was a strong belief that walking into the campus wasn't *allowed* with a real fear of being *arrested*. None of the next eight members of my family went to college (very few completed second level education). Now, even in the most disadvantaged communities, there will always be kids that are smart, highly driven or both. People who climb the educational mountain against the odds are exceptional. Today, some of the universities continue to sweep into disadvantaged areas and 'hoover up' the brightest children as a demonstration of their commitment to Access and social justice. While it is life changing for the chosen few, it does little to change the overall paradigm. However, even this limited intervention has an upside. We will see later that having role models – people 'like us' who attend college – is an important part of the marketing mix in disadvantaged communities.

While it's great that some students from disadvantaged areas are given the opportunity to attend college, targeting 'crème de la crème' students from poorer communities is a too-easy response from the third level sector. We can't be content with an educational system that only rewards gifted students. While the personal stories dotted throughout this book are inspiring, genius will find a way to climb Everest without support. Our targets are the normally bright students (both kids and adults) who populate every single social group – many of whom are currently left behind. In reality, when we speak about educational disadvantage, there are really two groups in our focus: (a) potential early school leavers who are most at risk of falling out of the education system, and (b) the regular schoolgoer who is doing okay but, by virtue of socio economic status, probably won't progress to college (as we will show later, there are different solutions for both groups).

The Huge Impact of Education

Following the family pattern, I left secondary school when I was 13 years old, having attended for just 10 months. It was young to leave full-time education, but not bizarre in an era where getting a job and earning money were highly valued. Indeed, in the 1970s, given the nature of the employment available, there was some opportunity for people who didn't attend college. There was (and still is) room for entrepreneurship, an ability to spot gaps in the market. But the main chance was to secure an entry-level job, work hard and get promoted. Years later, I observed this route to success being followed countless times within the multi-national sector. In the human resources community we even gave this a label – 'the back-stairs'. That was then. The current crop of early school leavers is seldom afforded an opportunity to prove themselves on-the-job. Entry-level roles are earmarked for graduates. Those without post-secondary qualifications don't even make it to an interview to tell their story – their CVs filed in the shredder. Educational qualification has become a passport, without which you can't get onto the pitch to prove yourself. As Bill Toner suggests, 'The early school drops-outs of today are the long-term unemployed of tomorrow'.

Reflecting back on that earlier time, the unspoken values shared by most families in our area were based on an unspoken 'Totem Pole' of status as follows:

1. *Office Job: If you secured a white-collar job you'd really arrived. For many years the height of my own ambition was to get a job where my hands weren't permanently cold!*

2. *Apprenticeship: Three of the five boys in my family became tradesmen – a status that bordered on posh at that time. The five girls went to work in various factories.*

3. *Any Job: Making enough money to pay your way was seen as progress, regardless of the job itself. It would be many years before I heard the terms 'career' or 'CV' – the idea that you would have to account for jobs held or that there should be some plan.*

4. *On the Dole: Being unemployed – for anything other than short periods in between employment, was seen as the lowest rung on the ladder – often equated with personal laziness. These were the guys (most often men) who waited for the pubs and the Bookies to open – a semi-permanent 'underclass'.*

While my educational journey started inauspiciously, I eventually went to trade school and then completed undergraduate and postgraduate studies in industrial relations. Being accepted as a student at the National College of Ireland,[59] despite the lack of either a Junior[60] or Leaving Certificate, offered a tremendous opportunity. The Jesuits, who ran the college at that time, had a strong ethos of providing second chance education, before that term became popular. Looking back, the impact of education on my life has been remarkable, opening up career, travel and earnings opportunities that would otherwise have been blocked. If the core argument is 'education has the power to change lives,' it certainly changed mine. Within my immediate family and community I've seen the evidence so many times: where education is stunted, it can have a lifelong negative impact. While there are several ways to measure success – and higher education is certainly not for everyone – the right to attend college should be open to all and actively encouraged.

Are we 'Over-Egging' the Benefits of Education?

The points made above are not universally accepted. Counter-arguments are sometimes put forward to suggest why people *should not* attend college.

1. There's too much emphasis placed on educational achievement to the detriment of a wider view of personal growth. Continually reinforcing this runs the risk of deepening a stereotype that the *only route* to success is through education, stigmatising people who don't attend college.

2. College should be the preserve of elite students – people with high intelligence who can *make the most* of the inputs and prosper. Encouraging children to go to college who can't cope, damages rather than enhances their confidence.

3. If everyone goes to college, who's going to clean the streets, shine our shoes and do the million mundane tasks required in a modern society? In North American parlance, if everyone aspires to become the Chief, where will we find the Indians?

The Middle Class 'Educational Taliban'

Without doubt, there are downsides to an over-obsession with educational achievement. Consider the following game that's played in Clontarf where I live (I suspect it's quite similar across all middle class areas). The game can be labelled: 'My son/daughter is doing great. How's yours doing?' While it's a year-round sport, this game flowers every August when the Leaving Certificate results are published. Essentially, the educational achievement of children has become a de facto national measure of parenting effectiveness. We don't ask if children are happy and well adjusted. We don't probe about whether they're progressing in life – along the route from dependence to independence. We don't consider if there's any evidence of a social conscience (unless they've won the Young Scientist of the Year for a social science project). No, we only enquire how many points did they get in the Leaving Certificate and whether they secured a place in a particular college.[61] A couple of years back, if I saw one particular local woman walking towards me, my instinct was almost to hide in the nearest garden rather than be regaled about how well her kids were doing and how some obscure (to me) aspect of the Leaving Certificate points system worked or didn't work. I suspect that this game is played equally strongly in rural areas, perhaps even a higher 'division' based on the statistics of the number of young people who go to college from farming backgrounds. Somehow, we've become obsessed by this national competitive sport in which the central mechanism to value children is through educational achievement. If children are not high achievers, parents live with the shame, within their wider families ('competitive cousins') and the local community ('brilliant neighbours'). Irish people sometimes argue that the UK is a stratified society, citing the Honours list ('Sir Anthony') and so on. Yet, when it comes to education, snobbery is alive and kicking in Ireland. It's like the joke about the mother in Cork standing on the seashore shouting: 'Help, help. My son, the first-class engineer, is drowning.'

Parental Preferences

Working at the National College of Ireland, I remember meeting one young person[62] – a potential college student – who was unsure of what he wanted to do. That's a long queue right there! Following two discussions, it emerged that he had a genuine interest in psychology and I advised him to follow that path – partly on the basis that what you study doesn't matter as much as people think. Many students shift to other disciplines when they enter the world of work. In the USA they say: 'Go to college to get an MBA. Then go to work to learn the rest of the alphabet.' The next day, his mother rang. In her own words, she was 'absolutely horrified' at this outcome. Her son 'needed' to become a lawyer – following in the footsteps of his father and his grandfather. She thought that I would 'talk sense into him' (the phone call felt like a negative performance appraisal). Of course, there were all the practical considerations. His Dad could help him with his studies, secure appropriate training, guarantee a job in the family firm and so on. But what struck me most forcefully during that conversation was not the mothers' concern about the future employability of her son. It was her deep status need for him to enter a recognised profession. Perhaps psychology wouldn't go down well in the Bridge Club! (I've had many similar conversations with fathers who, in similar vein, elevated prestige over the desire and competence of their children). Some parents live their lives vicariously – hoping children will follow an agenda that they themselves would choose if they could rewind the clock. Perhaps I'm particularly sensitive to this issue as my own crew (three kids) has been zig-zagging on the educational front (in reality, a bit more like Zig and Zag). But it seems to me that we need some better way to value our children and not reduce their life achievements to a single numerical score or a particular rite of passage.

Supporting the right of all children to attend college – if they choose to do so – is not the same as making 'attendance at college' the single way to evaluate success. However, many people get caught up in this competitive game. In part, it's understandable to want the *best* outcome for children and to push them to become the best they can be. In Catholic terms, perhaps this is a *Venial* sin and arguably better than the opposite – ignoring your children's academic achievements.[63] However, in some cases, the need for external validation trumps everything else and the educational success of children is elevated almost to a point of mental illness. There are many children in middle class areas better suited to working in the trades or physical roles that get swept away in a wave of parental expectation about going to college. If the ultimate goal is for our children is to be happy, finding a role where they can utilise their talent (whether hairdressing or medicine) certainly seems the best bet. The key question for parents is, 'Am I working on their agenda or on my own agenda?' Because some people can't make a distinction between their own needs and the needs of their offspring, this question is often muddled.

Are You 'Smart Enough' to Go to College?

The second question raised is whether college is really for everyone. Implicit in this is some notional cut off, a baseline ability, that's required for people to successfully complete post-secondary studies. Without this foundation of intelligence, perhaps people shouldn't attend college? It's an interesting, but misguided, argument. Dr. Kevin O'Higgins SJ, describes it as follows:

> I've worked with and taught kids in South America and Spain. In Ireland I've lectured in DCU and in NCI. Here's what I found. The kids in Ballymun are as brilliant as the best students I've met anywhere. The fact that many don't go to college is absolutely nothing to do with capacity. It's about history.

In recent years there's a growing recognition of different *types* of intelligence.[64] We all know *book smart* children, the ones who've read every Harry Potter story by the age of 10. Some are brilliant with people (emotionally intelligent) and demonstrate this from an early age. Still others have superb mechanical ability, fixing bikes, building tree houses and so on. So, which of these types is smart enough to go to college? The answer is: all of them. There's a *diversity of mission* across the education sector to cater for students of different abilities and orientations. An example of this is the movement within the third level sector towards embracing *skills-based* vocational courses that are not primarily academic, for example, the training of chefs.[65] While we have to recognise real differences in individual ability, the vast majority of people can be successful at college provided they are given the correct support. The trick is to overcome self-limiting beliefs about the degree of difficulty, particularly from people whose earlier experience of school was less than positive. In relation to recognising different types of intelligence, Tom Crean makes a colorful point:

> We know that a monkey and a crocodile don't have equal tree climbing skills. So, if the only thing we measure is tree climbing, the monkey wins ev-

ery time. We have to recognise the different skills brought to the table. Being fixated on academic ability undervalues the skills of too many children. We talk about it and everyone nods politely and acknowledges this. But we do fuck-all to change it.

From the Archives

At National School, a couple of the lads in my class were poor at maths. One particular student struggled, trying to get his head around long division. The teacher who had a reputation for being tough (his nickname was Hitler), stood behind him each day at the blackboard. For each failed attempt, and there were many, he lashed the kid full force across the back of his legs with a long bamboo cane. Physically hurt, and mentally scarred, I doubt if he remembers school as the best days of his life. While not as dramatic, many people were happy to walk out the school door for the last time, ending a chapter in their life where they felt unconfident and humiliated. Hopefully, things have moved on since then. In 2016, education seems closer to Disney than Dickens. Yet, despite the gains, we are not bringing everyone with us on the journey. Too many are still left behind. And too many of those are in working class areas. While that's factual, it has nothing whatsoever to do with baseline intelligence.

Self-Deprecation

When education focused on the so-called 3Rs (Reading, Writing and Arithmetic), intelligence was overly identified with those subjects. A couple of my siblings who may have had dyslexia (never formally diagnosed) incorrectly believed that, because they weren't good at spelling, they were stupid. I was never great at spelling myself – I've always clung to the line, 'you're not a real scholar unless you can spell a word at least two different ways' (reading this book without the aid of a computer spell check would be a very different experience). In pushing back against the belief that 'some children are not smart enough to go to college', Dr. Mary Liz Trant picks up the argument:

> In part this is just lazy thinking. Who doesn't like to teach bright kids who 'get it' straight away? More worryingly, this attitude can mask intellectual or social snobbery. Philosophically, why would you write off people who outwardly have less ability – don't they also need to reach their full potential? The challenge to educators is to help people of all abilities to maximise their talent, not to draw some arbitrary line in the sand that people have to cross before they can attend college.

It's common knowledge that Einstein's teacher at high school declared he would never amount to anything and he turned out to be pretty good at maths later on! The problem is that some students internalise these negative messages and carry them for life.

Off-Campus

We can view the *smart enough* argument through a slightly different lens. You may recall John Lonergan, the former Governor of Mountjoy Prison. He continually made the point that most prisoners come from disadvantaged areas, for example, from a small number of postal districts in Dublin. Indeed, there are some parts of Dublin that could be labelled as the off-campus of Mountjoy prison. Lonergan would ask, rhetorically, whether criminality was prevalent in these areas only? His core argument was that social disadvantage is a root cause in criminal behaviour. We could pose a similar question in relation to the education system: Are all the bright children in Dublin from Ballsbridge? The answer is no, they're not. Intelligence is evenly distributed across all sectors of society. While there's no particular gene for intelligence, a number of studies have shown what can labelled as a 'high level of heritability', in the range of 70-80 per cent.[66] Instinctively, we understand that if your father has brown eyes, you may inherit this. In similar vein, if he's highly intelligent, you might also inherit that trait. While this general point on inheritance is clear and applies to everyone, there's zero evidence that working class people have lower intelligence than middle class people as a group. Less education? Definitely. Less travel stimulation? That's often the case. Less confidence? In my experience, this one is a definite 'yes'. Less intelligence? Absolutely not. Performance at school is an outcome of a number of factors – children's baseline intelligence, whether their parents have talked, read and played with them, self-belief, behaviour, personality, well-being and their perceptions of the school environment. This rich mix of factors contributes to the fact that more working class children leave school early and fewer of those who stay go on to college.

The core argument here is not that *everyone* should go to college. Some people won't have the appetite for this journey and we have to respect that. Others won't have the discipline to see it through. But there's zero evidence to support a view that an entire 'class' of people shouldn't go to college because they haven't 'got the brains', the fundamental raw material to be successful in college. Yet, because we haven't yet found a way to 'crack the code' of educational disadvantage in particular communities, we sit and observe an enormous waste of human potential.

Mundane Tasks

The final pushback was that 'too many' people now go to college.[67] What does this actually mean? Is this a concern that we won't have enough people to do low level jobs like cleaning or security? Is the anxiety around mental health, that is, that over qualified people occupying junior roles will become bored? Does it mean that colleges are not producing the *right sort* of graduates, in other words, providing skills that don't match the needs in the marketplace? If we are producing *too many* graduates, will this lead to a glut, pushing the cost of labour downwards? Overall, the thinking here seems very muddled. Unquestionably, in a modern economy, we need people to do basic jobs. And, we've earlier made the point that 100 per cent college participation is unrealistic – so there will always be candidates for this type of work. However, the good citizens of Donnybrook (middle class) can offer up their children to do mundane jobs just as easily as the people in Darndale (working class). We should not assume that children from working class areas will continue the tradition of taking up unskilled, low paid employment, 'doing shit jobs for shit money', as one person described it.[68] We have to break the cycle where the place you are born automatically dictates the level to which you aspire, to move beyond this 'zip code' predictor of educational performance.[69] Now this point of view might be idealistic, naive even. But, why would we set our sights lower than this? There will always be enough *fallers* to ensure that the streets are kept clean. Our goal here is somewhat more noble: to maximise the intellectual capital of the nation. Perhaps you remain unconvinced and believe that all children have an equal opportunity to attend college: Then, consider the following:

Dublin Postcode: College Participation Rates[70]

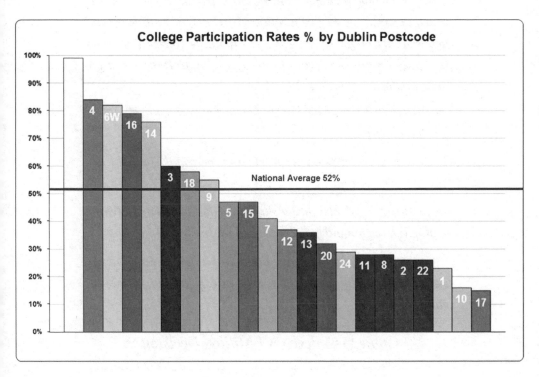

Making College 'Cool'

As President of the National College of Ireland (NCI) for just over three years (2007 to 2010), I gained some insight into how the higher education system works.[71] Philosophically, since its foundation in the early 1950s as a Jesuit-run college, NCI always had a positive bias towards Access and second chance education. Searching for ways to continue the tradition, we experimented with several ideas. One was called 'Adopt a School' where we established a bridge with selected secondary schools in disadvantaged areas – part of our 'target market.' By demystifying third level, the hope was that we might pave the way for students to see college as part of their future. I then linked up with the Donaghies Community School in Donaghmede, a working class area in Dublin 13. The principal asked me to give a talk to the Donaghies students and their parents about the benefits of attending college ('no good deed goes unpunished') and I put together a draft presentation, lining up the usual arguments:

Learning: By discovering 'how to learn,' you keep yourself up-to-date for a lifetime.

Confidence: College can improve your personal confidence – that's priceless.

Networking: Student relationships provide a lifelong network, helping you to gain independence from the 'mother ship.'

Overall, the pitch seemed solid but a bit dry. I needed a way to grab attention that had a bit more sizzle. Here's the actual presentation made:

Going to College = €1 Million Decision

Working Life: Most people work for 45 years (from age 20 to 65).

School Leaver: If you leave school without any qualifications you're likely to earn the minimum wage, that is, €8.30 per hour.[72] That equates to €330 per week or €17,000 per annum. In 45 years you will earn €776,000.00.

College Graduate: If you go to further or higher education and get a degree, you can make a starting salary of up to €30,000. That equates to a lifetime earnings figure of €1,350,000. That's a €575,000 difference – the price of 3 houses in the local area or 1 really jazzy house and a top end Ferrari sports car! But, as a college graduate you are also more likely to be promoted during your working life. That will take you well beyond your starting salary and the gap will widen even more.

The Deal: Going to college is therefore worth an extra €1 **million** *over a lifetime. That's one hell of a prize! That's the decision for you to make. Do you want to make an extra €1 million or not? It's your call! Because, while going to college won't be easy – if you successfully navigate your way through the Leaving Certificate – you will have already proven your capability to be successful in the education system.*

Other Reasons: Of course, I also added in all of the other reasons for going to college. Aware that some people in the audience hadn't been to college (many of the parents), I spoke with respect about exceptions. There are many historical examples of brilliant individuals who never made it through formal schooling. Entrepreneurial genius that spots an unmet customer need. Others exploit a physical gift through sports, becoming rich and famous on athletic rather than academic ability. Some will be born into wealth and inherit the red carpet. And, of course, there are people who successfully scale the education ladder, but lack the interpersonal skills or common sense to exploit this. I've met some academics that you wouldn't send to the local Spar to buy an ice cream! Yet, these exceptions actually prove the rule: 'The route to career success is almost always a solid education.' All other things being equal, the best way to put rocket fuel onto your career is to learn a trade or add a degree to your CV. If you are currently out of work and looking for a job, education can give you an edge over the candidate that's going to come second (there's a huge pro-education bias in the recruitment industry). Why wouldn't you give yourself that edge?

The Impact: Two years later, I met Peter Keohane, the principal of the Donaghies. He told me that after that night, the students didn't remember any of the wider arguments in favor of going to college but that they endlessly debated the €1 million figure. Was it real? Was it bullshit? The number had become tattooed into the mindset and eventually became the title of this book. As in all branches of marketing, Rule #1 is 'Know your audience.' Rule #2 is 'Help them to remember your pitch!'

Bottom Line

Despite our best efforts to date, we have failed the 10 per cent of children who fall out of the school system early – before they complete the Leaving Certificate. We have also failed to convince an audience of smart working class children, people with disabilities, older learners, Travellers and students from ethnic minority backgrounds that they could do really well in college.[73] The numbers don't lie: these groups are heavily underrepresented in third level, notwithstanding 20 years of Access plans. Orla Christle makes the point that:

> There has been progress, just not enough. For some students there's growing inequality as some communities rise and, in others, cycles of educational underperformance get continually repeated.

We now need to figure out what to do about this. The first step is to create awareness of the problem – that's been the goal in this opening chapter. The second step is to move beyond the social justice arguments into the cold land of economics. Because, economically, solving the problem of educational disadvantage makes perfect sense. When we turn our attention to the 'business case' for solving educational disadvantage, you may be as surprised as I was about how powerfully the numbers stack up.

Education Changes Lives:

Lynn Ruane
Trinity Access Student[74]

'Dear Santa, I would like a typewriter, Sellotape, a stapler and lots of blank pages as I'm going to be a writer'; 'Mam, I'm going to be a vet when I go older.'

These were two aspirations when I was seven years old. So, why didn't I become an author or a vet? Growing up I was surrounded by books, my bedroom was a library, I loved to read. In junior and senior infants I was probably above average, a couple of books ahead of the class; Ann and Barry seemed too easy. My first teacher was amazing and she nourished our group.

That changed in first class when we got the teacher that no one wanted. You couldn't ask questions. You couldn't move without her coming down on you like a ton of bricks. She was a bully and I firmly believe that she's responsible for many children having an early love of learning sucked out of them. From there on in, I developed a negative relationship with learning. School became low priority.

I continued to do okay in school but was never as enthusiastic as when starting out. My parents promoted and supported school, despite their own low educational attainments. Without wishing to sound boastful, I had the makings of a good student: the parents, the ability, the curiosity, but somehow school just didn't work for me. Some 'off switch' had been pressed.

Secondary was the hardest of all. Aged 13, I witnessed the death of a friend. Returning to school within a couple of days, sitting in a classroom full of trauma and pain, I was scarred. Everyone wanted to walk around it rather than come into my space. No teacher stopped to observe. That's what it felt like.

My story is not so different to so many others. That's the thing about schools in areas of social deprivation. So many kids arrive in the morning with a school bag full of pain and poverty. Teachers in those areas have to be better resourced and trained to work in this arena. Children want to succeed, their parents want them to succeed and the communities want to support. But where poor mental health and poverty are endemic, survival becomes the aim. Education in poorer areas requires a holistic approach based on a deep understanding of social context. We must arrive at a place where education is transformed from an industry to produce high points, to a place where the mind of a child can be nourished.

Chapter 2:

The Business Case: Money Spent on Access = a Great Investment

Q: *Does investment in Access provide a good return to Irish taxpayers?*

A: *Yes. There's a payback period after which graduates become net contributors to the economy*[1]

Some people dismiss the social justice arguments outlined in the previous chapter. They ask, 'why should anyone be supported to help them finish school or attend college?' Their core belief: it's up to everyone to make their own way in life. 'Cream rises to the top'; if the fundamental talent is there, it will eventually show itself. There's little point in pining for a utopian society that has never existed and which may never exist. Yet, even if you hold this 'survival of the fittest view', it's impossible to dismiss the business case for supporting Access initiatives. Getting as many people as possible to go to college offers an enormous financial upside to the economy. Here's how it works.

Personal Impact

People who don't attend college are effectively cut off from *full participation*, in terms of securing good employment and earnings. That's the obvious downside for individuals. But what's often missed in this debate is the incredibly negative societal costs that accompany this. The numbers are stark. The cost of putting someone through a four-year university degree is €41,140[2] while the lifetime benefit of this to society is over €1,000,000 as people become productive, tax-paying citizens (see Appendix A). In contrast, low levels of educational achievement can lead to inter-generational cycles of poverty, poor health and, in some cases, criminality. To use an extreme example, the cost of supporting a student for one year in college is 12.5 per cent of the cost of housing that same person in prison for a year, which costs over €80,000. As taxpayers, we collectively pick up the tab for people who *fall out of* the system. Stated another way, Access programmes which tackle educational disadvantage offer great value for money. There are a number of different strands to this argument.

Economic Sustainability

To make Ireland stronger, we need to unleash the talents of all of our people. Most people will be familiar with the economic dictum, 'A rising tide, raises all boats'. While this provides good imagery, it's actually a poor metaphor. A rising tide leaves some people behind, for example, those who are unable to swim in the new conditions. As a country we don't have much gold. Nor oil. With the exception of Kinsale and Mayo, we don't have much gas. Ireland's only natural resource is our people and we need to invest in them. In terms of making Ireland stronger, placing Access initiatives centre stage makes perfect economic sense as it underpins our competitiveness (the issues of social inclusion and fairness are really a bonus).

Changes in the Job Market

Commercial organisations in Ireland find it increasingly difficult to compete with low labor cost economies across the world. Because of high wage rates (in relative terms), we can't compete internationally on price. I've first-hand experience of this, having worked with several companies that closed down operations in Ireland. From a strategic perspective, is it possible to stop this hemorrhage of jobs? The consensus is that Ireland needs to move towards becoming what's usually labelled as a 'smart economy'[3] where a high percentage of the workforce are involved in tasks that require intellectual rather than manual skills. Here's the kicker. To secure employment in those sectors, candidates often need to hold third level qualifications. And, the real trick is getting these companies to locate here.

Competitive Island

Capital is the ultimate mobile commodity. Like a fisherman, Ireland needs a *lure* to attract this. To remain a compelling investment location, several things need to be in place.

Something Unique

We have to be able to market something unique (normally a combination of areas in which we excel). Certainly the companies that the IDA targets for investment are attracted to the fact that we have a unique 12.5 per cent corporation tax rate. As 90 per cent of the world's top pharmaceutical, banking and technology companies are already located in Ireland (most people will be familiar with high-profile technology brands such as Google, Facebook and LinkedIn) we are doing exceptionally well under this heading.

Solid Infrastructure

We need to have a broad infrastructure to attract capital, that is, transport, communications and so on. Solid progress has been made in this area in recent years. We now have a road system which is worthy of a developed economy, albeit the rollout of broadband countrywide remains incredibly slow.

Smart Workforce

At the heart of what we have to offer is a highly educated, English-speaking workforce with the ability to develop high-added-value products and services. It's not possible to build a smart economy without a smart workforce. So, producing highly skilled graduates and re-skilling workers from smokestack industries for jobs in the emerging sectors needs targeted investment.

Colleges play a vital role in the economic success of any country. High quality teaching and research outputs underpin future economic success and enrich the country in a host of additional ways (in keeping with the argument that Ireland is a *country*, not just an *economy*). The corollary is that the education sector needs continually to demonstrate high productivity to justify this investment and ensure that we can compete against the best in the world. It's not just about pumping more money in. The Irish health sector demonstrates that making huge additional investments doesn't automatically translate into superior outcomes.

The Magnificent 8

What type of industries are on our priority list to attract? The following areas feature strongly in investments secured to date:

1. Science: Pharmaceutical and bio-sciences (embedded now for over 30 years).

2. Software/ICT: Huge development capability based on our existing core competence in this space, for example, big data and analytics.

3. Education: Attracting overseas students and offering a unique experience, focusing on the USA and Asia in particular.

4. Agriculture and Food: Building on our image as a 'green island.'

5. Marine: Huge shoreline offers leisure and energy generation possibilities.

6. Finance: Despite recent problems in this area, we have an ability to rebuild a vibrant financial sector.

7. Tourism: It's not replicable elsewhere.

8. Arts: Building on our unique heritage and capability in an area of natural strength.

Focused Targets

With a limited budget, the government targets investments in areas of future strategic importance. At a national level, an example of this policy in practice is Singapore. It's a small island, not that much bigger than Achill, but catering for a population of just under 5 million people. In the early 1960s, the then Prime Minister Lee Kuan Yew decided, in the absence of any natural resources, that the country needed a basis to compete internationally. Singapore is now the fourth most important financial centre in the world. Obviously, the Singapore story is complex and the culture and political system don't provide an exact parallel with our own. However, the thrust of the argument is that a concentration of effort across a narrow range of defined areas pays dividends.

Employment Changes: New Jobs Require College Education

Over recent years, there's been a subtle but distinct change in the employment market. Today, a college education is increasingly required to secure employment. As manual jobs are exported overseas to low-wage countries, more and more Irish people are becoming *knowledge workers*, completing jobs that require specialist training. Unskilled or semi-skilled jobs, for example, packing boxes in manufacturing, get exported to Eastern Europe and Asia.[4] The European Union has estimated that by 2020, higher level qualifications will be required in 16 million additional jobs while the demand for low skills jobs will decline by 12 million.[5] The low skilled jobs that remain and which can't be exported (for example, security or cleaning) are paid at subsistence/minimum wage rates. All the research evidence points in a single direction. Labour force participation levels increase with educational achievement; people with a third level qualification are almost twice as likely to be employed as people who only hold primary level education.[6]

History Lesson: The Disappearing Jobs

In the early 1970s in Cabra West, staying in school until you completed the Leaving Certificate was almost an indication of genius. All of my peers had departed the education system long before then. The lads who did best secured apprenticeships; everyone else was lucky to get any job. In a similar vein, the girls took up employment at 14 or 15, many working in the local sewing factories that dotted Glasnevin Industrial Estate and Dominick Street. To the best of my knowledge, none of those clothing factories is in existence today. As Ireland became a high labour cost country, factory jobs began to be disappear. Today you are more likely to bump into

Mary Poppins than a sewing machine mechanic.[7] In future, what will the people from Cabra West (and every other working class area in Ireland) do to find employment? There are only so many retail opportunities in Arnott's or service roles in Starbucks. As the *type* of jobs changes, we have to educate our people to meet this changing demand. That's not some capitalist claptrap – getting the worker bees ready for the harvest.[8] At the heart of human dignity is the ability to secure employment and contribute economically. It's difficult to be self-actualised and reach your full potential if you are signing on for the Dole at Hatch 45. People 'Cap and Gown', not to collect a piece of paper, but to connect to a job. While the social welfare system supports people who get caught in the unemployment trap, this was originally intended to be a temporary solution.[9]

Case Example: Bin Men

Earlier on, I touched on a bit of my own family history. Here's another quick installment. When my father was younger, he spent several years working as a Bin Man. At that time (1950s) this was a physically demanding job. Household waste, including fireplace ashes, could be extremely heavy. The waste was placed into round steel bins and left outside domestic houses and business premises for collection. The Bin Man's job was to lift these bins, above shoulder height, and tip the rubbish into a truck, essentially just a large container with sliding doors along the side.[10] As each section became fully loaded, they moved along the side of the truck, putting the rubbish into the next available slot. Over time, the job changed. The use of black plastic bags, which couldn't take heavy rubbish, became more widespread. Around the early 1990s, 'wheelie bins' were introduced where the lift was completed mechanically by the truck. Each of these developments made this job physically easier. That's the good news. The bad news is that these changes decimated employment. According to Jim Lynch,[11] employment in that section of Dublin City Council declined by about 75 per cent

48

across those years. It's difficult to be precise as other factors were in the mix, including the introduction of a charge by weight system and privatization of refuse collection. However, there's little doubt that a huge chunk of these jobs disappeared forever. Jobs like 'Bin Man' may not have been glamorous, but they were sought after (one of the attractions was that the crews could finish early when the work was completed and they also received gifts at Christmas from householders and businesses).

Key Point: These jobs could be completed with minimum train-ing and no formal education. They were an outlet for early school leavers, an avenue that no longer exists for the almost 9,000 young people who currently leave school before the Leaving Certificate every year.[12]

Gis' A Job

There are other examples. To obtain a driver's license, everyone is now required to complete the Driver Theory Test. This means sitting at a computer screen and answering 35 of 40 questions cor-rectly. These '40 questions' come from a larger pool of circa 1,000 questions which have to be memorised (statistically, the chances of guessing 87.5 per cent of questions correctly is almost zero). So, how do you become a driver if you struggle with literacy or numeracy? The answer is that you can't and this job is closed to people who struggle in these areas. In early 2016, my niece was delighted to secure a temporary job in a foreign bank in the IFSC in Dublin. When the application arrived (via email and 7 attach-ments), she had to complete just over 50 pages of documentation. The unschooled and the unskilled can't even get a temporary role. In the past, while disadvantaged groups didn't make it to college they could access low-level jobs that didn't require much training but, 'Those type of jobs are scarcer than Rocking-Horse Shit.'[13] The choice has become stark. Finish your education. Then get a job. Or drop out of education and collect unemployment benefits. At a societal level, Ireland needs to develop its 'Human Capital' to secure these new types of employment. Unless, of course, we find oil in the Bog of Allen! We can rant about the downsides of globalisation and technological change. We can fantasise about glorious former times when car manufacturing plants dotted Dublin. Alternatively, we can take a leap into the future through education. As a small, open economy on the edge of Europe we have to recognise the world as it is, not as we want it to be.

Global Innovators

If 'Ireland Inc.' really wants to win on the world stage (as global innovators in strategically chosen areas in parallel with being great Riverdancers), the education sector has an enormous role to play. Without education, people are vulnerable to unemployment (can't get a job) and redundancy (can't hold an existing job which is open to *technology substitution* or low wage competition from overseas). All the evidence suggests that low-skilled work will continue to migrate outwards. In a high-tech (service) economy where the numbers employed in agriculture and manufacturing are continually declining, solving the educational disadvantage question has morphed from a 'nice-to-do' social justice question into a mainstream economic issue. The assumption here is that we want to avoid a two-tier economy where one group of tax-paying employees subsidise another (continually growing) group of people who are long-term unemployed. In addition to the brutal negative personal consequences, people who educationally underperform vis a vis their potential can become a financial burden on the state, sometimes for an entire lifetime.[14]

Pursuing a Dual Strategy

The concept of moving up the value chain was popularised by Michael Porter in his book *Competitive Advantage.*[15] Porter defined value as the amount buyers are willing to pay for what an organisation provides. Implicit in the notion of 'moving up the value chain' is a hierarchy with most value being created in higher end roles. From a job creation perspective, the value chain is really better understood as a *value pyramid*. Only a relatively small number of jobs are actually available at the very top-end (highest value creation activities, for example Pharmaceutical R&D) as against the larger volume of jobs available in the so-called middle-value added activities further down the pyramid (for example Pharmaceutical Manufacturing). At the bottom of this pyramid are service jobs which we've referred to earlier, in other words, you can't send your 'house cleaning' work to Bangladesh, it has to be completed locally (if it was possible to outsource cleaning roles, they'd be gone already). Nationally, we don't pursue a single job creation strategy; in practice; several strands are worked on simultaneously. Alex McDonnell takes up this point:

> To focus the bulk of our efforts on chasing high value added jobs is a bit like Toyota deciding it's only going to make Lexus cars and ignore the other market segments. Unless we plan to abandon people who, for the foreseeable future, are going to remain a majority of the workforce, then we have to find a portfolio of solutions that cater for the diverse competencies that exist in the Irish labour force and will exist in the near future.

But, even the jobs that Alex describes as mid-level in terms of added value – jobs like Engineering Technicians – require a college education.

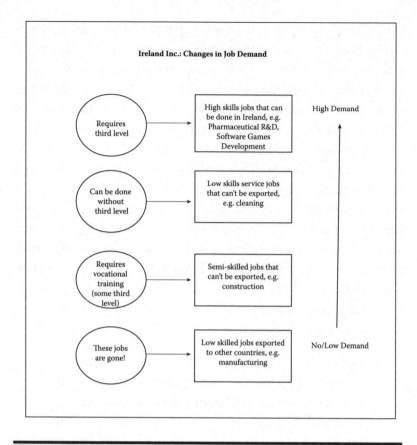

Ireland Inc.: Changes in Job Demand

Asian Experience

Some years ago I lived and worked in Singapore, completing a role that took me across most parts of Asia. At that time the relative cost of labour was as follows: If costs were baselined at €1 per hour in Ireland, the comparison costs was 30 cents per hour in Taiwan and 10 cents in China. A couple of years later, I was back in Guangdong province in China, the so-called 'denim capital of the world' where vast swathes of poorly paid workers produce a mountain of blue jeans. No matter how productive a clothing factory is in Ireland, it's impossible to compete against these low-cost, labour-intensive operations. The danger posed is that people who don't have the skills to shift into this emerging economy get left behind. People who don't attend college can't compete for high end jobs and face a lifetime of earnings marginalisation. You have to 'fish' where the fish are swimming. And the fish are swimming upstream to higher added value jobs completed by people who have access to third level (sometimes 'fourth Level,' that is, post-doctoral studies) education. In short, as Patrick Clancy suggests: 'Educational performance is increasingly synonymous with occupational performance.'[16]

You Only have to Fix this 'Once'

Access programmes that break the cycle of educational disadvantage offer a positive intergenerational impact. When an individual participates in continued education, this often influences his or her siblings to enter college. In one study, while over half of the participants in a UCC sample were the first in their immediate family to attend college, almost 45 per cent of these students' siblings have since entered Higher Education. A similar phenomenon has been reported across a number of colleges. In Trinity College, one study[17] suggested a *ripple effect* taking place within families (including cousins) as individuals pass on knowledge and understanding about the education system. When they graduate, some students remain in their original communities which can have a multiplier effect at a community level, demystifying third level education for others. Even those who leave and move to better areas, are known and become role models. There's a huge upside in encouraging as many people as we possibly can to take on the full educational journey, for themselves and for the generations which follow.[18]

Permanently Left Behind

Changes to the labour market are subtle and occur over time. Without being alarmist about the employment situation, logically the future economy will not provide decent jobs for people who can't complete value-adding roles. People who don't attend college[19] will tend to be employed in minimum wage roles or be out of work altogether. During the recent recession, many people had to re-skill. As jobs in the construction sector disappeared, architects, engineers, project managers and other professionals secured new roles. Under the government's Springboard initiative, thousands of people went back to college for intensive retraining in information technology and other fields. But, an important point is that these people were *already* college graduates. They had the baseline education and weren't fazed by a short, intensive period of re-training. In essence, their earlier training had equipped them for future change. After a short, bumpy period of career turbulence, they were able to move forward. In stark contrast, a huge tranche of Irish people – the Access groups identified earlier – are now in danger of being *permanently* left behind. One respondent noted that a high percentage of customer service and administration roles now require a degree to gain entry, despite the fact that these jobs are relatively straightforward. While organisations that over-hire may be storing up future problems (staff dissatisfaction and low morale), the point remains that people can't get in the door without the requisite qualification. Intermediate level jobs are essentially being 'hollowed out'. But, unlike buses, when you miss this opportunity, there isn't another one coming along anytime soon.

As the market requirements change from *brawn* to *brains*, we are witnessing the formation of a new 'sub-working class', that is, people cut off from participation in society because they don't have and can't get a job. While there was always a group people who were unemployed, the membership is becoming semi-permanent and the size of this group has the potential to expand exponentially. The medium-term danger lies in creating a disenfranchised group that has no economic stake in society. Education is the glue that can stop Irish society from coming apart. In parts of Manila in the Philippines there are many high-security estates where wealthy people live. These estates are guarded by security teams with all the usual paraphernalia: attack dogs, cameras, weapons, SUVs emblazoned with security logos and so on. Could this be a glimpse of Ireland at some future point? Will we erect high walls around Foxrock where you have to show a residents' permit to gain entry? I'm guessing that most people wouldn't want this visibly unequal

Irish society to come to pass and the recommendations (proposed later) will stop this scenario from evolving.

Government Spending Choices

There are always significant pressures on resources – competition for public monies between education, health, social protection, justice and so on. In practice, all public services are vulnerable to reductions in allocations, particularly where it's difficult to present a comprehensive picture of (a) how something contributes to socio-economic goals; (b) why a particular level of investment is important; (c) what clear outcomes will be delivered for the investment made. On all three fronts, we haven't managed to make a clear business case for investing in education. By focusing on the social justice arguments, Access has come to be seen as a special-interest topic, something to be lobbied for in pre-Budget submissions (except that there's no one lobbying on this particular issue). In the grounds of St. Anne's Park there's a large folly, defined as 'a building constructed primarily for decoration that has no practical purpose.' By ignoring the solid business case for investment to correct educational disadvantage the social justice arguments made are often seen as 'folly', that is, nice to do as surplus funds permit. What gets completely lost in this debate is that opportunities for individuals and families offered through education translate into a significant dividend for society as a whole, both socially and economically. The OECD captured this key point:

> ... an investment that can help foster economic growth, contribute to personal and social development and reduce social inequity. Like any investment, it involves both costs and returns. Some of the returns are monetary and directly related to the labour market, while others are personal, social, cultural and more broadly economic.[20]

Because we haven't yet been able to clearly articulate the business case, educational disadvantage limps along and is never systematically addressed.

The positive financial upside that goes well beyond an individual analysis. Based on a substantial body of work completed during the construction of this book, Dr Brian O'Kelly has estimated that the 'net benefit' to the state of someone completing their educational journey and taking up employment (versus spending a lifetime receiving unemployment benefit) is 'north' of €1 million. Not a bad return for an initial €50,000 investment! While it's difficult to calculate a precise figure (there are a range of variables), the financial benefits to society are of such magnitude that they cannot be ignored. Outside of education, very few initiatives could ever produce such a significant return from a relatively modest initial investment. Even if Brian's calculations are overstated (and he says he has actually been conservative in putting these numbers together), the upside for the state in pushing the education agenda is enormous. Bottom Line: Going to college represents a €1 million decision for each individual; it also has a €1 million+ upside for the state for each person who qualifies.

Who Takes Up the Available Jobs?

Let's briefly touch on a slightly more controversial point. One of my brothers, Peter, has been institutionalised for a number of years in a care facility for people with dementia. It's extremely sad, but Peter is well taken care of. The facility is spotlessly clean and there's a good link with all of the patients. While I've haven't audited this, my guess is that around 90 per cent of the staff in this very large care facility are non-EU nationals, mostly from India and the Philippines. In a similar vein, our two local petrol stations are staffed with Asian personnel, who are extremely customer focused and pleasant to deal with. The question is: Why are these jobs not filled by EU citizens? Based on the unemployment statistics, we know that there are enough Irish people available to do this work. So, will the Irish people 'not do' this work? Some other countries have addressed the question of filling lower-level jobs through immigration. For example, in Germany there is a heavy reliance on the migrant population, and it's similar in Dubai. I'm not being xenophobic here. While completing the education journey is the best option for most people, we know that not everyone will choose this route and there have to be alternatives. If you believe that there's more dignity for people in having a job than being in receipt of unemployment benefit (as I do), all available jobs should be firstly allocated to Irish and EU citizens. Being on the dole was never intended to become a lifestyle choice. It was meant to be a safety net, not a sofa! For example, in relation to community employment opportunities, one executive from the not-for-profit sector told me that about 5 per cent (1 in 20) of the people interviewed who get a job offer decide to take up the role. Essentially, they don't want a full time job. They have been 'sent' for the interview and have to comply with this but it's not compulsory that they take up the role offered. While this issue is slightly outside our current focus, there has to be a better mechanism to align people who are unemployed with available jobs. A graphic representation of these trends is detailed on page 60.

Education Changes Lives:

Norman Harte

Mature Student, University College Dublin

I come from a typical working class family in Artane. My Father was a labourer and my Mother was a home worker (making rosary beads at home while also taking care of the family). My Dad, who'd left school aged 12, wanted a better life for his kids. In particular, he wanted us to get an apprenticeship and would say: 'If you have a trade you'll never be out of work. And, if you can't find work at your trade you could always dig a hole until you do.'

My education was typical of the time. It was based on the idea of repeating what you learned. I left school with the Inter Certificate (now the Junior Certificate). To my surprise it was one of the best results achieved in the school and we were called in to meet the principal. My Mother, convinced I'd done something wrong, kept asking if I had cheated during the exam! At the meeting, I was offered a place to continue onto the Leaving Certificate, but I'd absolutely no appetite to stay. We thanked the Principal and left. Traveling home on the bus, I got a taste of inner city Dublin humour, my Mother said: 'Well son, you got one of the best Inter Certs in that school, so there's one of two things going on. Either you are one of the brightest in that school, which I find hard to believe, or the rest of them in that year are really thick.' Leave it to a Mother to have the last word.

I worked as a storeman in the music industry, posting records out to retail shops across Ireland. Shortly after, I became an apprentice electrician, the dream job. During the apprenticeship we had to acquire a range of craft certificates. So, back to school, but in a very different (more positve) learning environment. Later on, I joined a Trade Union and became active as a branch committee member and, for a time, was on the Dublin Trades Council. In this environment I met people from all walks of life, some with similar backgrounds, others with a more academic base. It had a huge influence. Continuing to dabble in part-time education, I studied CCTV installation, Fibre Optics and Trade Union Studies in the Peoples College. Eventually, I enrolled in a Human Resources Programme at the College of Industrial Relations in Ranelagh (now NCI). But through a combination of the arrival of our second child and being stony broke at that time, I dropped out after year one, much to the annoyance of my wife.

In work, the interest in learning continued. I was certified as a Trainer and a Facilitator and then got a job in the Equality Department, taking a distance learning diploma (Equality Studies) in Galway University. In 2011, when I eventually signed up for a BA in Business at UCD, I was 54 years old, finally 'scratching an itch' that had been bugging me for years.

University was a bit of a culture shock. We were informed that the secret wasn't just repeating, but gaining a deep understanding of the subject from a number of different perspectives (welcome to the world of academic referencing). When the text books arrived, I panicked; would I have time to read even one of these? The study guide supplied by UCD helped us to focus and a friend in the Trade Union movement calmed me down when he said: 'People can be well read. But the trick is to understand what you've read'.

The biggest barrier for me was learning how to write in an acceptable format, definitely the hardest nut to crack. I've always admired good writing, the ability to develop arguments logically. Under the direction of the course tutors, slowly but surely, confidence in our writing skills was built. When I graduated in 2015, my wife was standing there beside me. She'd been cheering me on, over all those years.

Looking back on the journey now, I'd say that there's never a right time. The main barrier to returning to education is overcoming fears and insecurites inside yourself. Continually asking, 'will I be up to the mark' and everyting that goes with that. I drive my own kids mad, talking about the power of education. Because I really believe that it's never too late to go back to college and change your life for the better.

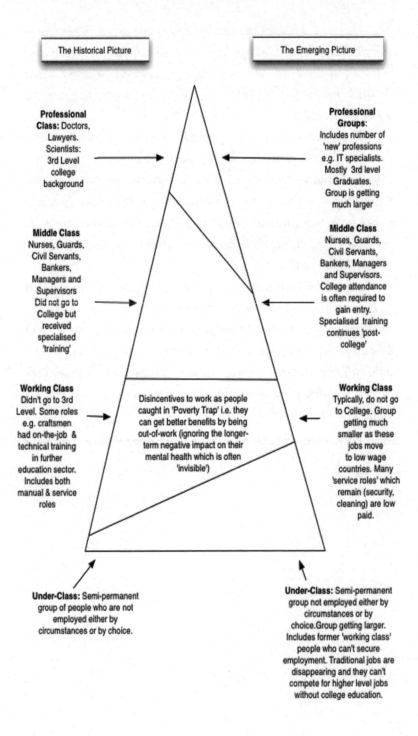

The Historical Picture

The Emerging Picture

Professional Class: Doctors, Lawyers. Scientists: 3rd Level college background

Professional Groups: Includes number of 'new' professions e.g. IT specialists. Mostly 3rd level Graduates. Group is getting much larger

Middle Class Nurses, Guards, Civil Servants, Bankers, Managers and Supervisors Did not go to College but received specialised 'training'

Middle Class Nurses, Guards, Civil Servants, Bankers, Managers and Supervisors. College attendance is often required to gain entry. Specialised training continues 'post-college'

Working Class Didn't go to 3rd Level. Some roles e.g. craftsmen had on-the-job & technical training in further education sector. Includes both manual & service roles

Disincentives to work as people caught in 'Poverty Trap' i.e. they can get better benefits by being out-of-work (ignoring the longer-term negative impact on their mental health which is often 'invisible')

Working Class Typically, do not go to College. Group getting much smaller as these jobs move to low wage countries. Many 'service roles' which remain (security, cleaning) are low paid.

Under-Class: Semi-permanent group of people who are not employed either by circumstances or by choice.

Under-Class: Semi-permanent group not employed either by circumstances or by choice. Group getting larger. Includes former 'working class' people who can't secure employment. Traditional jobs are disappearing and they can't compete for higher level jobs without college education.

Chapter 3:

THE IRISH EDUCATION SYSTEM: PRE-SCHOOL, PRIMARY AND SECONDARY

Q: *What does the 'education system' look like today?*

A: *It's labyrinthine! Some bits are great; other elements need work.*

When it comes to education, mapping what currently exists is a challenge. The sheer size and complexity of the system makes it difficult to understand or critique how the existing structures work. One respondent remarked: 'It's hard to get your head around this.' He wasn't joking. Our task in this chapter is essentially 'fog clearance'. The goal is to describe the mainstream education system. Before we drill into this, a couple of introductory points are worth making. Firstly, understanding what exists today is a necessary starting point. While this is arguably not the most exciting chapter ever written, it's not possible to evaluate the existing system until we understand how it actually works. Secondly, the sheer size and complexity of the education system acts as a brake on change. While it's relatively easy to review, evaluate, even to change individual pieces of the jigsaw, our task here is broader. We want to interrogate the design philosophy of the overall system. In the absence of this holistic review, piecemeal changes don't fundamentally tackle the problem of educational disadvantage. The system chugs along, producing the existing or marginally superior outcomes. Finally, while the task is to take a Polaroid snapshot of the existing system, I have to insert a caveat. While the points made are *directionally* correct, they will not be absolutely correct in every single educational institution or geographical area. I've focused mostly on practices within schools and colleges in the Dublin region. There's no intent to convey a Dublin is *better* message (my personal circumstances mean that Dublin is *nearer*). To make a start, let's take a high-level look at each stage of the education system in the order that students typically move through them. Firstly, we take a quick glance at the policies that govern the system.

Policy Making

State-funded educational policy, implementation and governance are led by the Department of Education and Skills (DES). The formal elements include pre-school, primary, post-primary, further education (FE) and higher education (HE).[1] At primary level, 3,200+ schools are controlled by patron bodies. A significant majority of these (circa 90 per cent) are owned by the Catholic Church but funded publicly through the DES. At post-primary level, there are 730+ schools. Around half of these are voluntary, that is, privately run secondary schools, the remainder being community schools, community colleges and comprehensive schools (post-primary level schools follow the same curriculum regardless of title). In terms of sheer numbers, it's certainly a wide remit with almost 4,000 individual schools.

Education Investment

In 2010, the average spend on education across OECD countries was 6.3 per cent of Gross Domestic Product (GDP), with some variation ranging between 5 per cent and 7 per cent.[2] With current spending at 6.4 per cent, Ireland hovers around the median. But, assessing educational *effectiveness* is broader than a simple financial equation. We need to understand how the money is actually spent and the outcomes produced. For example, Ireland spends circa €19.2 billion annually on health services (2015 figures) which is just over 12 per cent of GDP[3] versus an average European spend of circa 9 per cent. When it comes to putting money into health, we are well ahead of the game. While this might come as a surprise it's a fact that, relative to national income, Ireland is the second-highest spending country in the world on health.[4] So is everyone in Ireland *delighted* with this, jumping up and down with unbridled admiration about how well the health services are delivered? Quite the opposite. We are constantly bombarded by stories about patients lying on A&E department trolleys, awful misdiagnosis cases and a host of other breakdowns in the system.

Key Point

Investing sufficient money in an area is certainly part of the success equation. But financial resources need to be expertly deployed. It's not just a question of money. It's also a question of having a clear philosophy and solid implementation. The 'm' in **m**anagement is as important (or even more important) than the 'm' in **m**oney. While significant educational progress has been made in Ireland over recent years, the educational disadvantage question remains in the stubbornly difficult to fix category. Pouring more money into educational disadvantage, as a stand-alone response, won't provide the answer.

Different Streams

Throughout the Republic of Ireland, all primary school children follow a standard curriculum. At secondary level, this curriculum is taught at either *ordinary* or *higher* levels. While students normally choose subjects and levels,[5] in some schools the menu has quite restricted options to compete at higher level. Áine Hyland tells the story of visiting an inner-city second level school in Dublin in which no STEM[6] subject was taught at higher level in the senior cycle (that is, to Leaving Certificate). Let me repeat that in case you think it's a typo: *zero* higher-level STEM subjects were available. So regardless of how bright the kids enrolling in that school were, their choices were limited from day one. The number of Leaving Certificate points which they could aspire to (which determines what students can study in college) had an upper ceiling, pre-set by an educational institution which had set its sights that low. This 'separate but equal' idea (about the different types of second level schools) has been likened to the fiction used to justify the former system of segregation in South Africa;[7] perhaps a better label is separate and unequal. Robert Ward, Marketing Director in NCI, offered another vignette:

> I met a number of students from a working class school who were keen on coming to NCI and were on target to get the points. They were genuinely excited. Except when we realised that they were all doing foundation level maths for the Leaving Certificate. This meant they didn't meet the entry requirements for any college course. Nearly all courses at the time required at least pass level maths. Everyone in that school had been steered into doing foundation level. They were never informed this would effectively mean they couldn't go to any of the mainstream colleges. Setting low expectations from the start, the school had effectively barred them from third level.[8]

Compulsory School Attendance

The Education Act 1998 dictates that education is compulsory between the ages of six and sixteen,[9] in other words, all students have to complete the Junior but not the Senior cycle of education. Not everyone makes it that far.[10] In Ireland, around 1,000 students each year fail to make the transition between primary and secondary school – leaving school at around twelve years of age – despite the existing law.[11] Within the secondary cycle, around 3 per cent of children leave school without any qualifications at all, and approximately 9,000 students annually leave school before the completion of the Leaving Certificate. To put this another way, circa 10 per cent of the total student population who commence second level education don't make it to the finish line, the *lost group* that John Walshe identified earlier. These numbers represent the continuation of a long, negative tradition in Irish education. While the system works reasonably well for many students (we will return to this point later), it goes horribly wrong for this cohort of learners who never fulfil their potential. Take these numbers into other arenas. How would you feel if 10 per cent of the time the landing gear on airplanes didn't click into place? What would your response be if one in ten patients died during *routine* operations? Yet, somehow we tolerate this huge fallout from the education system, a tentative first-slip into what can become a lifetime of deprivation. Tackling education disadvantage is an effort to remove the tripwire from the path of students who are currently failing to stay the course. One respondent argued that, at some level, we tolerate this because we fundamentally believe that one system can't meet all students' needs. But hold that 10 per cent of 9,000 students number in your mind for the moment while we continue our journey through the current system.

No Fees

The education system (like the Health System) is twin-tiered. There are a variety of options for families who want to send their children to 'fee paying' schools. In state-owned schools, while there are no tuition fees,[12] parents pay for books, uniforms and often make voluntary contributions. At primary and secondary school level, supplementary welfare grants are available to people in receipt of long-term welfare benefits, or to those who can prove that the costs of education cause undue hardship. At third level, technically there are no fees, but about 50 per cent of students pay a 'Registration Fee' to cover the cost of exams and student support. This fee is currently €3,000 per annum (the charge is waived for the 50 per cent of students based on a means test). So, at least in theory, we have a free education system. In reality, there are very high costs of attending school – but let's stay with the no fees ideal for the moment.

EARLY CHILDHOOD EDUCATION

Early Childcare

In recent years, early Childhood Care and Education (ECCE) has become a topic of central importance and debate. With many families having two working parents, the cost of childcare is an issue that impacts huge numbers of people. In 2010, a free pre-school year was announced by the Government for all children (aged between three and four years). This provides universal care for three hours each day for all children, that is, it's not means tested.[13] With regard to Early Childhood Education, the implementation of this policy has been outsourced by the Department of Education and Skills (DES) and is run by private operators, jointly funded through a combination of public subsidy and by parents who use the facilities (many children are in childcare for longer than three hours each day with parents paying for the balance of time spent there). The free year of childcare is currently being extended to two free years before a child enters primary school. Before you drop this book and shout Hallelujah out loud, remember that this applies to all children, regardless of family wealth or circumstances. While politically popular, this change does absolutely nothing to address education disadvantage.[14] From a policy point of view, this move is reminiscent of the quip that 'politicians are people who become popular by giving other people grants out of their own money'; in other words, it drains money out of the system which could be spent on alleviating educational disadvantage.

Childcare Providers

At the time of writing, there are around 4,300 childcare providers in Ireland.[15] Some, but not all, operators try to make a distinction between child *minding* and early childhood *education*. As a minimum, anyone who drops their kids into a crèche wants them to be safe and happy. But the government want more than this, seeing this time as an opportunity for 'early learning'. From a ton of research studies, we know that younger children are sponges and absorb huge amounts of information, potentially giving them a head start before they enter the formal school system. In relation to early childcare education, the department's involvement is hands-off (other than footing some of the bill), a stance that's difficult to understand when all of the other elements of the education system are firmly under their remit. The fact that the DES has outsourced this huge 'chunk' of the educational system without the requisite governance mechanisms seems doubly strange.[16] The DES has not escaped criticism in the past along broadly similar lines. Fergus Finlay, CEO of Barnardos, who was interviewed during this research, previously commented that the DES:

> Must be the only Department of Education in the world who don't seem interested in education. They only seem interested in keeping the teachers' unions happy.[17]

In speaking with people quite familiar with this area, a number of specific criticisms were levelled at the way early childcare education currently operates:

a. No Curriculum: There is currently no standard pre-school curriculum; each school follows its own programme. More accurately, there is a suggested curriculum,[18] but it is not enforced. The guidelines are voluntary.[19] Let's hope that you are sending your children to an institution that knows what it's doing (hey, there's another thing to feel guilty about)!

b. Staff Qualifications: There are no minimum staff qualifications. Most (but certainly not all) staff working in this area are trained up to 'Level 5'[20] in childcare. There is a Level 6 programme but this focuses mainly on supervision of other childcare workers, not on learning per se. Some staff have Montessori or degree level qualifications, but this isn't an entry requirement. We wouldn't want an untrained nurse to take our blood or an unqualified taxi driver to take us home. But unqualified teachers to mind our children – that's deemed acceptable.

c. Teaching Practice: There's no agreed pedagogic practice. Each school decides this on a stand-alone basis. Given the points made, this is largely a subsidised child-minding (not teaching) service. Further, providing early childcare benefits for all children does nothing to correct the imbalance in the education system that's tilted against children growing up in disadvantaged areas. Could it be different?

Not New

Early childhood learning is certainly not a new topic. While there are differences in approaches, childhood education is underpinned by one common principle: the curriculum and practice must be adapted to the maturing needs, abilities and interests of the child. This was the principle embodied in the Kindergarten Program (Friedrich Froebel, 1782-1852), the first early childhood program to be widely adopted in Europe. The kindergarten movement was propelled by the industrial revolution and the introduction of women into the factory labour force. Maria Montessori's (1870-1952) early childhood program was also widely adopted in Europe and further afield. After World War I, early childhood education came to be seen as an important first step on the educational ladder. While there are commonly accepted universal needs in early childhood education, the needs in disadvantaged communities are quite specific, particularly the idea of getting parents (most often the mother), heavily involved. Maria O'Neill offered the following observation:

> With some parents you see it from day one. The books are bought and covered. It shows an interest. You can see that they want to make a real difference.

Disadvantaged Perspective

Phyllis Levinstein, a pioneer in the Parent Childhood Home Programme, started researching this area over 50 years ago in the USA. One of the initial questions tackled was, 'when should early learning start?' According to Dr. Josephine Bleach in the National College of Ireland, the correct answer is, 'in the womb'. Pregnant women need to become engaged around early learning practices before their child is born (the central feature of this type of intervention is a recognition of the importance of parents in the educational cycle). The imbalance in the education system for disadvantaged children is not hearsay; it's scientifically measurable. Today, children from disadvantaged areas come into a crèche (at age three) knowing between 400 and 500 words. That sounds impressive until you discover that, at the exact same age, children in advantaged areas already know 1,500 words. Unless there's an intervention, that head start advantage continues for life. But, when there's a positive intervention, kids who present with as little as 10 per cent of the language they should exhibit for their age can move back up to 100 per cent over the next 18-42 months. In other words, early intervention works and this deficit is fixable, assuming that the parents are on board. One person who works extensively in this space commented:

> In some disadvantaged communities, it's like guerrilla warfare. We have to sell the message from house to house, converting individual families to the benefits of education.

We know that children spend about 20 per cent of their time in school and 80 per cent outside of school. Confining learning to *within* the school walls misses a huge developmental opportunity. The good news is that there are well-researched models of best practice which can bridge the gap for these learning deficits. The bad news: this activity requires investment.

Preparing for Life

In 2008, with funding from Atlantic Philanthropies and the Department of Children and Youth Affairs, a programme called Preparing for Life commenced in a number of disadvantaged areas in North County Dublin. The programme was run by the Northside Partnership with the explicit aim of improving the life outcomes of children and families living in those areas. The design was based on the best international practices around working with families. A centrally important design feature was that the outcomes would be independently audited by the Geary Institute (University College Dublin), providing an evidence-based assessment. In simple terms, this would either work or it wouldn't. In order to make the design bulletproof, the researchers used a randomized control method, that is, some families were part of the programme and the outcomes were clinically measured against matched families who were not part of the programme. It ran for over five years in what Liz Canavan described as 'playing the long game.'[21]

The core design was to upskill parents in child development and promote positive parenting (nutrition, bonding exercises and so on). An array of measures were in place to assess outcomes, including health, social and emotional development, language development and cognition. While a full review of the programme is outside of our scope, here are a few highlights: At age four, children in the Preparing for Life programme were less likely to be overweight (23 per cent were overweight – in line with the national average – versus 41 per cent of the 'non-treatment' group). Incredibly, by age four there was a full 10-point gap in IQ between the children who received the Preparing for Life Programme and those who didn't, based on a standardised cognitive test: 13 per cent scored 'below average' on this test, versus 57 per cent of the children who didn't receive the programme. The cost: €2,000 per family, per year. In one of the longest and most rigorous studies of family intervention ever conducted in Ireland, this programme was scientifically proven to work.

Let's switch focus now and look at what happens when a child reaches the age of four or five and makes the transition into primary school.

PRIMARY LEVEL EDUCATION

The educationalists who met during the research phase offered a 'rule of thumb' as follows. At primary level, both the student's and the teacher's morale is generally high. There's less emphasis of *teaching to an exam*, allowing more scope for innovation around teaching practice. Dr. Paul Downes in St Patrick's Teacher Training College remarked, 'Generally, kids love primary school and they love their teacher.' Over fifty years later, I can vividly recall my primary school teacher (Mrs. O'Malley) and many happy years learning to read, write, draw and make stuff using exotic materials (such as Plasticine) which we didn't have at home. Young children are generally happy in school. And there's good evidence to support the idea that they are served well by a group of high-quality teachers.

Teacher Formation

In Ireland, the development of primary school teachers happens over three to four intensive years. Primary teacher training has perhaps the highest level of class contact time across the third level sector. It's hard to get into teaching and the course is demanding. In addition to mastering a wide range of subjects, trainee teachers also learn pedagogy (teaching approaches), how to lead a classroom, and to communicate effectively. In contrast, the formation of secondary schools teachers (subject experts in one or two areas) happens in a shorter timeframe, currently over two years.[22] It used to be said, perhaps unfairly, that people who completed a degree but were still confused about what they wanted to do in life became secondary school teachers. It was respectable, permanent and pensionable and offered that great carrot – the summer holidays. As primary school teaching requires very high points to gain entry,[23] this means that it's predominantly middle class students who go into the profession. There may even be a bit of intellectual snobbery at play here. According to Áine Hyland, teacher education was one of the *last* areas to open up to the idea that Access Students should be allowed entry on lower-points entry system. We will see later that social class is a definite factor in relation to the maintenance of educational disadvantage. Having someone 'like us' standing at the top of the classroom is an important role model for pupil motivation. It also has an important, albeit subtle, impact around the setting of high versus low expectations. Consider the following story ...

High Expectations

In 1964, a famous experiment, was conducted by Robert Rosenthal, Professor of Psychology at Harvard University, at an elementary school in San Francisco.[24] *The idea was to figure out the implication of teachers' bias, for example, being told that certain children in their class were destined to succeed. Rosenthal took a normal IQ test (Flanagan's Test of General Ability) and dressed it up as a different test. The cover read: 'Harvard Test of Inflected Acquisition.' Rosenthal told the teachers that this new test from Harvard could predict which kids were about to experience dramatic growth in their IQ. After the kids took the test, he then randomly chose several from a number of different classes with different teachers. While there was nothing to distinguish the children selected, he told their teachers that the test predicted these particular children were on the verge of an intensive intellectual bloom.*

As he followed the children over the next two years, Rosenthal discovered that the teachers' expectations really did affect the students. 'If teachers had been led to expect greater gains in IQ, then increasingly, those kids gained higher IQ scores.' But how do expectations influence IQ? As Rosenthal did more research, he found that expectations affect teachers' moment-to-moment interactions with the children they teach in a thousand almost invisible ways. With students that they expect to succeed, teachers give more time to answer questions, more specific feedback and more approval. They consistently touch, nod and smile at those children. 'It's not magic, it's not mental telepathy,' Rosenthal says. If expectations can change the performance of children, the question is how do we get teachers to set high expectations, particularly for children who are 'not like me' or those who may be experiencing difficulties in their wider life?

Immigrant Children

In a relatively short period of time, Irish schools have had to deal with a heterogeneous student intake.[25] Between 2002 and 2006, there was an 87 per cent increase in the number of immigrant children into the Irish school system. There are currently over 48,000 students from over 160 different nationalities in Irish schools. Around 10 per cent of the entire school population are the so-called 'new Irish'. Seventy per cent of these newcomer students are non-English (native) speaking, with the additional teaching requirement that this implies.[26] This pattern has significant educational implications. Smyth and others have noted the potential *ghettoisation* of schools where newcomers are highly represented in some urban and disadvantaged schools and under-represented in Gaelscoileanna (Irish-speaking schools). While 40 per cent of primary schools have zero newcomer children, they make up more than 20 per cent of the student body in some primary schools.[27] While the DES has provided resources at both primary and post-primary levels to support pupils whose first language is not English, there have been significant cutbacks since 2009 with a maximum of two English as an Additional Language (EAL) teachers per school, irrespective of the total number of EAL pupils. Bottom Line: The educational challenge faced by some schools has become significantly tougher. A centrally important point is that this steeper climb is often faced by schools located in disadvantaged areas who were already playing on an uneven surface. Despite the general gains made in education, in some areas educational disadvantage isn't getting better; it's actually getting worse – a point that applies at both primary and secondary level.

The Development of 'Alternative Schools'

Educate Together schools and the Gaelscoil movement[28] offer an alternative to the Catholic-dominated school system. The fundamental logic of the school system in Ireland is based on the principle of parental choice, in other words, that there is a competitive environment among parents for the best opportunities for their children.[29] But parental choice can be a fallacy when this involves driving small children several miles to a 'better school'. All things being equal, parents want their children to attend a *local* school. If a family doesn't have access to transport, there may be zero choice. Indeed, sending a child to a *posh* school outside the local area can have social downsides in terms of bullying and isolation. Sometimes, the local school is the *only* school. In order to understand their reasoning, I've spoken with several families whose children attend 'non-traditional schools'. While the sample size is too small to make generalisations, one interesting idea emerged: parents want their children to go to a *progressive* school. The Gaelschoils, in particular, have developed a reputation for high academic standards.[30] Also, they don't attract non-nationals who fail to see the value of learning through Irish. This opens up the intriguing possibility that the Irish-speaking schools are attractive to some parents because the other children are *like us*, that is, there is less racial diversity.[31] The current system for allocating resources to disadvantaged schools (DEIS, explored in more detail later) is a blunt instrument that doesn't take account of the wide variety of teaching challenges faced.

SECOND LEVEL EDUCATION

Where Should You Send Your Children to School?

To understand the current second level (post-primary) education system, it's worthwhile to take a (short) history lesson. For many years Ireland had two types of second level schools: (a) Secondary Schools, sometimes (mistakenly) seen as the natural home for bright kids, that is, those who were more academic, and (b) Technical or Vocational Schools (Techs) that offered an applied curriculum such as metalwork, woodwork, mechanical drawing and so on. At 12 years of age, children were streamed by 'interest/ability' and continued their educational journey along one of these two routes. The need for a vocational strand of education had been recognised as far back as 1930.[32] The 'Techs' offered two years post-primary education, allowing students to complete their 'Group Certificate'. Interestingly, at that time the Technical Schools also trained apprentices from a variety of trades.[33]

Church Resistance

One respondent argued that there was strong opposition to the establishment of the Vocational School system from the Catholic Church, which had a virtual monopoly on education up until that point. The compromise decision was that the teaching of the Intermediate (now Junior) and Leaving Certificates would be the exclusive preserve of the secondary schools. It follows that there was a marked difference in the curriculum between the two types of school. Secondary schools covered the basics (3Rs) plus the classics (Latin and Greek). Religion was not taught at that time in the 'Techs'. In effect, one educational route was being operated by the Church, the other by the state. The impact of this dual-streaming was to impose an educational ceiling on children who chose the vocational route. Educationally, the 'Group Certificate' represented a cul-de-sac. It would be many years before the idea of progression became part of the discourse in education – the idea that you could progress from a foundation programme and move onwards with your educational journey. At that time, children who chose the vocational route left 'Tech' with the 'Group Cert' and then looked for work. It was the educational terminal; the bus stopped here! As part of this separate streams idea, the teachers were affiliated to two different unions – the Association of Secondary Teachers Ireland (ASTI) and the Vocational Teachers' Association (later renamed the Teachers Union of Ireland (TUI), with a history of animosity between both groups across a range of issues.[34]

Two Educational Streams

Despite the somewhat inauspicious start, the Vocational Schools became successful. Apart from the attraction of a practical/vocational education, another reason helps to explain the enrolment growth. Up until 1967, secondary schools were fee-paying while the 'techs' were free. So, why did some parents pay for a secondary school education when Vocational Schools offered free education? For the exact same reason that parents today pay for grind schools – to give their children better opportunities. Despite the initial growth in student numbers, it soon became clear that the 'techs' were perceived as *lower on the totem pole*. The type of school that a student attended had a direct impact on future employability. At that time, the Leaving Certificate was a virtual *passport* into two secure and prestigious areas of employment – the Civil Service and the banks.[35] Arguably, the interests of many children (many more suited to a vocational education), were sacrificed on the altar of their parents' belief in stability, prestige or both.

Over time, Technical Schools essentially morphed into secondary schools and began to follow the same curriculum. While it's almost impossible to prove this, there is a strong sense that the teachers within the technical schools didn't like to be seen as part of the 'second division' of Irish education (everyone wants to play in the Champions League). Arguably, driven by the interests of the teachers (rather than the needs of the students), what had been two distinct forms of educational practice became virtually indistinguishable. We no longer had an academic stream running in parallel with a vocational stream; these educational tributaries combined into a single river. In Organisation Development, the technical name for this is *mission creep*, the expansion of a project beyond its original goals. The core question: is a 'one-size-fits-all' (standardised second level school curriculum) the right approach, or were we better served by having a dual approach? We now have a single curriculum for second level education, a system which doesn't meet the needs of a huge cohort of learners. All students are 'force fit' into a unitary system and then we seem surprised that (a) there's a huge drop out in terms of actual numbers, and (b) many of those who remain perform poorly. Recognising that the system doesn't work for a huge tranche of students, we have assembled a host of remediation initiatives – essentially welding additional 'wing mirrors' onto a car in which the engine has seized. We will return to this design flaw shortly; for the moment, bear with me on this short history lesson.

Developments in the 1960s

In the early 1960s the idea of a more centrally planned economy began to take shape and Ireland set its sights on membership of the European Union.[36] Rory O' Sullivan argued that during that period, the rhetoric of equality was imported into Ireland which led to an 'un-ease' with the two-stream education system which had been in place up until that time. If we conceptualise the secondary schools as a *blue stream* and the Vocational Schools as a *red stream,* there was an emerging argument for a *third way* in Irish education, that is, combining the approaches into what might be termed a *purple stream.* The Comprehensive (and later, the Community School) ideal was to offer both academic and vocational training under the same roof, in other words, two streams, one location.[37] Avoiding duplication of physical school buildings, having one principal and so on, seemed like a practical solution and a solid use of resources. But this *two streams* idea became subsumed and all schools began to offer the *same* curriculum, a single *blue stream* of education running across the Junior Certificate and the Leaving Certificate. The twin options (academic and vocational) – a pragmatic idea in place since the 1930s – became lost in a politically correct (but misguided) idea that all students should be offered equal opportunity, enacted through a one-size-fits-all curriculum. Forget about the needs and desires of individual students. It's analogous to designing an educational sausage machine that everyone gets thrown into. Most students survive (some thrive) and come out fully formed at the other end. Those whom the system doesn't suit get discarded as waste somewhere along the way. For students denied the vocational route (which has virtually disappeared) they are essentially offered an equal opportunity to fail. Arguably, the educational system was in better shape 70 years ago. We haven't made progress; we've actually gone backwards. With the history lesson completed (that's a promise), let's look at what exists today.

Junior Cycle

The Junior Cycle of education runs for three years. Students commence at 12 to 13 years of age and finish at 15 to 16. As with the later Leaving Certificate, English, Irish and Mathematics are compulsory subjects. In recent times a lot of work was undertaken to reform the junior cycle. The underpinning philosophy is that each student should leave school with a qualification, a centrally important idea which most educationalists support. However, in deciding how to measure achievement, there's a continuing belief across all levels of Irish education which could be described as 'test = best'. The Junior Certificate exam – originally designed in 1989 – quickly became a mirror image of the Leaving Certificate. The same criticisms could be applied. It was too high stakes, too dominated by rote learning and forced 'teaching to the test'. In October 2012, progressive new proposals were tabled by the then Minister for Education Ruairí Quinn which offered the potential to liberate students and teachers. In essence, the Junior Certificate was to be transformed from a high-stakes exam to a house exam run by the schools. Research by the Economic and Social Research Institute had shown that high numbers of students (often male and particularly those from disadvantaged backgrounds) disengaged during the Junior Certificate cycle. Many teenagers, it concluded, are 'ill-suited to an education system built around one terminal exam'. In addition to the changes to the examination system, students could 'mix and match' from a menu of traditional subjects alongside a range of new short courses (such as digital technology, Chinese culture). These elective subjects were to be chosen from a syllabus designed by the National Council for Curriculum and Assessment. The State Examinations Commission would continue to set papers in traditional subjects, but schools were free to mix these with their own choice of short courses. Overall, the plan was to move away from the current straitjacket with schools and teachers having the 'elbow room' to encourage critical thinking and provide more creative teaching. Wow! It sounded like real reform.

International Best Practice

This new design wasn't conceived on the back of an envelope. Benchmarked against the best, the reforms were broadly in line with educational practices in high performing education systems like Finland and New Zealand.[38] Clive Byrne, director of the National Association of Principals and Deputy Principals, suggested that teachers should be willing to correct their own students' Junior Cert exam papers: 'If we're in the middle of reforming it to ensure it's not a high-stakes exam any more, why not be a bit more courageous?'[39] Pushback from the teachers was around the focus on examinations versus continuous assessment, how these should be graded and by whom. The negotiations around Junior Certificate reform (even the very limited reforms around exam grading) became bogged down and have now been underway for over five years. At the time of writing there's no agreement in sight (the battle to date has included strike action). Eventually, one of the teachers' unions voted to accept a watered down version of the original proposals while the second, ASTI, has rejected it.[40] Ruairí Quinn's successor, Jan O'Sullivan, made it known that money and training were available to ensure schools were ready for the reform, and stated her own strong support for the changes: 'I'm absolutely determined that we will go ahead with this reform that has long been needed in the Irish education system.' In a statement, union president Máire Ní Chiarba said ASTI members were concerned about the lack of clarity in the latest plans: 'Teachers needed far more clarity and detail about how the process will operate' she said, adding, 'ASTI members are committed to educationally sound reform of the Junior Cycle.'

In industrial relations, like war, the first casualty is the truth. Here we see a multi-year negotiation with teachers' unions around a core educational reform. Through a process of whittling down, it's difficult to see how the original idea and what was eventually proposed were actually the same thing. Even this diluted reform still isn't in place. It raises the core question: Are we running the educational system for the benefits of the students or the teachers? While no one would argue against teachers being part of the design phase and having their voices heard, they shouldn't be allowed to stymie progress. The suggestion that more *clarity* is needed (after a multi-year negotiation) is disingenuous, *power* masquerading as *concern*. Meanwhile, back at the ranch, while the Government can't find the moxie to plough forward, children from disadvantaged areas continue to leave school in droves. It's simply not good enough. The best industrial relations experts in the country should be sent in like a SWAT team to resolve this. And the starting point shouldn't be to water down reforms to a point where they become acceptable to all stakeholders, that is, the least possible amount of change from the existing system. The starting point has to be the maximum gain for students.

Transition Year Curriculum

A transition year is offered by many (not all) schools in the senior cycle. It follows directly after the Junior Certificate. The goal is to provide opportunities for broader development, wider than *pure* academic development. For example, in September 2010, 'Exploring Options in Further and Higher Education' was launched.[41] This module aims to provide students with an opportunity to learn about available study options and careers. It was aimed particularly at those students who have little or no family experience of higher education. Paradoxically, challenging and more disadvantaged students (the ideal candidates for this programme) are often refused access to transition year by schools because of fears that they might be *disruptive*. On face value, having all students undergo this module makes perfect sense. Yet, practices around transition year differ across schools. In some schools it's optional; others don't offer it at all. Some parents are against it, seeing it as a 'doss year' in which the students take their foot off the gas (reinforcing the point made throughout that the central focus is scoring high points in the Leaving Certificate, rather than education per se). Broader arguments about development of the whole person fall into a bucket labelled 'Yeah, right!' There is no philosophical stance taken on the completion of the transition year by the Department of Education. Decisions around this are left up to the individual schools and students. It's a missing link in the educational chain.

Leaving Certificate

The Senior Cycle of secondary school is a two-year programme of study. Normally seven or eight subjects are studied with the results from the best six being counted for entrance into further or higher education. In most schools, papers can be taken at higher or lower levels. A student's grades on the best six subjects are summarised as a single score – with a maximum of 100 points awarded for each subjects (an extra 25 points is awarded for higher level maths), offering a theoretical maximum score of 625 points.[42] In practice, there are three streams for students completing the Leaving Certificate as follows:

Leaving Cert (LC)	Leaving Cert Vocational Programme (LCVP)	Leaving Cert Applied (LCA)
The 'mainstream' programme followed by the majority of students (67 per cent in 2013).[43] This provides the main entry route into higher education. This represents Level 5 on the National Framework of Qualifications (see later discussion points).	Designed to give a stronger *technical* and *vocational* focus, 28 per cent of students took this route in 2013. Includes the provision of 2 additional courses of study ('Work Preparation' and 'Enterprise') known as Link Modules. Also Level 5 on the National Framework of Qualifications.	This is targeted at students who are 'less able' academically but who still want to complete 2nd level education. This route does not qualify for direct entry into higher education (5 per cent of students in 2013 took this route). Level 4 on the National Framework of Qualifications.

The rationale for the different streams is to stop students quitting second level school without any qualification. Professor Áine Hyland takes up this point: 'It's important that everyone can qualify and take something positive from their school years. We don't want children to feel a failure at 18.' On first glance the Leaving Certificate Vocational Programme (LCVP) might look like it's replacing the type of vocational curriculum historically associated with the 'Techs'. The reality is that this is simply Leaving Certificate Light; just two of the subjects are changed – in every other respect this is exactly the same programme. This is not an alternative, more a slightly modified route. The Leaving Certificate dominates the Irish educational landscape. Rory O'Sullivan, a critic of current education policy, described this as follows:

> The Leaving Certificate sits like an 800 pound gorilla in the corner of the room. It has displaced the vocational

route which was perfect for some kids. Despite all the talk over all the years, no one can seem to shift it.

Cramming Schools

Critics of the current Leaving Certificate system highlight the fact that this is primarily an *admission system*. The core purpose is to gain the maximum number of points. This is in contrast to viewing education in a broader way, that is, providing students with thinking and problem-solving skills useable throughout life. The hunt for *points* has displaced the search for *learning*. And, according to many employers, there is a wide chasm between what's learned in school and what's needed in work. The final year in secondary school (in particular) focuses on cramming information into students in order for this to be 're-instated' onto an examinations page.[44] Extracurricular development of students (for example, physical education) is often ignored or seen as time wasted.

This rote learning doesn't prepare students for college where the emphasis is more on independent learning, not fact regurgitation. The high levels of predictability of the Leaving Certificate questions has led to a grind school ethos where students solely focus on the 'exam'. It's like cab drivers in London trying to pass 'The Knowledge', having to memorise 1,200 different routes (completely ignoring the fact that GPS has been invented). It has led to the growth of a number of actual grind schools and a large (mainly black) economy to meet the needs of significant numbers of students who are preparing for State examinations. This disadvantages students from less affluent backgrounds who can't afford to attend fee-paying schools or to pay for grinds, further tilting the system in favour of better-off children.

I'm not being holier-than-thou about this. At one point we had a stream of teachers coming to our house to help the kids with particular subjects. On an individual family basis, if you have the means, it makes perfect sense to maximise your children's potential. But from a 'systems perspective' my children, and similar students everywhere, had an unfair advantage over others who couldn't afford to pay for grinds and/or private schools.[45] Rory O'Sullivan, the principal in Killester College, described this as 'vending machine education' – you put €6,000 into one end of the machine and you get six As out the other end (from personal experience I can attest to the following: only the €6,000 part of that equation is assured). Lots of children survive the Leaving Certificate year with their parents on tenterhooks, minding them, providing special diets, tiptoeing around the house for 12 months, afraid of upsetting them. Entire households should be presented with T-Shirts bearing the slogan, 'We survived the Leaving Certificate.' The technical term for the current design of the system is as follows: *It's nuts.*

We need to teach students the skills to acquire and analyse data, not to soak up information and spit it back out as some sort of 'Human Google'. While the flaws in the existing design are widely known, somehow, we seem fearful of changing the system ('the divil you know is better than the divil you don't') or powerless to do this in the face of opposition from teaching unions, from parents who want to advantage their children and from those who survived the existing method and claim that 'it didn't do them any harm' (hardly a ringing endorsement). In terms of practical approaches, one school principal in Malahide has the following conversation with every Leaving Certificate class: 'The system is wrong. I know it's wrong and you know it's wrong. But that's the way it is at the moment. Now, my job is to help you get through it and here's what we need to do....'

While a potential candidate for a Teacher Bravery Award, she shouldn't have to make that speech. Few insiders have the guts to openly criticise the system.[46] There's pressure on everyone to collude with the current way of working. This overall point about the design of the Leaving Certificate applies across the board – to all students regardless of background. But, in relation to educational disadvantage, the negative impact on some students is massively *disproportional.*

Education Changes Lives:

Ger Robinson

Mature Student, Dublin City University

My memories of primary education in Ballymun are mixed. I had some really positive experiences with a couple of teachers. One of them, Mr. Killeen ('Killer') resembled and behaved like a bearded version of Basil Fawlty, bringing a measure of accidental comedy to the classroom. More negative memories relate to a despotic principal who never missed an opportunity to use the cane. When the ban on corporal punishment was introduced, he still managed to get the odd sly slap in. In fifth class I was suspended for telling my teacher to 'buzz off' (or words to that effect). Yes, I was that nuisance student from the dysfunctional family, constantly seeking attention.

The Comprehensive School (now Trinity Comprehensive) felt less oppressive, probably due to the ban on hitting students. Overall, I was capable, but had little or no interest. With significant alcohol abuse issues at home, I was often preoccupied with that and less concerned about schoolwork and grades. I was thrown out of the 'Comp' twice for messing – vandalism, break-dancing in the corridors, refusal to work, giving cheek etc. But I managed to get back in and sat the Inter-Cert (Junior Cert) which I failed miserably. It didn't help that I went on the 'hop' (no-show) for three of the exams. In the other exams, I scored well but my confidence was damaged and the overall experience of education was negative. To the delight of my parents, I immediately got a job in a sausage-making factory. Bringing home the bacon (excuse the pun) was the name of the game; education was simply a means to 'get a job.' It's a cultural thing – the benefits of education weren't discussed around our dinner table. From age 15 to 29, I moved from one menial job to another, slowly beginning to regret not staying in school.

When my son Eoghan was born, I decided to give it a second shot. My younger sister had studied for a degree at St. Pat's in Drumcondra. At that time, it was practically unheard of that a 'Munner' would go to college and I was really inspired by this. I linked up with NCI and completed a foundation course in Social Studies. Looking back now, that course was both a cultural and an intellectual shock. When our sociology lecturer, Michael Barry, would join the students for lunch, I was literally terrified to speak for fear of 'saying something stupid.' An exposure to Marx explained the melancholia and alienation I'd come to associate with years spent doing menial labour. It was truly liberating to learn this. In spite of my post-code stigma (and other insecurities) I passed the year.

The baptism of fire at NCI pushed me to take on a degree (theology and philosophy) at All Hallows College (DCU). Unlike the bigger universities, All Hallows was an intimate learning community and studying philosophy was like coming home (I probably was always a bit of an odd kid). A first class degree and a medal for academic excellence came as a total shock. In fairness, the medal should have gone to my partner and mother of our three children who worked tirelessly minding the kids and allowing me bury myself in the books. In parallel, I received huge support from Kevin O'Higgins, a Jesuit and fellow philosopher living in Ballymun.

In 2015 I obtained a slot on the Ph.D. programme (Philosophy) at UCD. Unfortunately, 10 weeks in, I've had to withdraw because I didn't qualify for the SUSI funding. That's the reality for students coming from my social background. Capital (material and cultural), rather than aptitude or capability, so often determines their fate. The saying education opens doors is certainly true in my case. It's definitely opened up new career options. But, more importantly, it has opened my mind in terms of social awareness and self-belief. I've witnessed, first hand, the power that education can bring in disadvantaged communities.

Chapter 4

TACKLING EDUCATIONAL
DISADVANTAGE: CURRENT SUPPORTS

The Education Act 1998 defines education disadvantage as: 'The impediments to education arising from social or economic disadvantage which prevent students from deriving appropriate benefit from education in Schools' (Section 32:9). The issue has been on the policy radar since the 1960's with numerous national, regional and local initiatives launched to level the playing field. Consider the following: while circa 11 per cent of students have *significant* literacy problems on leaving school, those who live in disadvantaged areas have 3 times the national average. Recognising that something fundamental had to be done to address this, the Department of Education and Science established the DEIS schools classification. It was certainly a bold move.

Delivering Equality of Opportunity in Schools (DEIS)

The central pillar in tackling educational disadvantage is the designation of particular schools under the Delivering Equality of Opportunity in Schools (DEIS) classification. Disadvantaged schools[1] have been formally identified since 2005. Here's how Mary Hanafin, the Minister for Education at that time, described the initiative:

> I believe that the emphasis in DEIS on targeting resources at those most in need, on providing greater support for teachers working in the most disadvantaged schools, and on promoting greater cooperation between the home and the school and between

different State agencies and departments, will make
a real difference to the lives of those young people
that most need extra help.[2]

At primary level, indicators include levels of unemployment
and lone parenthood, the numbers of Travellers and large families,
eligibility for free book grants and local authority housing. These
factors combine into an overall *scale of disadvantage*.[3] Secondary
Schools are also categorised as DEIS (disadvantaged) or non-DEIS.
Socio-economic indicators (medical card ownership) combined
with measures of educational outcomes (junior cycle drop-out and
Junior Certificate performance) are used.[4] DEIS schools generally
have a higher proportion of students from lower socio-economic
groups, newcomers (immigrants), students with disabilities and
Travellers.[5] The same authors note a higher incidence of serious literacy and numeracy problems, emotional and behavioural
problems, absenteeism, lower student motivation, problematic
student-teacher relationships and less parental involvement. Tom
Crean[6] offered the following statistics:

Factor	National Average	DEIS School Average	% difference
Days Absent from School	7.5%	10.3%	27%
Children Suspended from School	4.1%	9.6%	57%

Supplementary Funding

To understand the imbalance between different types of schools,
let's just look at one issue – supplementary funding. Most schools
in middle class areas look for supplementary funding from parents. Because of a tax-break for the schools, a €250 contribution
from parents is actually worth €500 to the school. It follows that
schools in wealthier areas receive significant income to fund additional services. In working class areas, it's more difficult to get

voluntary funding from parents who have less disposable income. So these schools offer *less* services and become more *unequal*. For example, guidance counselling is an entitlement for all children. It shouldn't be a luxury only provided in schools that can afford this. However, the career guidance staffing levels are so poor in some schools, it's the equivalent of having one nurse available in a general hospital. Sometimes, there's no nurse at all. In 2012, guidance provision was slashed to the effect that some schools have almost zero provision. And, that's just on the *career side*. Many children don't just require education, that is, being stuffed with facts. Their wellbeing and development also requires emotional care, as we see from daily reports of children in crisis, the number of suicides and so on.

In practice, the guidance counsellors role has three dimensions: (1) personal/social development, (2) educational guidance and (3) career guidance.[7] When the available time is reduced, as it has been across the system, it turns into a reactive 'fire brigade' service, where crisis intervention becomes the norm rather than the exception. With the overall shortage of resources, many schools prioritise academic achievement over emotional care and the counsellors are given an academic timetable. The result: care available for vulnerable students and those with mental health issues is heavily compromised. The extra income in the fee-charging schools (and in middle class schools who have a 'voluntary income source') allows these extra resources to be in place. Meanwhile, the climb for disadvantaged students becomes steeper.

Emotional Support Services

There is a strong need for access to a counsellor or key staff with appropriate skills to provide emotional/therapeutic support in a respectful and confidential context, and a strong need for schools to be able to respond to trauma (for example, bereavement). Dr. Paul Downes was heavily critical of existing emotional support services for students. He suggested that the language most often used is Pastoral Care. The current system requires students who have a problem to report this to the school chaplain, career guidance, year head or the principal. It is akin to being asked to go to your boss in work and confide all your personal troubles. Something which we wouldn't expect of adults is also unacceptable for children. The kids don't feel that the service is independent or that any of the above actors would mediate on their behalf. In explaining the history, he suggested that the religious orders initially fought against the establishment of a proper counselling system as psychology was seen to conflict with theology. While I didn't drill into this point in enough detail to come to a reasoned view, the take-away impression from some of the schools visited was one of benign neglect rather than an anti-counselling policy. In contrast, the central importance of counseling services is recognised and well established across Europe, even in countries that we mightn't consider to be as economically advanced as Ireland.[8] A centrally important tenet across all branches of counselling is to maintain confidentiality around the issues raised by a client. Paul Downes provided an example of a response to the issue of confidentiality he received in one school: 'Our School has a very clear policy on confidentiality. Teachers don't tell the kids that they are talking about them.'

Classification System

The criteria for having a school designated as DEIS was initially based on a 'self-reporting' system completed by the principal in each school. On mature reflection, the general consensus is as follows: where the principal was totally honest about student performance, they received less support. Some principals, who decided to be economical with the truth, achieved more support for their schools.[9] Thirteen years later there have been major shifts in demographics. Some areas have been considerably gentrified while others have experienced an influx of immigrant children, posing additional resourcing challenges. While there are current plans underway to re-classify schools, any new system will have winners and losers. Certainly, the decisions made in this space are not straightforward. For example, in the original thinking the overall weight of argument was in favour of recognising concentrated disadvantage. When a school is located in an area of social deprivation, there's a belief that this has a cumulative downwards pull on education achievement which makes sense. However, we also know that about 45 per cent of disadvantaged children live in non-disadvantaged areas (pockets of disadvantage in more affluent areas) and these children don't receive additional support. There's no neat solution available here, just a need for agreed criteria to identify the level of disadvantage in particular communities.

DEIS Investment

A total of 670 primary and 195 post-primary schools are currently part of the DEIS School Support Programme, circa 23 per cent of the total number of schools in the system. In 2012 over €158 million was made available under this scheme for additional teaching and other forms of support. To ascertain if that money was well spent, a number of evaluation reports have been completed.[10] The research findings show that the initiative has had a positive effect on tackling educational disadvantage. For example, almost all of the schools demonstrated significant improvements in attendance rates. Achievement gains were also found in literacy and numeracy levels in primary schools.[11] To understand how additional resourcing impacts education, let's take an obvious example. If children arrive for school hungry, they can't study or learn. The introduction of Breakfast Clubs, providing students with nourishment in advance of studying, helps to address this.

Breakfast Clubs

On first sight this is a problem that looks like it has been solved. But, according to Dr Paul Downes, it's a fig leaf solution where children in need fall through the gaps. And not all children are involved. Some principals don't bother with this as there's extra paperwork and administration involved, and they elevate the needs of the institution over the needs of the children:

> Look across the water. Even the most right-wing Tory politicians never spoke about removing school dinners. Here, we don't have that debate because the school canteen facilities just don't exist.

The provision of food for children isn't a new idea. In my own time in primary school we were given a lunch, a particular type of sandwich issued like clockwork on each day of the week along with a small bottle of milk. To this day if I eat a current bun, I automatically think that it's Wednesday! I have no memory of ever feeling poor because of this. That was the system in place and we simply accepted this. Should we be doing less for children going to school today than we did in the early 1960s? Would that fall under the heading of 'social progress'?

Challenging Behaviour

That some children have poor attitudes towards school is perhaps less than surprising. But well beyond cheekiness or poor study routines, some behaviour can be extremely challenging, including bullying, fighting, coming into school drunk or under the influence of drugs. Picture yourself standing at the front of a class of 28 students where three of the students are disruptive. Should your loyalty be toward the three or the remaining 25? Many teachers opt for the larger number and are happy when troublesome students disappear from the classroom. School principals face exactly the same dilemma. Should they try to 'hold' individual (troubled) children and get them through the system? If these kids fall out of the system, the immediate impact on the school may actually be *positive*, with other children and their parents breathing a sigh of relief. But the impact on the child and society generally may be worse. While not every early school-leaver becomes a criminal, a huge percentage of criminals are early school-leavers.[12] Early intervention is key.

Early Indicators of Educational Underperformance:

It's generally accepted that there are three clear indicators of educational underperformance: Poor attendance, low academic achievement and early school-leaving.

1. Poor Attendance

Absenteeism is accepted as a strong predictor of early school-leaving and provides a clear signal of children at risk. There's solid evidence to support this. While the national average of school days missed through absenteeism is 14, in disadvantaged areas this increases by 50 per cent to 21 days.[13] In 2013, The National Education and Welfare Board (NEWB) was set up to develop a more cohesive approach to school attendance and address the related problems of absenteeism and early school-leaving.[14] A recent DEIS evaluation report noted the difficulty for a teacher in improving a child's literacy and numeracy when they are regularly missing. Absenteeism has a dramatically negative effect on an individuals' attainment levels and also causes extensive disruption to the learning opportunities of their classmates. When a child has high absenteeism, gaps in concept and skill development are inevitable.

2. Poor Academic Achievement

Research has shown that dominant educational practices disadvantage those from lower socio-economic and minority groups.[15] Low teacher expectations in relation to certain groups (along the lines of the Harvard experiment cited earlier) along with ability grouping, play a particularly damaging role. When ability grouping is used, students are educated in a highly differentiated system from an early stage. In the senior cycle, classes are based around the 'level' at which Leaving Certificate papers are offered (higher, ordinary or foundation), making progression to further or higher education extremely difficult for some students who simply can't get the points to enter college. While the overall goal is to promote positive educational outcomes, we have to recognise that simply keeping some students in school is an outcome in itself.

And the Result Is ... Zero Points!

Some people question the value of a child completing the second level cycle and emerging with very low points.[16] How can this be? Was that a complete waste of time? A score of zero or very low points can be viewed another way. Rather than seeing this as an academic 'failure', the success might have been containment. For some children, spending five years in an environment with role model adults (teachers) is positive. Alongside this, there is the subtle influence of a peer group who want to get something from the education system. To understand this perspective, we have to ask: what was the alternative? What would that same child have done over those 5 years if they hadn't been at school? Some years ago, I ran the Dublin City Marathon in a record-breaking time of 5 hours and 10 minutes, perhaps a candidate for one of the slowest times ever recorded. However, I ran the full 26 miles and I'm still boasting about it. Completing secondary level education for some children represents a similar victory. It's not about the score, the number of points achieved. The victory is in completing the circuit. That's not an argument to aim low for disadvantaged children. It's a recognition that the aim point for individual students needs to be set in different places. A child's personal educational journey cannot be summarised into a single, numerical measure. Even where the score is zero, the journey may have required incredible perseverance.

3. Early School-Leaving

The Education and Welfare Act 2000 addresses early school-leaving. Early school-leaving is strongly linked to socio-economic background[17] and membership of the Travelling community. A high proportion of early school-leavers come from semi-skilled and unskilled manual backgrounds.[18] While Travellers have almost full participation at primary school and a high transfer rate to secondary levels, they have quite poor post-primary attendance and retention rates. A significant majority leave school around the Junior Certificate and less than 20 per cent complete second level school.[19]

Focusing on Travellers

Participation in higher education by Travellers has long been part of the national access policy. A national target was set for 27 people to attend third level in 2014, rising to 60 people in 2016. This was the first time that a target was established for people from the Traveller community (the need for a numeric target had been identified in consultation with Traveller representative groups). But, we know that the problems with Traveller education begin long before this. Currently circa 13 per cent of travellers complete second level education vs 90 per cent of the general population. The question = why so little progress has been made with this particular group? This group have been the most difficult to change (that is, shown the least numerical growth in educational participation) of the five target groups identified over the course of the previous three national access plans. It's a multi-faceted issue: poor literacy levels among the community, the living circumstances of students, marginalisation experienced by Travellers in earlier education and so on. In a more recent pruning, there was a savage cut in the number of teachers working with Travellers. Without some powerful interventions to meet the targets set, nothing will change and we will be carrying this forward to be inserted into the next national plan.

To tackle the core educational disadvantage issues listed, several structures has been established within the DEIS schools. The main elements are...

Strand #1: Home-School Community Liaison Scheme

Established in 1990, this programme is normally led by a teacher on secondment for a five-year period. Home-School Community Liaison Officers work with *all* children in DEIS schools and with their parents (offering parenting education and individual coaching). The original goal was for parents to have a voice in running of schools, but practices around this seem very varied. The remit of Home-School Community Liaison Officers is to work with all children in a school, not just those at risk of leaving or underperforming. The thinking is that the best students will influence the others; there's no stigma around services when everyone is involved. Two general criticisms can be levelled at the existing system: (a) Home-School Community Liaison staff are too often on the side of the teachers rather than advocates for the children – they have come from the teaching ranks and return to the profession when their stint in this job is over;[20] (b) the level of parental involvement differs widely. When asked about their understanding of school policy one parent asked: 'Was that about keeping the rooms tidy?' In working class communities, parents were traditionally expected to be 'of service' to schools and they 'tacitly accepted that role'.[21]

One Problem: Two Groups

I mentioned earlier that, under the general heading of 'Educational Disadvantage', it's useful to think about two separate cohorts of children who have very different needs. Most of our attention thus far has focused on the low hanging fruit – children from disadvantaged areas that don't have a family background in education and perhaps don't fully understand the benefits of this. The role for educationalists is to recognise this, set high expectations and help these children to maximise their potential. The second group are, figuratively, higher up the tree, that is, further out of reach, children who present with challenging emotional or behavioural difficulties. While politically incorrect, this group is often labelled the 'mad, bad and sad'. These more difficult children, are targeted in the school completions programme where a list is made (the listing is never made public) of children who require special attention.

STRAND #2: SCHOOL-COMPLETION PROGRAMMES[22]

The School-Completion Programme Co-ordinators work with children (and parents of children) who are at risk of falling out of the education system or those who need additional support to stay involved. There are currently 124 School-Completion Programmes in place linked to specific DEIS schools. Each coordinator is responsible for a number of primary and secondary schools' (from 2 to 11 schools, depending on size) in a catchment area such as Clondalkin in Dublin. It makes sense. Logistically, the co-ordinator doesn't have to spend a huge amount of time travelling and they get an intimate understanding of the issues in a particular area. Each programme is locally managed, that is, headed up by a School-Completion Programme Co-ordinator and typically governed by a local committee of volunteers (while the co-ordinator works with the schools, s/he doesn't report into any particular school).[23] This system is in place since 2003 and is currently overseen by TUSLA, the child and family agency, governed by Department of Health.[24] For reasons that are not immediately clear, some School-Completion Programmes Co-ordinators report to the Educational and Training Boards and some programmes are set up as Limited Liability companies (if you are finding it difficult to follow this, get on the queue; the current structures and the underpinning rationale are both unclear). While the overall trend in school completion is positive (over 90 per cent of all children now complete the Leaving Certificate), in DEIS schools the number of 'non-completions' is 'twice as bad' as other schools. The result: thousands of children leave school every single year before their second level education is completed. The presenting issues in dealing with children in this catchment group are enormously varied. Family issues can range from not understanding that a child has to attend school 'every day' (not just two or three days each week) to addiction or other mental and physical health issues.

Impossible to Teach?

Inevitably, some children are labelled 'impossible to teach'. Where behavioral issues become severe, the school eventually has to take action. At the mild end, sanctions include detention, extra homework or summoning parents. When these tools have been deployed and, if there's still no significant behavioural change, sanctions get ratcheted upwards. The norm is to put these students on 'reduced hours' or onto a 'rolling suspension'. When these are in place, a student is nominally in school. They may arrive and sign-the-book, but go home 20 minutes later. Or they may not come to school at all as the rolling suspensions effectively disbar them from attending. Technically on the books, these children are not actually in school. In the United States, Fine reported how some students in disadvantaged schools were essentially coerced out when they reached the statutory leaving age or were actively discouraged from attending school, a process he described as 'exporting dissent'.[25] An important point here is that while a student remains registered the school continues to receive a capitation grant (currently €345 per student per year) from the Department of Education and Skills. So there's both a monetary and a staffing ratio incentive to schools to maintain the numbers. But, it's overly cynical to see this as an issue of financial manipulation. From discussions held with several secondary school leaders, there is often an embarrassment factor, a sense that the 'school has failed the child', sometimes a reluctance to formally admit this. In some cases where sanctions continue to roll forward, time takes care of the problem. The child eventually reaches the ripe old age of 16 and can now *officially* leave school. Eureka, the problem is sorted! Except, of course, the societal problem in terms of an under-educated, disruptive young adult hasn't gone away and so often resurfaces in the criminal justice system. Those outside the school management system are critical of the level of fallout. One committed advocate of children's rights argued: 'The schools just can't deal with this, not in the current model.' But, while it's easy to criticize, those tasked with directly managing the problem, don't see any easy answers.

High Anxiety

Lets state the obvious: dealing with difficult children is time consuming. Teachers and principals are tasked with getting the main body of students through the system. Disruptive children add massively to the workload, often soaking up a hugely disproportionate amount of time. In some cases, these children can be physically threatening, even violent. They may be coming from dysfunctional families, bringing negative baggage into school each day. Calling in the parents isn't always the solution. Some 'take up the cudgel' on behalf of their child (that's not always a figure of speech). Some children suffer from underlying psychological or psychiatric conditions, which may not be easy to diagnose and schools don't have the in-house expertise to unravel this.

Getting psychological or psychiatric assessments typically takes more than a year in the public system. Even when assessments have been completed and the school now has a label, what happens next? Disruptive behaviour doesn't magically disappear as soon as the diagnosis becomes clear. Alongside personal safety issues, there's the ever-present threat of legal action. Concerns about the school being sued, in parallel with anxiety around personal/school reputation damage, provide a constant source of worry. And, of course, school leaders are responsible to a variety of stakeholders. Every day in the staffroom, principals are reminded of their duty of care to teaching and non-teaching staff. All school principals in Ireland are promoted from the ranks, so they primarily identify with their group (teachers). A large part of their success in the school leadership role is dictated by their ability to keep staff on-side. All in all, it's a potent mix that leads to high anxiety for the school leaders tasked with dealing with this cohort of students. In the world of school management, 'uneasy lies the head that wears the crown.'[26] While all school principals are former teachers (which probably makes sense), the best teachers don't always morph into the best leaders. Significant personal developmental work needs to be conducted with school principals to allow them carry out this difficult, multiple-stakeholder role, which often poses contradictory requirements.[27]

Confidence Impact

For the students who leave the education system, non-completion often further drains their self-confidence. We've already highlighted that, in former years, children who left school early could secure a job. Sometimes it was a prized apprenticeship, sometimes just a starter job that nevertheless offered structure and income. Now, leaving school without completing the Junior and Leaving Certificates, often leads to a sense of despair. Tom Crean, School Completion Coordinator in Clondalkin said:

> Students who don't complete school often speak about a strong sense of loss. They regret not finishing. They carry this with them all the time, feeling that there's something missing in their lives, that they are branded as a failure.

Design Philosophy

School-completion programmes are built from the 'bottom up' to meet local needs. However, in reality, the needs are very similar across the country. One Coordinator said: 'Kids in Galway, Limerick or Wexford present with essentially the same issues. The only difference is their accent.' In recent times there was an attempt to install a 'best-practice' approach (labelled 'One-Child, One-Team, One-Plan') but this has since fallen by the wayside and the programmes have reverted to local-design, that is, whatever is deemed appropriate by the local co-coordinator. The strong consensus is that the role has become more paper driven (to demonstrate financial governance) with less time spent doing the actual job. Government funding comes with rules. No one in the public sector wants money to go missing on their watch and the pendulum has swung from light to heavy across all governance topics. While there's always a need for control, the bureaucracy imposed saps the energy of the people working on the front line and strangles services.[28]

Declining Investment

In 2008, it cost around €32 million annually to run this service. The current spend on the school completion programmes is €24 million. Annual cuts to the service of the order of 7.5 per cent have reduced funding with no respite in sight. For example, three National Coordinators had led this service, but these positions were culled in 2015. Has it had an impact? Professor Patrick Clancy who's been working the educational disadvantage stream for 20+ years, makes the point that there's always a time lag in the data, perhaps as long as five years. So the impact of the most recent recession will not have shown up yet. With less investment in public spending across a range of areas, Ireland may well have seen a reversal in the positive trend of second level school completions and third level participation which has not yet come through in the numbers. There is zero room for complacency here as more lives are blighted by unemployment and some are completely derailed through involvement in crime. These children are essentially drowning, one at a time, away from any media spotlight. And, the lifeguards are slowly being removed from the beach.

Perhaps you think that this is melodramatic and there's no support evidence? In 2014, the Higher Education Authority (HEA) prepared a report for the Minister for Education on the operation of the third level system. That report warned of the huge risks inherent in significant declines in public funding. Funding per student dropped from €11,800 in 2007/2008 to €9,200 in 2013/2014.

The forecast was that the per capita investment would further decline to less than €9,000 in 2015/2016, an absolute decline of almost 25 per cent over this short period. While efficiency savings can always be made through better asset utilisation, you can't get a quart from a pint bottle. Taking this amount of money out of the education system is the equivalent of cutting off your right leg as part of a weight control programme.[29] But, in the absence of a compelling vision or a counterbalancing voice, it's death by a thousand cuts. Meanwhile, the rest of us don't even notice this. We're too busy designing placards to protest about water charges!

Absence of a Clear Strategy

I've already made the point that **m**oney is one component in the design and successful execution of a project. Arguably the second 'm' (**m**anagement) is even more important. We have seen that each School Completion Project runs on a stand-alone basis with the duplication of effort that this implies. In the absence of a support system, some co-coordinators have set up informal clusters to meet and swop best practice ideas (and, perhaps, to re-charge their own batteries). There's no model to follow, no measurable outcomes or quality control of the process. It doesn't make sense. To take an example from the food business: McDonalds don't employ chefs to dream up customised menus. The bill of fare is standardised to meet a particular need. While it may not be cordon bleu, it is consistent. The same point applies to this area.

Despite the fact that there are some really committed people in these roles, it's ridiculous to allow such an important pillar of the education disadvantage system to be wholly dependent on the quality of the person doing the job, a point that applies across many of the DEIS initiatives. While resources are being pumped into schools, one respondent argued: 'Some of these schools have failed miserably to really address the problem.' To support this, he offered the following story: In one disadvantaged school, the principal used available funds to purchase coats for every single child in the school. When questioned about the rationale, she said that they: 'Didn't want anyone to be singled out and made to feel poor.' Yet, the essence of the leadership role is to make difficult choices.

Decisions need to be made around the allocation of resources to particular children. Those decisions are seldom black or white. In the absence of clear guidelines, it's down to individuals to do the best they can.

Skills Required

In order to be successful in the School Completion Coordinators role, a range of skills are required. The person has to have some understanding of programme design to meet the needs of this cohort of learners. Secondly, the person needs to have the connection skills ('street cred') to establish links with these children and their parents. Thirdly, the School-Completion Co-coordinator needs to be an advocate for the kids within the schools. In some cases they stand up for the children, against a school system that would like to suspend or disappear them under the heading of a rolling suspension.[30] Overall, it's a demanding job that requires a mix of skills. However, while the other two legs of the system (Education Welfare Service and Home School Community Liaison) are both staffed by full-time people (most often teachers on secondment), this part of the structure in populated by people on temporary contracts who are poorly paid, get 26 days a year holidays (that is, they don't have the school holiday entitlement enjoyed by teachers) and have zero pension entitlement. How come? Because, this system was established as a stopgap, despite the fact that it's still running several years later. TUSLA, the employer, won't address this, as they would have to engage an additional 124 people and face up to the responsibility of these people not having pensionable jobs. So, why are people attracted to these jobs in the first place? There are a variety of reasons. Some are wholly committed to working with disadvantaged children and families and concentrate on this area full-time. It's a calling in the best sense of that term. There are some teachers among this group, attracted by the idea of a 'break from the classroom' or who enjoy the freedom of movement and autonomy offered by the role. Others want to stamp this onto their CV, believing it offers career advantage if they apply for more senior posts. But, for the non-teachers, this isn't an easy space if they crave security. Many, many times, I've met people working in the not-for-profit arena who provide the glue that binds the system together. While admirable, we shouldn't exploit their personal commitment and passion and reward them with inferior conditions.

Becoming Disaffected at School

In broad terms, schools are set up to deal with normal children and operate best when everyone conforms to the rules. Academically, some children are easy to teach while others struggle. The school task is to get all of them over the line. But, like horses running in the Grand National, not everyone completes the course. There are fallers along the way with students in the 12-15 year old age bracket most at risk.[31] Recent research has found that students become disaffected during the early junior cycle and begin to disengage.[32] The most often cited reasons are negative relationships with teachers (especially amongst males), boredom, falling behind with academic work and poor attendance. Far from being the best days, for some students school represents the worst days of their life. Many talk about 'hating school' and some perceive that they are treated differently by teachers depending on whether or not they are expected to progress to Higher Education. Research has consistently found that those from lower socio-economic groups report more negative school experiences than other students.[33] The negative experience often combines with a lack of family educational success. It gets bundled into an 'anti-education mix' that damages self-confidence and lowers expectations about future achievement. An argument made throughout this book is that approaches that over-focus on rote learning cause many students to mentally withdraw from school.[34] Students, along with many others, are critical of what is perceived as a dependent-creating, examination-focused approach. In one report, Duncan,[35] a second year undergraduate access student, labelled this the 'read, remember and regurgitate' approach, suggesting a new (negative) meaning for the 3Rs.[36]

Disaffected students vote with their feet. They start to miss days at school; some stop attending altogether. That's when they come to the attention of the Education Welfare Service.

STRAND #3: EDUCATION WELFARE SERVICE

The third leg of the educational disadvantage system is *enforcement*. All schools are obliged to record attendance; absences of 20 days (or more) get red-flagged.[37] The legislation provides a range of penalties for parents around non-school attendance including fines and even imprisonment. In practice, this is more threat than punishment. Most of the parents sent to jail are released almost immediately due to prison overcrowding. While it's difficult to establish the exact number of parents imprisoned, in 2015 146 SAN's (school attendance notices) were issued in relation to 102 children.[38] Does this act as a deterrent? The views on this are mixed. One person commented:

> Where a parent has to be dragged into court to get children to attend school, that's telling you something about the home environment. This might look good to the 'law & order' brigade, but it has zero impact on the ground.

The range of initiatives detailed above (all three strands) are designed to keep students in school. Despite these measures, a number of children slip through the safety net and leave school before completing second level education. To target the fallers, a number of additional systems are in place.

Early School-Leaver Programmes

The central goal in Youthreach (Government programme to cater for early school-leavers) is to encourage unemployed people to return to structured learning.[39] The target audience are young people (aged between 15-18) who've left mainstream education. Essentially, Youthreach provides an alternative to school. Somewhat controversially, students who attend Youthreach are paid a state funded allowance, currently running at €40 per week.[40] In parallel, Foroige have set up an 'Early School Leavers Programme', which targets a similar group of children but they are not paid to attend.[41] A critique of Youthreach addresses two specific points: (a) the curriculum for these students needs to be very different than the 'mainstream' curriculum which caused them to drop out in the first place. The argument here is that kids hanging around the street become bored so they can be attracted back into the education system. But, by mirroring the mainstream curriculum, the Youthreach education system risks losing these children a second time, perhaps forever.[42](b) Foroige believe that 15-18 year olds should not be paid to attend school as this 'rewards bad behaviour' and children should be encouraged to stay in mainstream schools for as long as possible.

With Youthreach the government have set up an alternative to school that's actually more attractive. The monetary incentive is a pull factor, encouraging students to leave. Where students want to make money there's a requirement to find a legitimate way to satisfy that need. But, arguably, a flat payment for attendance doesn't make sense. In a related criticism, the St. Vincent de Paul Society (SVP) advises caution, suggesting that Youthreach should not be used to remove underachieving or problematic students from mainstream schools. One person, who didn't want to be named, made a very strong case that there's no 'vision' for this particular cohort: 'No one is exercised by this. There's no champion for these kids, no one making a fuss. These are the forgotten group in Irish Education.' Undoubtedly, these are a difficult (but not impossible) to reach group. Significant progress can be made, provided their needs are understood. This group certainly requires a particular *type* of curriculum and specialist leadership skills (it's not a teaching job that everyone can do). However, where these conditions are met, this group of children can definitely make progress and there are hundreds of individual success stories to prove this.[43]

System Evaluation

On paper, the range of structures in place to address educational disadvantage seems comprehensive. But, of course, we understand that the number of initiatives in place is no guarantee that the problem is being tackled effectively. The answer to that question depends on how well the system operates i.e. the needs are understood, design of high quality programmes and so on. Further, a simple overview of what exists doesn't address the question of whether the same outcomes could be achieved for less i.e. answering the value for money question. We return to these specific issues in the recommendations.

Education Changes Lives:
Naomi Lester
Nursing Graduate, Trinity College

My name is Naomi. I'm 23 years old and live in Coolock. My Dad came from Sheriff Street, in inner city Dublin. He worked all his life as an insulator. My mother came from Coolock. She's a housewife and keeps us all on track. In primary school, education didn't really seem like a big deal. I liked school but didn't think about its importance. My Dad always said: 'If you don't have education these days you've nothing. It's your passport to the world.' After primary level he went straight to work so he was clued into the importance education long before the penny dropped for me.

In fifth class, a representative from the Challenger Programme[44] spoke to our class and encouraged us to join. It made me think about the future. In first year in secondary school, our group from the Challenger Programme visited Dublin City University (DCU). One of the nursing lecturers showed us around and asked if anyone wanted to be a nurse. Intrigued by everything, I said YES and she let me check the pulse rate on the practice mannequin. After that I was hooked. To you, this might seem like a small moment. But it was a big moment in my life, one that was literally life changing.

I studied hard and stayed focused for the Leaving Certificate. With 420 points, I was accepted into General Nursing in Trinity

College. As the first one to go to University, it was a huge moment for me and for my family. The financial side was definitely a worry but a grant covered the registration fees; otherwise, we couldn't have afforded it. To be honest, I was nervous about Trinity, always associating it with very wealthy people. I thought I'd be ostracised. Although there were a lot of wealthy people in Trinity, there were a lot of ordinary people too (like me) and we made great friends.

The course was tough. During the day we worked on the wards doing 12-hour shifts as part of the training. Studying happened at night and a weekend job in the local bowling alley helped pay the bills. The fact that I had such great family support got me through. I graduated in September 2015 and am now the proud holder of a 2:1 BSc. (degree in general nursing). I really love working on a Cardiothoracic Ward. We look after patients who've had bypass, heart valve or major lung surgeries. At some future point, I'd love to do a community nursing masters. The financial side of it is an issue but I'll save hard and push on to this next dream. I know what's out there now and that it's achievable.

Sometimes I have to pinch myself. Yes it was a struggle and I'm proud of the journey. But I know that I've been lucky too. The Challenger Programme - built around the core idea that you can do this – made a huge difference in my life. I really hope that it continues to positively impact the lives of others going forward.

Chapter 5

GOING TO COLLEGE:
FURTHER AND HIGHER EDUCATION

GOING TO COLLEGE

Career Guidance

The importance of career guidance in the educational arena can't be overstated. Information about the further/higher education application process (how to apply), available options (courses), routes (methods of entry) and the costs (financial supports), are critically important to young students and adults considering continuing their education journey. Students from a working class background who have financial concerns (or literacy problems) are much more reliant on data being provided through the school system. Very different experiences of school-based guidance are reported amongst working class and middle class students. Lower non-manual group students report being directed away from Higher Education, towards apprenticeships and further education courses and generally register negative experiences of the process. In contrast, middle class students report generally positive experiences of information exchange. Availability of information and advice on continuing education is one factor. But, arguably, even more important is the underpinning belief, that is, *this is the right option for me.* Without any experience on which to base their decision, a student is almost wholly reliant on teaching and guidance staff to provide a steer towards the best option. So, what might be happening here? Why are radically different conversations underway with students from disadvantaged areas and those from middle class areas? There are a number of factors at play.

At second level, people involved in career guidance are regular teachers who've undertaken additional training. Some are attracted to the individual coaching aspect of the role – a *pull* towards career guidance. Some are attracted by the thought of getting away from the classroom (not a happy place for all teachers). A stint in career guidance can be both a classroom sabbatical and a way to bolster professional skills. Given the importance of career guidance for students, one question is whether all teachers should rotate through this role for at least one full academic year? There's a second issue under this heading. The Irish Guidance Counsellors (2013 conference) found that less than 10 per cent of classroom guidance practice hours were spent working with Junior Cycle students. We have shown earlier that for many students, *later* guidance is *too late*; they may already have left the school system.[1] While providing earlier career guidance would not, as a stand-alone issue, prevent early school-leaving, it would certainly be part of a jigsaw of initiatives to support this:

> Children and young people who have difficulties with school attendance now ... will find no solace or consolation in the acceptance that this and other vital services in education will be funded incrementally and gradually. It is now and only now that their right to education can be fully delivered.[2]

Completion of the CAO 'Form'

Prior to the completion of the Leaving Certificate, students complete the CAO form and submit it (mostly electronically, occasionally in hard copy) to the Central Applications Office in Galway. The 'form' is complex as the current design offers up to 20 choices.[3] Ten of those choices are courses at Level 6/7 (National Certificate Level or Ordinary Degree level), which typically run for two to three years. Ten of the choices are reserved for Level 8 programmes (Honours Degree) which typically run for four years. The CAO form has to be completed by February 1, in other words, about five months in advance of the student sitting the Leaving Certificate exams. Thereafter, students have a *change of mind* option where they can re-order their choices or even make completely new choices. In the 1990s, circa 50 per cent of the choices made were for Level 6/7 programmes. By 2012, that number had changed and 72 per cent were choosing courses at level 8. This underscores the point made earlier that there is a continuous upwards qualifications drift as students target more advanced programmes to secure future employment. The height of the educational bar continues to move upwards, as it has done throughout history. For mainstream students and for 'Ireland Inc' that's good news, allowing us to compete internationally for increasingly complex work. For educationally disadvantaged students, it simply means that the passport to a decent job becomes ever more difficult to secure.

An ongoing debate is whether the CAO form is confusing. My experience is that it's not the form per se, it's the choice that's confusing. Normally, each third level college produces (a) a prospectus that details the range of courses and (b) a syllabus outlining the exact topics studied within each course. All of this information can be accessed on college websites. In some cases, these websites are complex and difficult to navigate. Looking up the syllabus online to gauge programme content can be confusing (it's definitely time consuming). The context here is that this selection is completed at a time when the students are teenagers (that is, sometimes generally confused about life), when they should be investing time in studying for their final exams, are caught up completing mock exams and so on.

College Campus

Students who physically visit a college get a sense of the campus and can pick up a hard copy of the Prospectus. Some will prefer the open space and range of facilities offered by large campuses like UCD. Others prefer a more intimate setting, perhaps with smaller class sizes and less confusing geography. If a student's parents have been through third level, they can offer support with course selection. They are more likely to know (or be related to) people in professions chosen by their children and can arrange for them to talk to the student directly. They can actively help in completing the CAO application, with a higher likelihood that they have a computer and internet access. Students can also be physically shuffled around to see a range of campuses and make a more informed decision. So, even at the choice stage, middle class children are advantaged in making the call about which course to complete and which college to attend. And, making a good call at that point supports later retention rates. In contrast, where parents don't have a strong educational background, lack confidence in their writing ability or can't access computing/transport, the which course/which college decision can be baffling. The topic of career guidance offers low hanging fruit in terms of a potential fix. It's an obvious place where resources within the second level system or community educational resources can bridge this information gap. Later in this book we provide an 'educational roadmap' to help students navigate the system.[4] But, a gap that's less easy to bridge is the confidence shown by middle class parents, pushing for the best solutions for their children – even when things go slightly awry.

Almost There

As a new and inexperienced President in NCI, I was contacted by a well-known businessman. His son, having chosen NCI as a place to study, had underperformed in the Leaving Certificate and didn't achieve the required number of points. The question was straightforward. Could I help him in any way? The intent wasn't to game the system, but simply to understand if anything could be done within the existing rules. Not knowing how the CAO worked, I spoke with the Registrar. The answer was swift and clear. The student didn't have enough points to get in and that was that. He could re-sit the Leaving Certificate the following year and try to secure more points. It seemed like game over. From talking with his father, I knew that the 're-sit' option was about as attractive as having root canal work completed on his teeth. We needed something creative. It turned out that NCI ran the exact same programme on an evening basis, a fee-paying option normally attended by mature students. This course was not part of the 'free fees' CAO system and not subject to the same rules. We suggested that the student complete the evening course. His dad stumped up the money, the student signed up and successfully completed the degree. All perfectly legitimate and a positive outcome. However, what struck me forcefully was the confidence of the father in putting the question and his expectation that all avenues would be pursued on behalf of his son. He was right. The middle class advantage is not just money. It's also about assertiveness.

College Entry

The majority of students enter college following the completion of the Leaving Certificate examinations held in May/June of each year. Assuming that the student can achieve enough points in the Leaving Certificate to secure their chosen programme, this is the most direct entry route.[5] The entry system, administered by the Central Applications Office (CAO), is streamlined.[6] In 2013, the CAO system regulated entry into 1,325 individual courses.[7] While the system is very efficient and transparent, it doesn't deliver perfect outcomes for all students. The points required for individual programmes change from year to year (depending on demand) with some students having to accept their second or third choice. There's general agreement that allocating college places based on Leaving Certificate results is outwardly fair in the sense that no one can jockey the system. All exam papers are marked anonymously, with each student identified by a number. The rules are transparent and apply to everyone. Yet this outward fairness masks a structural inequality that's more difficult to detect. Like an iceberg, 90 per cent of the discrimination is below the waterline, hidden from view. We know that students who are most likely to score well come from middle class areas, the overwhelmingly majority of whom subsequently go to college. So this outwardly fair system actually produces a heavily biased outcome; the odds are stacked against working class children long before they commence the Leaving Certificate cycle. It's hardly a surprise that middle class kids do better in exams and that more go to college. They have access to role models, space to study, extra tuition/grinds, more computers, a peer group where the norm is to go to college and so on. In short, the education system mirrors the general inequalities in society. But, do we simply 'wash our hands' and walk away? Or is there something concrete that can be done, something that stops somewhere short of a political revolution? Park that thought until we come to the recommendations section. For the moment, we are staying with the college entry question.

Programme Difficulty

There's a general misconception about the Irish educational system as follows: The man on the street believes that a course of study which requires high points will be more difficult to complete. That's factually incorrect. A course requiring 555 entry points, for example, the BA in Psychology in Trinity College (2015 figures) is pitched at exactly the same level of difficulty as a degree requiring 350 entry points in an Institute of Technology. The difficulty of individual programmes can be likened to basketball hoops – the height of the hoop is 10 feet regardless of whether you are playing in the National Basketball Arena in Tallaght or a schoolyard in Waterford. The same idea applies to diplomas or degrees.[8] In short, the difficulty of individual programmes is broadly comparable across the entire system regardless of the number of points it takes to gain entry to a particular course. The high points required for some courses reflects the law of supply and demand, nothing more. Where there is a small number of places and high demand (for example, architecture), the points to get in are sky high. It doesn't actually mean that architects need to be smarter than the rest of us![9]

UNDERSTANDING 'LEVELS'

The National Framework of Qualifications

The National Framework of Qualifications (NFQ) was designed to map individual courses of study on to a coherent National Framework. The NFQ, launched in 2003, consists of a system of 10 award levels. Levels 1-6 were awarded by FETAC (Further Education and Training Awards Council); levels 6-10 awarded by HETAC (Higher Education and Training Awards Council).[10] A centrally important purpose of the NFQ map was to highlight opportunities to transfer and progress from one education level to the next,[11] that is, the map was designed to facilitate student mobility.

Simplifying the Journey

Like a rail network, the Irish education system is complex. There are lots of places to 'get on' and 'get off'. The NFQ map would also help people navigate their journey. Prior to the development of the NFQ, it was almost impossible to understand the *status* of awards made by numerous providers and how much weight to attach to them. For example, were all of the accounting bodies operating to the same standards, or was one type of accountancy qualification superior to another? The NFQ helped to communicate the point that having a 'Level 7' qualification (or any other level) is the same regardless of the institution that issues the award (albeit you can't legislate against informal snobbery and some educational institutions still rank higher on the status totem pole).[12] Despite the excellent work completed in this area, my sense is that the 10 levels are not widely-known or understood outside of a narrow group of specialists who work in the sector. While the NFQ has achieved its *simplification* objectives, it's a long way short of fulfilling the promise that this would help students *navigate* the system. We return to the general issue of marketing in the concluding section.

THE ROADS LESS TRAVELLED: ALTERNATIVE ROUTES INTO HIGHER EDUCATION

Running alongside the Central Applications Office (CAO), several additional routes into Higher Education are available. These alternative routes are an overt recognition that some 'structural unfairness' is embedded in the current design of the Leaving Certificate points system. Like the handicap system in golf, this is an attempt to make the game fair. The five alternatives routes are:

Route 1: Higher Education Access Route (HEAR)

The target is under-represented socio-economic students. Relevant students (for example, those coming from DEIS schools), compete for entry into participating colleges on reduced Leaving Certificate points. For example, the requirement to study Arts in UCD – 345 points in 2016 – was reduced to 320 points for HEAR students.[13] In addition to a reduction in the number of points required, a range of financial, academic and other supports are also made available to students taking this route. Example: Some colleges provide scholarships for qualifying students.[14]

Route 2: Disability Access Route to Higher Education (DARE)

This route caters for students presenting with a disability. Once they gain entry, a range of supports can be put in place to help students cope with the rigors of college life. Many colleges now employ a Disability Officer and have a Fund for Students with Disabilities. Other developments include AHEAD's (Association for Higher Education Access and Disability) Charter for Inclusive Teaching[15] which includes recommendations on reasonable accommodations (key argument: good pedagogical practices benefit *all* students).

Route 3: Further Education

Further education colleges offer an alternative path for (a) students who've completed the Leaving Certificate and (b) mature students who want to re-enter the education system.[16] Post-Leaving Certificate Programmes (PLCs), completed by younger students who didn't achieve high points in the Leaving Certificate exams, provide a bridge into third level education. Where a student achieves a solid result in their PLC exams (normally a distinction), this provides an alternative route into college. Even where students don't move onto third level, completing a PLC is an additional successful element of their educational journey. Deirdre Giblin describes this as follows: 'While it might not be a posh college, there's a huge upside in being able to communicate college attendance, a positive for the student and the parent.'

Route 4: Mature Entry

It generally surprises people that mature students in Ireland are defined as people who've reached the ripe old age of 23. The thinking here is to catch people who didn't make their way into college directly after the Leaving Certificate. Students who didn't achieve high points in the Leaving Certificate can set that result aside, which allows a second bite of the cherry. Normally, there are a number of designated places for mature students who gain entry on a 'reduced points' basis.

Route 5: Direct Entry

Some higher education institutions have developed pre-entry 'Access' courses (sometimes called foundation courses) to prepare students who don't meet *traditional* entry requirements. The courses are usually several months to one year in duration. Progression on to an undergraduate degree is the next rung on the education ladder for students who successfully complete foundation programmes and who wish to continue their studies. Foundation courses provide opportunities for students to become familiar with college life. By providing tuition in areas like mathematics and academic writing, students are prepared for college. Sometimes, additional support is provided on personal (there's often a strong focus on confidence-building) and financial issues. People who work in the 'access space' are normally very attuned to this type of student and their particular needs. In constructing this book, I heard dozens of positive stories about lecturers and other educational staff 'going the extra mile' for access students to ensure their success.

THE FURTHER EDUCATION SECTOR

The further education sector, part of the Irish landscape for circa 50 years, essentially occupies the space between second level and third level education. It's a huge arena with upwards of 192,000 learners participating at any one time.[17] A significant proportion of these students come from the disadvantaged groups identified earlier. So, education disadvantage and further education are intimately connected. Currently, there are four types of programme on offer (1) Post-Leaving Certificate Courses, (2) Vocational Training Opportunities, (3) Labour Activation Programmes and (4) Short Programmes, sometimes aimed at hobby students, that is, people who want to study a topic for intellectual stimulation or just for fun.

Historical Backdrop

In the early 1970s, the oil crisis and subsequent recession led to a large increase in unemployment. When Ireland joined the European Union (1973), this opened up a number of grant aid possibilities to address this problem. While there had always been shifts in employment, the impact of microprocessor technology had a profound impact on the *type* of employment becoming available. Essentially, unemployment started to shift from *cyclical* to *structural*. An emerging group of adolescents and adults couldn't access the jobs market without further education and training. Lacking the skills to participate, they needed to re-train and a range of courses were developed to up-skill this group. What initially began as a 'Pre-Employment Course' eventually morphed into a range of Post-Leaving Certificate courses which are still in place today. The significant difference between 'then' and 'now' is that younger participants, around 15 or 16 years old, completed these programmes throughout the 1980s whereas the age profile has now changed to 18 or 19 (participants complete the Leaving Certificate before signing up for a PLC).[18]

Post-Leaving Certificate Programmes

The focus of PLCs is to integrate general education, vocational training and work experience – a *learning by doing* approach. Programmes typically run for one to two years fulltime and students graduate with a Level 5 award (these courses are pitched at the same academic level as the Leaving Certificate).[19] Post-Leaving Certificate programmes (PLCs) account for the bulk of intake students into further education and they typically study for 21.5 hours a week.[20]

Vocational Training Opportunities Scheme (VTOS)

Some students are registered on Vocational Training Opportunity Schemes (VTOS),[21] which run for around 30 hours a week (6 six-hours a day for five days) and last for up to two years. The target group here are 15-20 year olds, unemployed, early school-leavers. This is full time education, delivered in further education colleges or community training centres, funded by the Department of Education and Skills.[22] The goal here is to provide unemployed people with employability skills to prepare them for paid employment.[23]

Labour Activation Initiatives

One interesting (relatively recent) development was the provision of financial support to students on part-time courses under the Springboard scheme. The then Minister for Education and Skills, Ruairí Quinn, launched Springboard in May 2011. Labour Activation targets unemployed adults, offering a route to reskill and get back into the workforce. Many of the people targeted had lost their jobs during the recession. College places were provided on a no-fees basis to students (the colleges were paid directly by the exchequer). A centrally important point was that students were also able to keep their social welfare supports in place while studying.[24] Springboard offered almost 6,000, part-time places in higher education leading to certificate, degree and post-graduate awards. Feedback on the initiative from participants, colleges and industry representatives has generally been positive.

To take just one measure, the formal evaluation reported that over 40 per cent of participants returned to employment within six months of programme completion.[25] On one level, the Springboard initiative highlights an inconsistency in government policy. Providing funding for part-time students who wish to reskill while, at the same time, reducing funding for undergraduate students doesn't make sense (in fairness, the economic crisis has forced the Government to make tough choices). Interestingly, the Springboard initiative was led by the Access Office in the Higher Education Authority. This is a small group (fewer than six people) who co-ordinate all access activities across the third level sector. This already tiny resource was essentially *raided* to provide expertise for the Springboard initiative. While labour activation is an important pillar in government plans to 'get people working', it doesn't make sense to asset strip this tiny section and worsen the plight of educationally disadvantaged students.

Further Education Discussion Points

A review of the further education system raises two important discussion points: Firstly, is the underpinning philosophy clear? Secondly, are the available resources adequate and the administration simple?

Missing Philosophy

Within the sector, the importance of the work is understood: 'Colleges have developed a very significant role in the education landscape, providing career-specific certification for many sectors, including some that are not represented elsewhere.'[26] It has also become a growing feeder stream for people moving into higher education. In 2001, 2,903 Central Applications Office (CAO) applicants presented with FETAC (now QQI) qualifications; by 2012, that number had risen to 15,288 students, an increase of 527 per cent.[27] Despite the above, it's difficult to understand the philosophy which underpins the further education sector. At the time of writing, further education is defined as anything that's *not* secondary education or higher education, that is, the sector is defined by what it isn't.

In public discourse, further education is arguably the forgotten link in the education chain. When he was Minister for Education, Ruairi Quinn called further education the 'Cinderella' of the education system. It's as if we were discussing the Irish road network and the only roads under consideration were the motorways (higher education institutions). In public commentary on post-secondary education, higher education is virtually the only option ever discussed. Further education, a sector which accounts for nearly €1 billion spend per annum, rarely merits a mention. Rory O'Sullivan labelled it *terra incognita*, undiscovered land. The sector is part-funded by the exchequer and partly through the National Training Fund, a levy on employers, so it's not crystal clear exactly who owns it (albeit the Department of Education and Skills have a clear responsibility for this area). While further education colleges offer a broad range of courses (full-time and part-time), the student body attending is quite diverse. Some students actively try to up-skill as a way to re-train for employment. Some re-enter the education system for personal confidence, for example, to improve English or baseline maths as a 'second chance'. There's also a large chunk of students attending just for fun, for example, learning to play the violin or speak Spanish. The variety of student motives and the wide range of services makes it difficult to succinctly capture the underpinning philosophy (although the further education system plays an enormously important role in addressing educational disadvantage).

Administration Complexity

For the moment, let's park philosophy and look at what actually happens in practice. In attempting to unravel the types of further education students and how the funding system works, what quickly became apparent is a hopeless complexity. On the good news front, there's been a recent smart change in the rules. When studying, a person can continue to receive social welfare payments and doesn't have to be 'available for work'. That criteria had been used to limit the payment of unemployment benefit. The unintended consequence was to keep unskilled people unemployed for longer periods as they couldn't afford to lose social welfare benefits and wouldn't return to education, a roadblock that's now been removed. The bad news is that a huge chunk of administration time is taken up, with senior people applying for funding to a variety of government agencies under different programme headings with endless 'form filling'. The system is crying out for business simplification. For example, where a student presents with a disability, a claim for this person is made by the individual institution. Multiply that single task by the number of students in further education who present with a disability and you begin to see the scale of the problem. It would be much simpler to estimate the overall numbers of students with disabilities who apply (based on a per cent of the population) and make a single payment. Rory O'Sullivan, frustrated that so much time is taken up in administration said: 'Last week I had to fill in a 16 page form for a €1,000 grant. It would drive you mad. Perhaps I should take the Naomi Campbell line, saying, "I'm not going to get out of bed for less than €10,000."'

Resource Inflexibility

The further education sector is essentially a training system for both younger students and older adults, which is being strangled by the school year. For no good reason, their training year essentially mirrors the school year for younger children – with elongated holidays and a very restricted time calendar for teachers – without any outward logic for this. Overall the further education sector is hugely important as a stepping-stone for people wishing to continue their education journey (often disadvantaged students who are taking this zig zag route). It's currently planned that Solas will become the new co-coordinating body for the further education sector. Hopefully, the confused mission and the administration complexity detailed above will be placed squarely on the change agenda for Solas.[28]

TACKLING EDUCATIONAL DISADVANTAGE WITHIN HIGHER EDUCATION

Let's start with the good news. 'Access' initiatives are becoming more centrally embedded across the third level sector. For example, the current UCD strategic plan sets out to 'attract and retain a diverse student group' and similar sentiments can be found in many college strategies. Beyond formal strategy, there is strong anecdotal evidence of senior executive support. Fiona Sweeney, who runs the Access Programmes in UCD, stated that her department gets great support from a Registrar deemed to be pro-student generally and very proactive on the access question. However, while we are familiar with the line 'an organisation is a shadow of its leader'[29] access initiatives shouldn't be overly dependent on the person in the chair at a moment in time. University leaders, coming from diverse backgrounds, are not automatically pro-access in outlook. Progressing educational disadvantage is bigger than any single executive and needs to become hardwired into each organisation across the sector. And, of course, there are national level questions that sit above the individual institutions. While there are a number of separate strands to this, let's start with college fees.

Abolition of University Fees

In 1996, the then Minister for Education, Niamh Bhreathnach, abolished tuition fees to 'increase access to third level education for all students'. Doing so would 'remove important financial and psychological barriers to participation at third level' (White Paper 1995:101). No evidence was cited to support the assumption that more access students would actually attend college. Since that time there has been an enormous expansion in the number of students completing third level, but actually little evidence of narrowing the gap between middle class students and the disadvantaged groups listed earlier.[30] Arguably, the unintended consequence of the abolition of fees has been to allow wealthier families divert spending into fee-paying second level schools and grinds thereby further widening the educational disadvantage gap: 'Bearing in mind that most low income students would typically not have been paying university fees (since most would have been in receipt of the Higher Education Grant)... The logic of this apparently escaped policy makers at the time.'[31] Perhaps the unspoken logic was not publicised.

More cynical observers have commented that the forthcoming general election (which took place the following year, in 1997) may have been part of the rationale. What's clear is that the decision to forgo college fees was hugely popular.[32] Parents who'd been making an investment in education were now subsidised by general taxpayers. In hindsight, it's difficult to see the logic of replacing private funding of education with public funding without any material (other than political) gain. There's no obvious wisdom in subsidising families who can afford to send their children to college and who will ultimately benefit from it. Regardless of whether you believe (a) access to third level for disadvantaged students was the fundamental rationale (even if this didn't pan out) or (b) you hold a more cynical view that real politic drove this decision, the net effect was to drain a huge amount of income from the third level sector – money that had to be replaced by the exchequer.

Declining Third Level Resources

There were mixed views on the 'free fees' initiative within the third level sector. Many universities didn't support the abolition of fees as they hypothesized that *central money* would come with the hidden price of control over their autonomy, historically jealously guarded. Worse still, the fear was that future governments might renege on the required funding, putting the sector into a resource squeeze. That fear was well founded. Since the fall of the Celtic Tiger, the Irish public sector has been under enormous cost pressure. In 2009, the 'Employment Control Framework' froze employment levels. As new posts couldn't be filled, the effect was that between 2007 and 2011, non-academic staff numbers declined by 10 per cent (academics by 3 per cent).[33] Since that time the annual registration charge has also come into play. It currently costs €3,000 per annum for a student to attend college (this is still heavily subsidised, well below the actual costs of a third level education which is around €10,000 per annum). Access activities run by third level colleges are costly and expenditure cuts have made this work particularly challenging. In short, the abolition of third level fees offered the outward illusion of progress on access without the magic actually happening. By starving the third level system of income and subsidising all students (not just those who couldn't afford to pay), abolishing college fees actually *damaged* the opportunity to tackle educational disadvantage.

Multiple Approaches

Under the general heading of college preparation we see a phenomenon which is repeated time and again across the educational sector. There's no agreement on the best methods to tackle educational disadvantage. For example, in University College Dublin, no foundation courses are run. The college does a lot of outreach work in disadvantaged communities and certainly seems committed to the general provision of access, but doesn't deploy this particular method. A couple of miles down the road in Trinity College, foundation courses are a central building block of the 'access system'. Here we see the local nature of decision-making around promoting access. Given the historical autonomy of the universities, a cookie-cutter approach to access may simply be unworkable. But it's difficult not to arrive at the conclusion that there's too much *innovation* and too little *implementation*. While I have sympathy with the general ambition to give scope to local decision-making, there's a trade off between localism and the need to develop shared methods that benefit from economies of scale through collaboration on a cross-institution basis.

What 'Should' Happen?

Third level colleges have a complex assortment of Access initiatives in place.[34] These typically consist of pre-entry activities, aimed at the five under-represented groups listed earlier. Assuming that these students can overcome the early hurdles and actually get into college, a range of post-entry supports become available (personal, financial, academic, career). As far back as 2006, the evaluation of the Higher Education Access Programmes[35] highlighted the need for institutions to (a) develop clear plans around links between their programmes and community/other education providers, (b) the involvement and commitment of all staff (not just those employed in the access office), (c) clear progression routes to higher education for targeted groups, (d) clear targets, including timescales, for the admission and graduation of specific groups and (e) a systematic approach to data mining to monitor success. On face value all of the above seem eminently sensible. The 2008-2013 National Plan[36] reinforced the importance of the post-entry stage and suggested building a third level research network to share best practice. One interesting target suggested was that all socio-economic groups should have an entry rate of at least 54 per cent by 2020 (based on the principle that no group should have a participation rate less than three-quarters of the national average). While it's difficult to argue against any of these suggestions, the words 'money' and 'mouth' spring to mind. Access activities need to be resourced. Ferdinand Von Prondzynski, former President of DCU, making a similar point, said:

> Policy makers sometimes argue that the access problem requires a high level of commitment from university leaders. There's no question that this needs to be in place. But, in addition, there needs to be an interlocking series of supports that are resource intensive. Unfortunately, access isn't 'free'.

It Can Be Done

Some foundation programmes are run outside of the formal college sector. For example, the Jesuit involvement with third level education goes back to the sixteenth century. In more recent times, there's been an involvement in Ballymun for 35 years and the JUST Programme (Jesuit University Support and Training) has been running for 10 years. The central aim is to encourage more people to enrol in university-level studies and JUST offers personal and academic support to those who've decided to take this life-changing step. In the past 10 years, Ballymun has managed to 'move the needle' of people who attend college from about 2.5 per cent (of secondary school leavers) to circa 10 per cent. While this is still well below the national average, it demonstrates that movement is possible and gives great hope for the future. The people in JUST (the project is run from a building in the centre of Ballymun) are rightly proud of their 'First 5 PhD's' and there are numerous students who've completed both undergraduate and Masters degrees. All of this achieved in an area that boasted the 'Worst Secondary School in Ireland.'[37] In one year, the highest performing child in that particular secondary school scored 290 points in the Leaving Certificate. Everyone else came in below that score, with several children receiving zero points in the Leaving Certificate, often through no-shows at the exams. JUST, working with the

Society of St Vincent de Paul and the local BITE (Ballymun Initiative for Third Level Education) project provide 10 scholarships annually and there's an emerging competition to be selected. The project was independently funded by the sale of a former university residence (Hatch Street in Dublin) with the proceeds invested in an educational trust. But it isn't just about money. The project director, Dr. Kevin O'Higgins SJ, lives in the community. Overall, the JUST programme represents an extraordinary, sustained personal commitment by both religious and lay people.

Investment in Access in Third Level Colleges

To help align institutional strategies with national priorities, Access is given a weighting in terms of core funding. While, over the years there have been many changes in how this works, the current system is as follows:[38] higher education institutions receive a grant per access student at the level of 130 per cent of normal intake students. This is a recognition of the additional teaching and learning costs involved in working with this cohort of students and supports the employment of Access, Disability and Mature Student officers, the front line of an institution's access programme.

Working with Schools and Communities

Higher education institutions who are committed to the access agenda often work with DEIS primary and post-primary schools to improve progression to college. At a basic level, this work includes guidance and information support ('what are the higher education options?' and 'how do you get in?'). Sometimes specific academic support is provided, either at the school or on campus (for example, revision bootcamps in preparation for the Leaving Certificate). Access staff may visit schools and community groups to 'sell the message' and school pupils visit the campus for events and open days. Post-entry, some colleges provide student-to-student mentoring or shadowing (buddy system) during orientation. At the higher end, some institutions provide professional development and networking opportunities for primary and secondary schoolteachers and

principals, support school-based curriculum enhancement projects and facilitate teachers to undertake research.

Engaging Parents

Some of the access initiatives include parents. For example, UCD
works with parents of school-going children (cleverly seeing the
parents as mature students, a potential double reinforcement of
the social capital within a family). Overall, there are many ways
in which a college can be made less distant (and less intimidating)
and more relevant in the life of a student, a school or a community.[39] While hugely laudable, all of this work is completed against
a backdrop of declining resources. Consider the following: it's very
difficult for staff who work in this area to *prove* the value of what
they do for their *particular* college. The payback argument becomes mired in debates around 'who would have gone to college
anyway' (even without additional support) and the fact that some
second-level students will decide to go to colleges other than the
one that has provided the direct support. While there's a general
benefit to the exchequer, it can be almost impossible to prove a
payback link to the college supporting the initiative.[40] Perhaps the
most publicised third level access programme in Ireland is run by
Trinity College. Here's how it works...

Trinity Access Programme

*I sat in Goldsmith House, where the Trinity Access Programme
(TAP) is located, listening to some fairly flat Dublin accents (exactly like my own). There was a lot of noisy chatter, par for the
course with young students everywhere. Those working class accents highlight an emerging diversity on a historically conservative campus. The TAP story is impressive: this is an access programme that delivers. Let me declare a bias at the outset. I became
acquainted with the Trinity Access Programme many years ago.
As a former Trinity access student (it was completely informal
in the 1980s), I had a particular interest in how this new official*

system worked. In 2001, the numbers were disappointing. Trinity College had circa 40 access students across the entire campus. It seemed like tokenism. The take-away impression – the first time I looked at it – was that a centrally important element was access to high net worth donors. Educational disadvantage seemed like a front for securing philanthropy, a brass plaque of concern to suck in monetary support. Roll that clock forward to today and I'm delighted to have been proven wrong.

23rd Anniversary. *The TAP Programme, in place for 23 years, has come of age. In 2016, 256 access students registered in first year, just short of 10 per cent of Trinity's student intake. Across all years, the number of access students rises to 978. Those numbers don't lie; access is starting to gain traction. The numeric gains are driven by a system that includes a number of interlocking elements.[41] It's worthwhile to take-a-peek under the bonnet of TAP to see how it works. Interestingly, there's zero insider-trading here; third level institutions are completely open about sharing practices in the interests of the common good.*

How do you get in? About two-thirds of access students come through the HEAR route detailed earlier. Because Trinity is high status (and, therefore, a popular choice), the number of points required to gain entry to all courses is high. Under the HEAR route, students qualify for points reduction ranging between 10 per cent (lower points courses) and 20 per cent (highest points courses). The remaining access students come in via a 1-year Foundation programme run on campus and at three off-campus locations across the city. Up to 90 per cent of students who start the foundation programme, complete the course. Of those who move into the college proper, over 90 per cent of those complete the degree, scoring an average 2.1 rating.[42] These are the exact same 'working class' students some argue shouldn't go to college as they don't have the brains to be successful (highlighting the fallacy of the Leaving Certificate points system as an ability measure). The retention rates for access students are seriously impressive. If Trinity College is hard to get into (high points), it also seems hard to fall out of (for access students). Supporting this broad point, Fiona Sweeney (speaking about UCD) suggested that student retention is: 'At least as strong and often better than normal intake students. Access students are minded a bit better, particularly in the crucial 1st year.'[43] *For the first time in their lives, this group experience being advantaged. And, it works.*

Staffing Levels: The TAP programme has 12 full-time staff. While I didn't meet everyone, there's a mix of social classes, several coming into the role as former access students themselves. People who've made a similar journey push students, in an encouraging way. Six of these full-time positions are sponsored by commercial organisations, highlighting strong links with the business world. Dr. Cliona Hannon leads the effort. In a former life, I worked with General Electric, an organisation with a well-deserved reputation for developing talent. One of the core beliefs in GE was as follows: 'You can't send a technician to do an engineers' job.' Difficult projects, like running an access department, require strong and committed leaders, people who understand the social, human and cultural theories which underpin this work. Without doubt, the leadership, bench strength and staff numbers in TAP help to explain the programme's success. In some of the smaller, third-level institutions, there's often a single person staffing the access fort, dealing with social deprivation, disability, the specific needs of travellers and so on. With low resources, it's hardly surprising that nothing of consequence happens. One respondent, cut to the chase: 'The access department has to be something more than 'one man and his dog.'' In Trinity, we see a programme resourced for success in terms of time, expertise, money and passion.

Corporate Links: Strong relationships have been built with a number of Corporate Sponsors. For example, Trinity work with five of the 'Big Six' law firms and secure direct training placements for law students. While no firm will guarantee employment, the stamp of the Trinity Access Programme opens the door to opportunity and the students take it from there themselves. Stated another way, the historical discrimination against working class students is reversed and this actually stacks the odds in their favour. Of course, like closet racism, there's undoubtedly still some discrimination (not everyone is in thrall to that flat Dublin accent) but this represents a real step forward.

Pathways to College: A number of outreach elements are in place, including some standard fare, for example, summer programmes for potential students. In line with the arguments made elsewhere, there's a belief that students need 'hard information' about how the education system works. They are motivated to progress when they have a better understanding of what they want to do. A crucial element of the TAP programme is that career guidance is given to 13-year-olds, letting them see the rabbit at any early age.[44]

Mentoring: Children relate well to role models, people who came from their own community. Trinity works with second level schools to help them find and establish relationships with alumni who've been successful. Most second level schools have little contact with former pupils, other than a tiny number of stars (for example boy band members or inter-county GAA players). While all mentors have to be vetted (child protection guidelines), these offer a rich resource to the schools. It's a simple idea, one that could be scaled nationally. Dr. Cliona Hannon argues: 'People want a structured way to give back to the communities they live in or grew up in.'

Leadership Through Service: Trinity College works with Transition Year students, helping them to choose and execute projects without the involvement of adults. The central driver here is to provide a sense of agency. In one example, students in Inchicore built a '21st Century Classroom' with sponsorship from Google. Their impressive achievements were later replayed at an internal company conference offering everyone a feel-good hit around what can be achieved. Companies use corporate social responsibility programmes to bind staff, supporting retention rates by making staff feel that they work for an organisation that stands for something (a huge potential win/win).

21st Century Teaching and Learning: TAP is working to develop a more modern form of teaching and learning, a centrally important idea addressed throughout this book. The underpinning philosophy is democratisation of the classroom, giving more power to the students. To make this real, Trinity have developed a post-graduate programme (Level 9). In 2015, 87 teachers (many from DEIS schools) were enrolled in the programme, offering an enormous potential ripple effect when these teachers return to their classrooms. While our focus has been on Trinity College, there are excellent access initiatives in place across the sector.

Improving Teaching Methods

The teaching methods in place across higher education institutions is a sensitive topic. One criticism of outdated teaching methods is captured in an old joke. Rip Van Winkle wakes up after a long sleep and makes his way around the city. He sees people speaking into mobile phones and is at a complete loss to understand what's happening. Overhead, planes make their way across the sky and Rip is mesmerised. Then he stumbles through the gate of a university and goes into a theatre when the lecturer stands at the front of the class delivering his sermon. Rip van Winkle says, 'Thank God, at last I know where I am.' Colleges have been around for many centuries. In some cases, the teaching methodology hasn't changed all that much. Lecturers individually prepare and deliver their notes. But this is changing with some terrific innovations in teaching practice. As a snippet, consider the following notices issued to UCD students:

- **Tuesday, 23 February**: 6.00 pm in New Theatre 1, Newman Building. Title: *Plato Would Make French Films but Aristotle would make Hollywood Movies.* The lecture promises to be a fun and engaging way for undergraduates and postgraduates to engage with these two prolific Greek philosophers from a perspective they may have never thought of.

- **Wednesday, 2 March: Student Legal Convention:** Hosted by Miriam O'Callaghan, featuring discussions on rights of accused in criminal cases, media and law, social inequality and surrogacy. The SLC will hear from Fr. Peter McVerry, Colm O'Gorman, and more.

Improved Pedagogy Benefits Everyone

Great learning and teaching practices positively impact *all students* and are an important factor in supporting retention.[45] In recognition of this, most Higher Education Institutions have established 'Learning and Teaching Centres' focused on enhancing the learning experience for *all* (not just access) students. Several offer Postgraduate Certificates/Diplomas in Teaching and Learning, where academics can upskill and the programmes are generally well subscribed. The institutional self-evaluation reports (submitted to the HEA) contain many examples of excellent learning and teaching practices.[46] They also generally support student evaluations of teaching (at some point, someone has to ask the *customers* what they think). At this moment in time, work in this area is voluntary. Academics who participate in improved teaching and learning do so on a voluntary basis. While it's difficult to get precise data, anecdotal evidence suggests that it's the *best lecturers* who keep getting better. There is a tranche of poor lecturers across all of the colleges who don't participate in continuous improvement and there's no sanction against this group (nor reward for those who continually upskill). Many years ago there was an old line about Dunlop's, the tyre manufacturers in Cork: 'Once you get your leg in, you're right' (in other words, no one was ever fired, regardless of subsequent performance). In many ways that statement reflects the performance management systems in place across the third level sector with 'pockets of excellence' (in terms of teaching practice) operating in parallel with some brutal teaching which students have to endure.

College Foundations

I was struck by the fact that colleges with the 'most advanced' access programmes generally also have the most active foundations – the arm of the college that secures philanthropic contributions and engages business organisations. Given the *cost* of access, perhaps this finding is not surprising. Establishing a working foundation is extremely difficult. Finding the right person to lead it is often the single most elusive hiring assignment across the entire campus. Fundraising has become a science and the underpinning expertise is scarce. There's enormous competition for professional foundation staff across a range of good causes, such as medical research. Under this heading, the larger colleges are certainly advantaged. Even if a smaller college could set up a fully functioning foundation on day one, it can take several years before the work yields fruit. Interestingly, in relation to securing access students, there's no real competition between the colleges. Educational disadvantage is so widespread, there are plenty of students to go around!

Retention: Getting In and Staying In

The current rate for completion of college programmes is 83 per cent.[47] The general rule of thumb is as follows. Courses that require the highest number of points for entry purposes record the highest level of completion rates. In the Institutes of Technology, 43 per cent of students don't complete their programme of study which makes the drop out rate more than double that in the universities. Is that because the programmes on offer are more difficult? No, it's because the students who enter on lower entry points generally require more support to complete their journey. Prior educational attainment is the strongest predictor of successful progression in higher education.[48]

Why Students Drop Out

Several studies have ascertained why students drop out of college. The most significant factors include:

- **Unclear aspirations:** Particularly around the type of job aimed for.

- **Poor research:** Students didn't understand the course content.

- **Underestimated workload:** While this is normally on par with secondary level workload, because some of this is self-directed, students can feel it's more stressful (particularly in year 1 during the transition).

- **Specific difficulties:** Often with maths (the high failure rates on maths-intensive programmes bears this out).

- **Staff relationships:** Some report negative relationships with staff and poor general communications within college as the reason for leaving.

- **External reasons:** Financial, personal or work-related problems.[49]

The centrally important point here is that a number of studies have shown that where access students receive institutional support, retention rates are on par (or better) with students who come through the normal intake.[50] The conclusion from one study was as follows: It's not access, per se, which causes problems with student retention; the problem is a lack of attention to the needs of a more diverse range of students.[51] The challenge for all colleges is to meet the needs of an increasingly diverse student body rather than expecting the students to conform to the traditional model (without, of course, lowering overall educational standards). As a minimum, even if the system stays as is (and we return to that particular argument later), the trick is to get students to successfully complete first year. After that, all the evidence suggests that they are much more likely to stay the course.

Post-Entry Retention Practices

Higher Education Institutions offer a range of interventions to support retention. Some of these are aimed directly at access students; others apply to all students. Supports include financial (transport, childcare), assistive technology, accommodations for students with disabilities, learning supports (diagnosis and additional tuition) and so on. This can also include peer support, the provision of study skills, career development advice, and general student support such as counseling. Post-entry supports enhance retention. If we think of a college as a business, some make huge customer retention efforts and hate to lose a student. Other colleges implicitly accept a 'survival of the fittest' philosophy with massive fallout. A really well run access programme is a delight. But, some colleges seem blasé on retention, offering poor direction and zero oversight.

Mixing the Tribes

The importance of students from under-represented groups feeling that they *belong* in college is well documented in the literature on student retention. The need to foster positive peer relationships and build social networks between different student groups (to improve the student experience and support retention) has emerged as an important finding. But how do you achieve this? A college can't force students to have particular friends. The single best method seems to be through inclusive teaching approaches where students work closely together on projects. Keane[52] reported significant distancing behaviours on campus from some groups of students. Access students in her study tended to 'stick to their own' on campus, rather than integrating with traditional entry students. They talked about feeling safe and comfortable with other access students and of sensing other student groups were exclusive and distant (albeit, a lack of engagement and networking with other students may ultimately be a form of self-sabotage). Interestingly, both access and traditional entry students in that study talked at length about some wealthy, snobby students (termed 'the Abercrombie and Fitch' type and the 'Plastics') who, they believed, exhibited social peacocking behaviour to establish their status through physical appearance, clothes and material possessions.[53] While the brand names may be new, the phenomena itself isn't.

Fitting In

Part of my undergraduate studies involved a number of encounter weekends held in Kilkenny. Attendance was compulsory. From memory, a lot of the 'encounters' were with pints of Heineken. Most of the people studying the industrial relations stream were from working class backgrounds, with a significant minority involved in trade unions, definitely not the target audience for Louis Copeland pinstriped suits. While the general focus was on learning (and socialising), one woman in our year changed her outfit about three times every day. It led to a number of other women commenting that they 'didn't realise we were studying fashion' (alongside some more pointed comments). This issue of 'fitting in' is perhaps more important than we pay attention to. In my experience, access students often have lower levels of self-confidence, relative to their traditional entry peers. This lack of confidence can lead to students experiencing significant stress and over-work when completing assessment tasks. The good news is that all of the available evidence suggests that these hurdles can be overcome when the correct supports are in place.

Summary of the Key Arguments

Working class students who make it to college are more likely to go to an Institute of Technology rather than a university (because the universities require higher points to gain entry). As they are more dependent of government funding, the Institutes of Technology don't have the resources to spend on 'post-entry' access supports. In contrast, universities often have more money/personnel dedicated to student retention. It follows that through a combination of lower entry points and poorer post-entry support working class students are more likely to drop out of college. In short, it's harder for working class students to get into college and easier for them to drop out. **Good News**: We know what to do about this. There aren't too many new ideas that haven't been tried and tested somewhere across the sector. **Bad News:** The design and delivery of these systems is completely ad hoc. It's down to each individual institution to do what they feel is best.

Too Much Innovation?

I've now had the opportunity to review a wide range of higher education institutional efforts to improve access and retention. What's striking is the range of innovation across the sector. For example, one college had a 'Learning on the Streets' initiative, specifically targeting young Travellers. If you can't bring Mohammad to the mountain, then bring the mountain to Mohammad! In a project funded by CITI (Financial Services) called 'Future You,' UCD students act as mentors in DEIS schools. And on and on and on it goes. While these initiatives can be brilliant in concept and/ or execution (a) there's a large design cost (time and money) surrounding each programme, (b) staff have to be trained to run each specific initiative and (c) when key personnel move on, particularly if an initiative has been championed by a single individual, stuff often gets abandoned. Is there a better way to do this? My overall sense is that there's too much innovation. The needs of the different categories of access students are well known and generally stable over time. They don't change on a week-by-week basis or differ too much across the regions. It would certainly be possible to build a 'model' (best-practice) access programme and ensure that it becomes embedded in each third level institution. Focusing time and effort on implementing the model is a better use of resources than continually designing new initiatives, some of which run into the sand. When it comes to tackling educational disadvantage, I'm voting for less innovation and more delivery. A best-practice model for the third level sector is detailed in the appendices.

MONEY, MONEY, MONEY:
HOW THE FINANCIAL SUPPORTS WORK

Student Income

To get themselves through college, students raise funds from different sources. It can come directly from their family or in the form of an education grant (scholarship, student assistance fund etc.). Alternatively, students can generate income from employment or take out a repayable loan with a bank or credit union. Euro student data (2011) showed that one-third of Irish students (26 per cent of full-time students and 72 per cent of part-time students) work in parallel with studying. Students living away from home reported a 43-hour week (17 hours of classes, 15 hours of personal study and 11 hours of paid employment). Of course, these are average times and some students work more or fewer hours than this. Critically, students who reported working for more than 15 hours a week during term, spend around 8 hours less per week on study time.[54] Logic would suggest (and the evidence supports this) that a student who works more studies less. Because of their financial circumstances, we know that students from disadvantaged socio-economic backgrounds have to work more. So the lower academic achievement problem that working class students bring into college is compounded by lower study inputs and, often, financial concerns. In an interesting twist, a couple of studies have shown that many Irish employers are not overly focused on the 'institution' that someone graduates from.[55] Perhaps there's an inherent recognition that working class students have essentially faced a tougher climb and, on that basis alone, are worth a shot in the jobs market. It is worth repeating a core point. There will always be exceptional students that make their way through the system through some combination of smarts, resilience and luck. The concern here is for the cohort who struggle to climb the mountain. For those students, the educational system essentially needs to play the role of a sherpa, assisting the climb. And, without doubt, finance is a key component in this. The first port of call is around making the system understandable.

Financial Supports

The Higher Education Authority promotes awareness of financial supports for students and prospective students through regular updating of *www.studentfinance.ie*. This website has played a key role in widening awareness of the supports available for further and higher education.[56] Students can apply for a means-tested maintenance grant, which supports living and educational costs. There's now a single grant administration authority, Student Universal Support Ireland (SUSI), with a dedicated website focusing on the student maintenance grant.[57]

Maintenance Grants

Introduced in 1968, maintenance grants address the financial barriers to participation in college. Eligibility for the grant is means-tested, based on family and/or personal income.[58] Maintenance grants aim to assist with living expenses, such as rent and food and are available at different rates (adjacent and non-adjacent). Approximately 41 per cent of students are in receipt of a maintenance grant and have their fees (€3,000 student contribution) paid.[59] In 2000, an additional Special Rate of Maintenance (top-up) grant was introduced, targeting students from households with the lowest income levels and those in receipt of long-term social welfare payments. In 2011, 24,666 people received income support to attend full-time courses in further and higher education, an increase of 213 per cent on the numbers in 2008.[60]

Additional Financial Support

Students can apply for additional financial support through a range of schemes (including the Student Assistance Fund, the Fund for Students with Disabilities, and the community-based Millennium Partnership Fund), all of which are administered by the National Access Office under the European Social Fund (ESF). The Student Assistance Fund provides financial aid for third level students who experience hardship. Students apply at institutional level; funding covers living and academic expenses (for example, textbooks). In addition to the above, there are a range of bursary and scholarship schemes available, targeted at students from lower socio-economic groups and students with disabilities, funded by various groups.[61]

Declining Grant Levels[62]

The serious pressure on State finances led to a range of reductions in student finance. First announced in Budget 2010, the downwards trend continued in subsequent years. The cuts included:

- Doubling of the distance requirement to qualify for a non-adjacent grant

- Abolition of automatic entitlement for mature grant-holders

- Abolition of maintenance entitlement for 'Back to Education' participants

- Abolition of maintenance for postgraduate students

- Reductions in fee support for postgraduate students (except those on social welfare income up to a limit of €22,703).

The overall point is that the economic crisis has had a negative impact on the availability of resources for student support with corresponding reductions in the amounts available and a squeezing of grant eligibility criteria. In Ireland, we *talk* about tackling education disadvantage; we then *walk* a very different line. In the recommendations section an attempt is made to ensure that policy direction and actual practices are aligned.

BY-PASSING THIRD LEVEL: GOING DIRECTLY TO WORK

Some people decide to leave school after completing second level to take up a starter job. Others are lucky enough to secure a formal apprenticeship. Apprenticeships offer a very significant training experience in their own right, normally running over a three to four year period. The twin benefits of the apprenticeship route are employment and income. Depending on the particular trade, demand for skilled craftsmen (and women) can be very high practically guaranteeing employment. An old story illustrates this. A dentist noticed a leak underneath his sink and had to ring four plumbers before he could get someone to come out. The plumber sourced the leak, replaced a small rubber seal and the problem was solved. 'That'll be €180.' The dentist said, 'But, you're only here 15 minutes. Jesus, I don't make that kind of money myself', to which the plumber replied, 'I know. I used to be a dentist!' On the income side, additional money can often be made doing 'nixers', that is, black economy jobs where no tax is paid. The apprenticeship route is not as well trod; a decline in our core manufacturing base has closed off many traditional options in areas like fitting and turning. While still an excellent option, the opportunities to progress this route have declined (the number of apprenticeship places plummeted during the recession from 29,000 in 2007 to 5,711 in 2013).[63] That was certainly the case until very recently.

The New Apprenticeships[64]

We tend to think of apprenticeships along traditional lines, car mechanics and carpenters. Since 2009, when Ireland began competing in the World Skills competitions, Irish teams have won 10 Gold Medals, 2 Silver, 1 Bronze and 25 medallions of excellence – so we have some form here.[65] In more recent times there has been a huge effort invested in designing what are termed the 'new apprenticeships'. These changes have been driven by Solas.[66] The underpinning design philosophy is sometimes referred to as the 'German Model'. To simplify: the lessons from Germany are that all routes into employment are valued. College, in its traditional academic configuration, is not suitable for everyone. In fact, the new apprentices may be more valuable than traditional graduates; the practical nature of the training allows them to hit the ground running when they complete their studies. These New Apprenticeships, targeting a range of industries, are pitched between levels 6 and 9 on the National Qualifications Framework (NFQ), in other words, they start modestly but run close to the top end of the educational spectrum. Essentially, these are white collar, knowledge worker jobs, different to our traditional understanding of an apprenticeship as the learning of a craft (such as welding, cabinet making or brewing). While it's too early to judge results, this is a new and very welcome development in the Irish education landscape. This style of training is likely to appeal to access students who can immediately see the practical application of what they are learning and how this leads to employment.

Lifelong Learning

Part of the government strategy around broadening access is to encourage lifelong learning. The target audience here are older learners. It could be someone who has always had low education attainment or whose skill base has become outdated. Part-time and flexible programmes (such as distance learning) have a role to play here. In terms of provision, there's been significant progress made, including the quadrupling in the number of part-time, short duration, distance and e-learning programmes.[67] In terms of work-based education, the focus is on understanding the needs of older workers in industry, the mature learners who represent one of the five education disadvantage categories listed earlier.[68] Where sophisticated HR departments are in place, the educational needs of this group can normally be assessed locally.[69]

Training Resources

All organisations are faced with a choice of where to spend their training resources. In simple terms, there are two steps required:

1. A *method* to identify the training needs of the workforce.

2. A *menu* of off-the-shelf courses which are easily accessible.

Making the method and the menu available nationally (backed with government support) would go a long way towards meeting the needs of older workers who are seeking 'second chance' education opportunities.

Education Changes Lives:

Nicky Kehoe

Mature Student, Trinity College

Having sat the entry exam for the local secondary school, I waited every morning for the postman to deliver the letter confirming I'd secured a place. It never arrived. My father went up to the school to enquire, but he didn't tell me what was said. I'm guessing that he was trying to shield me from the fact that the results were poor. I was 12 years old.

Growing up, I was probably academically average. I was certainly high-spirited, even a bit wild. But growing up in a household that was full of books where reading and debating was encouraged, I was definitely inquisitive. During primary, I attended St Finbarr's in Cabra West. Denoted as a working class area at the time, Cabra had a lot of poverty and unemployment. Most of the teachers were good. With up to 40 students in each class, their main role was to keep order. Overall, they did their best but the large numbers didn't lend itself to positive learning. In the yard, if you showed any kind of weakness, bullying could be a problem. Those who had an older brother to look out for them were lucky. But there was also a kind of freedom there. It had its own momentum and I think most of us enjoyed primary.

I was sent to the local vocational school (Tech). While the classes size were about the same, there was a noticeable sense of freedom within the school that encouraged pupils to learn. In the 1970s, most young people in working class areas left school around 14 or 15, working at whatever they could get. Bringing 'a few bob' into the house was the name of the game. In families where the fathers had trades, lads like myself often took the same road, whether we liked it or not. Economically, a trade was consid-

ered a good way of making a living. I just about passed the Group Certificate and this gave me a start in the building industry as a bricklayer. Third level was never an option, not even on the radar. We focused on survival; educational aspirations was something for others to think about.

Around that time, I became acutely aware of the political struggle within the six counties in the North of Ireland and the inequalities and injustices experienced by the people living there. Developing a deep interest in political struggles worldwide, I became involved. It led to two long terms of imprisonment for republican activism. In prison, there were a number of educational opportunities and I took courses in creative writing, poetry, drama and art. These were hugely enjoyable, building confidence in our academic ability and general communication skills. Courses were delivered by some really great tutors, people who were both passionate and knowledgeable. I owe a debt of gratitude to those people and I'm happy to be able to express this now.

With a love of the community where I grew up, I stood as a candidate in the Local City Council Elections in 1999 and, subsequently, in the General Election in 2002. After eight years as a Dublin City Councillor, I left and returned to the building industry for a short time. But work was scarce and I decided to try my hand at computers, returning to the education arena. In 2009, my wife Marie suggested going back into education on a full-time basis. As a mature student, Marie had completed an honours degree in Trinity. To be honest, I was sceptical but she was adamant that I'd be able for it and would even enjoy it. Sometimes, you need someone else to push the point.

After successfully completing the Trinity Access Programme, I decided to study History. While it was challenging, overall the experience was brilliant. A love of history along with being reasonably well read on the subject stood to me. Completing essays, working in groups, the endless classroom debates, they were all highlights. I'm not downplaying the fact that I had to work hard at this stuff. But, with the help of teaching staff, my wife Marie and a friend who was a previous history graduate, I finished the course. After a four-year (sometimes hard) journey, I was awarded an honours degree and had a great sense of achievement and personal satisfaction. With the right preparation and encouragement, third level education is definitely achievable. Any student, regardless of class or background, can do this.

It brought me back. Earlier, as a general election candidate in 2002, I had been asked by a student group in Trinity College to participate in a question and answer session. I remember saying to the audience that when access to Trinity College (and all other universities) was available to everyone, then Ireland would be moving in the right direction. The Trinity Access Programme has been hugely instrumental in supporting people from different socio-economic backgrounds to enter college and that's to be greatly welcomed. Despite this, and similar programmes elsewhere, it's still a fact that a woeful lack of school resources are major impediments to young people in disadvantaged communities finishing their education. The inequality in the system has to change.

Education is the key to solving a lot of problems we face in society. Free education should mean free education. Drama, sport and music should be core subjects. Smaller classes and guidance teachers should be the order of the day. A wide choice of practical and academic courses should be available with creativity actively encouraged. We have to recognise the many learning styles and that not all students are suited to the academic-only route. Overall, education is a lifelong quest, it's not confined to the classroom. I found out it's never too late to start. Hopefully, I will stay open to learning.

In November 2013, during the graduation ceremony, I wondered what would my father think if he could have been there on the day. I'm fairly sure that he (and my mother) would have been proud. That's a feeling that should be open to every father and mother across Ireland.

Chapter 6

Diagnosing the Root Causes of Educational Disadvantage

Q: *What causes educational disadvantage?*

A: *There are several strands. It's partly economic (poverty). Partly sociological (family and community). Some of it's explained by individual psychology. Wrestling with this complexity is important – before we break the cycle, we need to understand it.*

Strand #1: The Family Agenda

The Constitution of Ireland (1937) declares parents to be the primary educators of children. It's not just an Irish phenomenon. Type 'education + parents' into Google and you'll get a million hits. Traditionally, parents were responsible for the socialisation, moral training and leisure activities of children while teachers took on their academic progress.[1] The role of schools has expanded and many now take responsibility for children's moral education in the formal teaching of religion. However, we know that children only spend a couple of hours each day (and not that many days) in school, so the influence of the family on their development is enormous. We can't expect schools to *fix* an educational disadvantage problem when students only spend about 20 per cent of their time in school. What happens in the family is critically important.

Family History

According to Dr. Kevin O'Higgins, the issue of educational disadvantage needs to be understood in a historical context. Some of the families in the poorer areas of Dublin have 'inter-generational' non-attendance at college. In many cases, their grandparents lived in tenement slums in Dublin. After the professional classes decamped to London (following the Act of Union in 1801), the landlords moved in. Georgian houses that had provided accommodation for single families, were subdivided and often housed up to 100 people. It soon degenerated into a slum environment and Ireland 'topped the table' in terms of physiological, sociological and psychiatric problems. Alcohol was part of the mix, offering a way for people to seek temporary escape. Sprawling city council housing estates, built after the Second World War, displaced those inner-city populations to new areas. The new urban wastelands often had few community facilities and little sense of place. Arguably, while the quality of the housing stock improved, social poverty worsened. In their All-Island Deprivation Index, academics at Maynooth University have colour-coded geographical areas using blue to highlight affluence and red to denote social deprivation. In line with population growth, those red areas now extend to new parts of the city. While working class people are now living in new areas, they face old social problems.[2] Roll the camera forward by five or six generations from those tenement days and we encounter a group of people with very little family exposure to college. There's a saying in Ireland that, 'You never know what's going on behind someone's hall door.[3] What we know for sure is that it's difficult for families who don't have a tradition of education to instill a passion for this in their children. The solution here, and we will look at some specific ideas in the next chapter, is to go behind the hall door, that is, get parents more directly involved in the education of their children. Where working class parents are

classified as 'the enemies of education' (how one respondent de-
scribed the current situation), there's very little chance of moving
the needle forward.

Intergenerational Impact

How does this short history lesson add value? In order to change
something, we first have to understand it. George Santayana reminded us: 'Those who cannot remember the past are condemned
to repeat it.' Earlier we mentioned John Lonergan, the former
governor of Mountjoy Prison. Many times he made the point that
his *clients* were the sons or even the grandchildren of former prisoners, in other words, criminality is *intergenerational*. The exact
same point applies to educational disadvantage, a cycle that's long
in the making. Even if, by some magic decree, we could put all the
needed educational supports in place tomorrow, changing family and community cultures will come slowly, perhaps over two or
three generations. The alternative, of course, is that we do nothing and absolutely nothing will change. Unless we intervene, an
updated copy of this book will be written 50 years from now. The
only difference will be the author! While there's little doubt that
turning around the fortunes of families living in disadvantaged
areas is a long-term commitment, we have to start somewhere.
In the words of the Chinese philosopher Lao Tzu, 'A journey of a
thousand miles begins with a single step.'

Family Context

While neighbourhood dynamics can have a significant impact on
educational outcomes, the family environment remains the centrally important layer. The family unit is the protective environment within which a child grows and develops. In 2004, the Centre
for Early Childhood Development and Education (CECDE) noted:

> A child does not experience disadvantage on his/
> her own, but in the family context. The child's future
> is affected by the number of risk factors associated
> with a family's experience.

A child's early formation, education and development take place in the family. While children thrive in a loving environment, poor parenting skills/capability can have a lifelong positive or detrimental effect.[4] On one level the tasks seem simple enough, for example, reading to a child or playing games, particularly during those early, formative years. But these are not simple tasks for all parents. For example, the parents of Traveller children can find it difficult to engage with the education system as many have had a 'negative experience in school, illiteracy and the widespread experience of exclusion.'[5]

Bigger Issues

Of course, some families face bigger issues than educational disadvantage. They can literally be life and death, running the gamut from suicide to involvement in gang crime and murders. Upwards of 1,000 children each year are taken from families (for a variety of reasons) and put into state care. Contrast this with a 'view from the bridge'. At the other end of the social spectrum you have families who are fourth and fifth generation Belvedere or Blackrock College graduates. Making allowance for poor grammar, these are people who've 'never not been' to university.[6] When children grow up in a specific context, they learn the rules of the game. In some families, educational success is simply not part of the mix. It's like the Leonard Cohen lyric: 'Everybody knows the dice are loaded.'[7] The dice are loaded against children born into families where the view of the education system is negative and where there's zero experience of college. Sean Dowling[8] takes up this point:

> Normally, someone needs to plant the seed of ambition and argue the benefits of education. A kid, given a plausible vision of what could be, can dare to dream. Kids often become ambitious following a visionary conversation that suggests a path to a fulfilling job. Of course, that assumes there's someone around to have that conversation with.

Having access to people who've gone to college puts this on the *possibilities list*. If no one in your orbit has ever been to college, it's a leap into the unknown. But, not everyone buys the bleak picture sketched above. For example, Ann Louise Gilligan argues:[9]

> Many children who live with the injustice of poverty live in houses of enormous love, care and fun. Parents who have had few educational opportunities themselves often have an instinctual capacity to educate themselves and their own children and encourage their development in creative ways.

It's a useful caution against too easily accepting the stereotype. Not every working class family has low educational achievement, nor is every middle class family a breeding ground for high fliers. There can be huge individual differences. However, the numbers don't lie. Growing up in a 'Red' area significantly impacts your life chances; it's back to that Lottery of the Womb. The role for policy makers is to recognise the inherent inequity in this and put mechanisms in place that actually level the pitch.

Parental Aspirations

There's a subtle but important point at play here. Working class families are not less ambitious for the success of their children. Every parent wants their children to do well, across all family types. What working class families lack is the 'how' (*how* the system works, *how* to make key contacts and so on) coupled with a belief that they are advocates on behalf of the child. Dr. Josephine Bleach offered a simple example in one of her PhD findings:

> In more affluent areas, many parents had a friend who was a teacher. Or the woman down the road or a sister-in-law was a teacher. If a child encountered a problem, they would tease this out with their contact and then approach the school. In disadvantaged areas it works differently. If a child had a problem in school, some people would ring the Department of Education and then be surprised that nothing happened.

Josephine runs the Early Learning Initiative in the National College of Ireland. A former primary school teacher, she worked in DEIS schools for many years. Later she worked as a Home-School Liaison Officer and also as a School Planning Co-coordinator. So she's been heavily involved in the question of educational disadvantage for most of her working life. I asked her if working class parents had lower aspirations for their children:

> The short answer is no, they don't. Every parent wants his or her child to have the best chance in life. There's absolutely no difference on that score between disadvantaged and more affluent areas.

The follow on question was easy. If aspirations are broadly similar, how come the *outcomes* are so different?

> It comes down to the 'how'. Firstly, middle class people – and I'm generalising here – know more about how the education system works. They put children's names down for particular secondary schools six years ahead of time, having already mapped out their educational journey.

So planning is the key?

> It's deeper than that. When I worked in DEIS schools the mothers would often come into the class and help. They would defer to the professionals – the teachers – who were seen as 'qualified'. In middle class areas there was a much stronger push to understand why John or Joan wasn't making progress. There's a sense of entitlement around the education process and a feeling that they can steer this.

She offered an example where parents become involved in the running of schools:

In DEIS schools, the level of volunteering to support the teachers was very high, certainly on par with volunteering in middle class areas. But in disadvantaged areas the parents were there to support. In middle class areas they were there to check the teachers, to serve on boards of management and so on.

Another respondent (a teacher), supporting this broad point, stated:

The general problem in disadvantaged areas is managing the children. In middle class areas it's managing the parents.

Aiming High

When Darina Shouldice was Home-School Liaison Officer in Darndale she took numerous parents on tours of Dublin City University. It was a foreign world. It hadn't occurred to some parents that their children, even the ones who were extremely bright and capable, might go to university. During the course of this research, several people recalled specific conversations when someone (a parent, a teacher, a priest) essentially 'gave them permission' to dream about their educational future and how this changed their life. So, while the aspirations *are similar, somehow the* expectations *are lower and this gets transmitted to the children.*

Is Educational Disadvantage Just Another Name for 'Poverty?'[10]

There's a close link between educational disadvantage and poverty. Research evidence indicates that individuals from poorer socio-economic backgrounds are more likely to underachieve in the education system vis a vis their peers from higher income backgrounds.[11] Middle class children have much more income spent of their development across a range of activities. At the extreme there's the so-called hot housing of children by 'Tiger Mums' (and Dads). But even in *ordinary* families, it's not unusual to see flowcharts dictating the week's events where children complete tennis lessons on Monday, Lifesaving on Tuesday, Horseriding on Wednesday and so on. Many times I told my kids I was ordering a 'taxi' sign for the roof of the car to use the bus lanes to drive them to various activities (I suspect it's a common refrain from middle class parents). Contrast this with parents who take children out of school to help with the family business at particular times of the year. Is that neglect or economic necessity? It raises the question: Can you solve education disadvantage without solving poverty?

According to Barnardos, in 2014 11 per cent of children under the age of 17 in Ireland lived in consistent poverty. That's one child in nine (132,000 children) based on the 2011 census. Children in these households suffer deprivation, including going 24 hours without a proper hot meal, not being able to afford heating in the home and so on. The longer a child is deprived, the greater the deprivation they suffer in later life. Studies by UNICEF show that children from poor households are much more likely to do poorly in school, become teenage parents, spend time in prison and have difficulty finding or keeping jobs.[12] Overall, research in Ireland has demonstrated[13] that poverty is the most common indicator of educational disadvantage. It's not a coincidence that the countries with the best education systems, those we admire and wish to emulate, are the regions with lower poverty indices, for example, Scandinavia.

But poverty, while centrally important, only explains part of the educational disadvantage story. For example, we witness poverty in every part of the world, sometimes in extremes like the *favelas*[14] in South America. Yet some of these outwardly poor communities have a rich network of music, dancing and looking after their grandparents and extended families. In other words, strong social rules regularise behaviour. Some use the social glue of religion and, like my own family of origin, cling to the hope of a better future in the afterlife. In the sprawling housing estates in north and west Dublin (the same points apply across all cities in Ireland), this 'social web' has virtually disappeared. In some cases, it has been overtaken by a drink/drug culture which focuses on the immediate high. When hope arrives in the shape of a pharmaceutical product to medicate life, it's not a huge next step to taking an illegal drug, leaving communities blighted with the problem of addiction. This mirrors a similar trend in the UK, captured in the lyrics to the Rolling Stones song 'Mothers Little Helper':[15]

> Kids are different today, I hear every mother say
> Mother needs something today to calm her down
> And though she's not really ill, there's a little yellow pill
> She goes running for the shelter of a mother's little helper
> And it helps her on her way, gets her through her busy day

Cultural Impact

It's not just about money. Many families in rural areas face levels of poverty that match those of urban areas. Yet secondary school completion rates and college attendance were historically much higher in some rural areas. If income/poverty levels are similar, how can we explain this? According to Professor Patrick Clancy, the local *culture* plays a huge role in this. While economically poor, many rural communities were hugely pro-education. In some counties, for example Leitrim, there was so little local employment that people had to compete nationally for jobs in banking, nursing and the gardaí. In Dublin, which had more local opportunity for employment, those who fell out of the education system early had a better chance of securing employment. The pro-education philosophy was therefore a practical means to an end in rural communities and this became self-reinforcing/replicating over time.

> While much of the problem of early leaving and under-achievement is linked to socio-economic disadvantage, it is also the case that we cannot discount the importance of cultural factors. The high admission rates from Western counties [to third level], which are linked to high retention rates at second level, reflect a cultural orientation in many families, which, despite meagre resources, foster and realise

high educational aspirations. The high levels of social segregation and polarisation which occur both in housing and in education in large urban areas inhibit the development of high aspirations for many working class children.[16]

Airs and Graces

In the 1960s, Bill Toner SJ grew up in Drimnagh, a working class area in Dublin 12. He made the point that his mother occasionally ridiculed a neighbour who had hopes that her daughter would go to 'Uni', deeming the woman to have 'airs and graces'.[17] There was something in the culture that made his parents believe that going to university wasn't for 'people like us'. Indeed, during that era, pragmatism was at play. Jobs secured by working class people required little formal education or training. At that time the underpinning belief was: 'a bird in the hand is worth two in the bush'. Securing a job today and making money made more sense that training for a job tomorrow. Ancient history? A similar logic is at play in 2016 where some children drop out of school early to take up employment.[18] But, we've shown earlier that the jobs market has fundamentally changed. For example, in order to secure the modest role of driver, a person now has to sit the Driver Theory Test and achieve an 87.5 per cent result, answering 35 of 40 questions correctly from a possible pool of over 1,000 questions. So even driving a van, a relatively simple job, requires good literacy and comprehension skills. But somehow this fundamental shift in the job market is not understood in all communities. The consequence is that individuals, families and entire communities will potentially be disadvantaged as people fail to secure even baseline employment. As an illustration of how the family environment influences education, consider the following:

A Tale of Two Cities: How Children are 'Educated' Differently

Tony starts school at 4. He is a normally bright and inquisitive child.	Coleen also starts school at 4. She is also normally bright and inquisitive.
No one in his extended family system has ever been to college. They aren't *against it*, but don't know how the education system works.	Both of her parents went to college. They are 'pro-education' and prepared to invest in this over and above shorter-term investments.
There are almost no books in the house. Newspapers are bought occasionally. Most news is gleaned from TV.	The house is full of books. Both parents read newspapers and regularly 'read to' Coleen at bedtime.
While Tony's parents love him, they hold the view that 'a child should be seen but not heard.' They don't want to overindulge him and are strict in some areas (e.g. around using bad language).	Her parents feel that Coleen is a 'mini-adult' and she becomes part of the decision-making cycle in the home. They are somewhat indulgent about behaviour but strict in other areas, for example, study routines and bedtimes.
His teachers feel that he has capability but are concerned about his lack of concentration and focus. He seems to spend an inordinate amount of time watching TV.	Her teachers feel that she has good academic capability. They definitely like the fact that she's well behaved in class. Coleen is 'easy to manage.'
His parents drop and collect but there's very little interaction with the teaching staff. His teachers view Tony's parents as polite but distant. They're not really involved in the school. His Mam did volunteer on the Sports Day, helping with the food and drinks but his dad has little contact.	Her mother and father assume that she will be going to college and discuss her overall educational performance with the teacher. They are demanding of the teacher in the sense of wanting to address specific educational needs that they've noticed. Her Mother has joined the Parents Committee and does some fundraising for the school.

Tony has begun take up a role as the class clown. He likes making the other boys laugh and the attention that accompanies this. Sometimes he can be outrageous in his efforts to do this. The teacher has 'spoken to' his parents about this in a formal meeting.	Coleen has settled into a solid pattern of schoolwork. She is attentive and detailed. If anything, her teacher is slightly concerned that she becomes 'overly-worried' if there are mistakes and she doesn't get an 'A' result on each test.
As school becomes *difficult,* Tony becomes *distant.* It's not a place where he experiences success – quite the opposite. He can't get much support at home with homework as his parents don't always understand the material themselves. He has no idea about potential jobs (a lot of the information he hears about work is broadly negative, that is, 'working for the Man.'	Coleen starts to develop ideas around careers and what she might do in the future. Her parents encourage this and plan 'educational trips' to copperfasten this. With a strong interest in animals, she has the path worn out to the Natural History Museum and the Zoo. Her parents ask the local Vet is she can spend time there, informally helping out. Her future is becoming clearer.
Tony's parents are appreciative of the teaching staff. But they never actually mention this. His dad has a lingering resentment about being 'spoken down to' when they were called in about Tony's behaviour and generally avoids the school.	Her parents bought an expensive bottle of wine and chocolates and presented them to the teacher at Christmas. Both signed a nice 'thank you for your expertise' note. To the teacher, they seem like 'really nice people'.

Fiction? The HEA (2006) evaluation highlighted the importance of high teacher expectations, that is, the need to work with teachers and career guidance staff to raise expectations and aspirations, with regard to progression to higher education for students from disadvantaged backgrounds.[19]

Parental Roles

When it comes to education, many families adhere to traditional roles with mothers taking centre stage while 'fathers continue to be absent or shadowy figures in their children's education'.[20] But some families just can't cope. Early school leaving and 'not going' to college becomes part of a Life Script[21] for individual members who become disempowered, sometimes medicated and welfare dependent. *Education immobility*, the association between the educational levels of individuals and their parents, is higher in Ireland than any other country in Europe.[22] Breaking this negative spiral, supporting mothers and fathers and helping them to support their children, requires a focused and consistent commitment at central government level to address social and community challenges. At present there's a complete absence of an overall conceptual plan to address this (it's hardly surprising that we don't have a plan to do something when the baseline problem isn't acknowledged). What we have is a range of government initiatives which ping-pong from left to right every couple of years as the political scene changes.[23] In relation to the lack of a political response, the cynics say, 'same circus, different clowns.' But that's all too easy a response. It's up to the educational policy makers to craft a vision for a 'better tomorrow' and then push for political support. Support for a better tomorrow is only possible when the shape of this and the route to get there are made crystal clear.

STRAND #2: THE COMMUNITY AGENDA

Social Class

Discussions about the impact of the family on education need to take account of the community in which the family is resident. To paraphrase John Donne,[24] 'No family is an island.' This brings us into the heart of somewhat uncomfortable territory. While educational disadvantage can be openly discussed, social class seems risqué.[25] We know that low-income households lack the money and sometimes the means (transport, knowledge of how the education system works etc.) to compete on a level basis. Indeed, because of low levels of educational attainment, some parents in disadvantaged areas lack the confidence and self-belief to help their children. In contrast, middle class parents believe that they possess similar or even superior educational skills and prestige to the teachers.[26] The impact of social class on education has been well researched and the findings highlight major differences in educational attainment between people from different social groups. In simple terms, working class students with the same IQ as their middle class counterparts are less successful in the educational system. But, slightly more controversially, there's a view in some quarters that working class people actually decide to spend their money differently, elevating short-term issues like house redecoration, holidays or entertainment over longer-term investments like education. It's not that they don't 'get it'; they make a deliberate choice not-to-follow the educational path. When it comes to educational disadvantage, are people in working class areas the authors of their own misfortune? To give substance to those arguments, there are always heroes, people who've forged great careers from inauspicious beginnings. These are held up as beacons for what can be achieved. It's all down to moral fibre, right? A lot of people like to think that they've climbed Everest alone, like the old joke, 'He's a self-made man who worships his maker.' But what's often forgotten (or deliberately ignored) is that many people have had the benefit of that invisible sherpa. When you add in the factors of genetic disposition (you broadly inherit your intellect) and social determinism (where you grow up helps to set your values), the scope for self-determination is quite constrained. I'm personally more inclined to the view expressed by Howard Gardner, the American educationalist, who cautioned not to over-romanticise poverty: 'For every career it assisted, it blighted one hundred.'[27] The arguments here are somewhat complex (buckle in for the next couple of minutes).

Value Systems: Time Horizons

One of the factors that separates working class from middle class communities is a shorter time horizon.[28] Economics provides part of the explanation. Where money is tight, people living on a day-to-day basis tend not to plan too far ahead. While this can be interpreted negatively as immediate gratification, the working class culture is strongly rooted in the 'here and now', because it had to be. Over time, a pattern of more immediate (survival) spending can become habitual, even when circumstances have changed for the better. While this may be factually correct, the core charge of fecklessness is hard to shift. In the 1960s, the American sociologist Herbert H. Hyman described the value systems of different classes,[29] arguing that the lower classes create 'a self-imposed barrier to an improved position': (1) Members of the working class place a lower value on education as a route to personal achievement, for example, seeing less value in continuing school beyond the minimum age; (2) in evaluating jobs, working class people emphasise stability, security and immediate economic benefits and reject aiming for high-risk occupations (limiting their job horizons) and (3) compared to their middle class counterparts, members of the working class believe there is less opportunity for personal advancement.

Closer to home, the British sociologist Barry Sugarman[30] took a different tact. He suggested that the differences in attitude and outlook between the two classes resulted from the nature of manual and non-manual occupations. He claimed middle class jobs provide an opportunity for continuous advancement in income and status, which encourages planning. In contrast working class jobs reach full earning capacity quite quickly. The absence of a career structure in many working class jobs meant that individual effort has less chance of producing improvements in income, status or working conditions. Collective action, in the form of trade union pressure, offered a more effective strategy than individual effort. So, differences in the nature of jobs (as distinct from differences in the nature of people) explain the attitudes and behaviour reported. Since they had less control over the future, less opportunity to improve their position, and less income to invest, working class people tend to be fatalistic (acceptance of a situation rather than making an effort to improve it) and become present-time orientated. Immediate enjoyment makes more sense than making a sacrifice for future reward. Following this logic, early school leaving provides the immediate reward of a wage packet, adult status and freedom from the disciplines of school.

In yet another classification, Tessa Blackstone and Jo Mortimore[31] offer the following observations: (1) Working class parents have less time to attend school because of the demands of their jobs. Manual jobs typically involve longer and less regular hours than non-manual jobs.[32] (2) Working class parents may be very interested in their children's education but are put off going to school because of the way teachers interact with them; they feel ill at ease or even subject to criticism when they visit schools.[33] Over generations, these attitudes and orientations become an established part of working class culture, that is, children from working class areas became socialised and accept these beliefs. And, of course, these points apply to people who have jobs. Where people are unemployed or completely welfare dependent, the sense of hopelessness worsens and the short-termism is likely to be even stronger. When people who hold common views live in close proximity, these 'beliefs' become shared, continually reinforced and strengthened in conversations. While somewhat invisible, this socialization process applies to everyone, whether you live in a corporation housing estate in Cork or are part of a headhunting tribe in Indonesia. In short, you believe what your tribe believes. Or you leave. And, it's more than just beliefs. In some houses there are physical limitations, with less personal space. In a small house with a number of children, having a designated study area for each child simply isn't practical.

Class Subcultures

While there's good support for the view that social class influences educational attainment (including differences in parental encouragement of children), this perspective has been criticised on the basis of the implicit moral superiority in the arguments, that is, (a) poor people are themselves accountable for their impoverished circumstances, and (b) if only they would think ahead and make a real effort/sacrifice now they would reap the benefits in the future. We've already reviewed the idea of victim blaming and don't need to repeat the arguments here. An alternative view is that the working class orientation may be *realistic* rather than *fatalistic*. Working class people might defer gratification if they had the resources to defer, and might be future-orientated if the opportunities for successful future planning were available. From this point of view, members of the working class share the same norms and values as everyone else. Their behaviour is not dictated by a distinctive psychology as if they were some separate life form. It's simply that their situation propels them to follow the norms and values embraced by members of their own class, and these are different to those held by middle class people (please don't misinterpret *different* as some sort of secret code for *inferior*).

Overall, while there are alternative explanations around *why* educational achievement is lower in disadvantaged areas, the core point that class differences strongly influence outcomes is accepted. Most people, instinctively, accept that the local culture influences a child. Where the culture supports education, children will grow up with a pro-education bias. If that culture is neutral or anti, the education aim point will be lower. To some extent this is stating the blinding obvious. However, it's a useful insight into a potential key lever to promote education in disadvantaged communities. The challenge is to make education cool and actively supported, across all communities. The Goal: The new working class heroes will be the ones who stay in school, a cultural shift that can be strongly influenced by community leadership. So, how do we build community leadership assets?

Developing Community Leadership

In the early 1980s, the Irish government was faced with a housing shortage, a challenge not dissimilar to the homeless crisis faced today. The solution chosen at that time was to encourage people living in local authority housing to free up the unit by moving to a purchased house. To incentivise this, the government offered grants (from memory, IR£5,000) to the families who moved on. Outwardly, this made perfect sense, providing an additional local authority house for a relatively small cost. However, the unintended consequence of this policy was that some communities were decapitated in terms of local leadership. The most upwardly mobile families left poorer neighborhoods to go to better areas. Sociologists even have a label for this – 'The Reproduction of Advantage' – where the most talented or ambitious people continually leave poorer communities.[34] If you were looking for a single example to illustrate the need for joined-up thinking, this is as good as it gets. Of course, there's always mobility with families moving to more attractive areas. But today former local authority houses are being sold to house purchasers, that is, the families that move out are essentially being replaced with 'like for like'. Building community leadership, through sports and other clubs, and continually reinforcing the power of education through these fora, is a key strand in tackling education disadvantage. And, we have some experience to build on.

Whole Community Development

A variety of governments have recognised that communities don't develop equally and have tried to intervene.[35] One example of this was the RAPID programme (Revitalising Areas by Planning, Investment and Development).[36] The areas designated for RAPID development were predominantly local authority housing estates. No surprise there. Local planning generally followed a standard format: an overview of the area, an assessment of needs, a future vision alongside detailed action steps to make this happen. Under RAPID, the themes selected were quite broad, for example, Older Folks, Youth, Disabled People, Travellers, Employment, Health, Security, Housing, Environment, Infrastructure and Education/Training. Recognising that there's often an 'implementation deficit' (plans get *developed* but *results pay the bills)* an entire implementation architecture was designed. Area Implementation Teams were set up with social partnership-type memberships (representatives from State Agencies, Local Development Agencies, Community members, Drug Task Forces and so on). Individual task groups were established to progress specific initiatives and a Local Area Coordinator was appointed (employed by the County/City Council) to provide ongoing direction.

Governance Structures

Sitting above this local apparatus, city/county Monitoring groups (Regional Level) and the National Monitoring Committee were composed of members from the Social Partners, National Departments and Agencies. There was also full-time staff (National Co-coordinator, Liaison Officers, Information Officers and administrators). In terms of community infrastructure, this wasn't a 'knee bone' or a 'thigh bone'; it was an entire skeleton. The plans made in local areas were both comprehensive and complex. For example, the Tallaght plans in West Dublin (combining three RAPID districts) listed 73 individual actions.[37] Some projects required massive expenditure, for example, the redevelopment of existing housing stock. Others were more limited in scope – the provision of recycling facilities, a library and so on. Each individual strand was written up as a project, submitted for central vetting and (if approved) allocated to the government department charged with that particular area of activity. There are multiple stakeholders involved, for example, (a) Government Ministers and their departments (b) local authorities (c) community and voluntary sector organisations, often working with both paid and volunteer staff and (d) individual communities.

Did it Work?

RAPID helped to prioritise the needs in each area. It involved the local community in drafting plans from the bottom-up, progressing what is generally accepted as best practice in civic engagement. The most often reported downsides to this process was (a) bureaucracy/slow speed, particularly around implementation and (b) local structures had to fit with the Government Departmental structure; otherwise, plans were ignored and 'died on the vine.'

Government/Political System

Politicians certainly become involved in community development initiatives like access to education. Some have a huge personal commitment to this area. Maureen O'Sullivan, the Dublin inner city TD, springs to mind, perhaps reflecting her background as a former teacher. But, an over-reliance on local political support for access initiatives raises two potential issues. Firstly, and most obviously, TDs come and go while access supports need to remain in place over many years. In designing the overall solution, we should view local political support as a bonus rather than a centrally important element of the access machine. Secondly, and more worrying, some TDs seek to politicise issues. If they are in power, they want to highlight what's working well. If not in power, they want to highlight what's broken and assign blame. Access problems become a political opportunity to score points rather than something that needs to be understood and resolved. Of course, we need political support at a national level to secure support and funding for educational disadvantage. But educational disadvantage should not be overly dependant on the political system.

Local Authority Versus Community Services

One difficult question posed is whether the voluntary sector is better value for money than the public sector? A criticism levelled at Local Authority staff is that they 'switch off' (outside the narrow time-band of 9.00-5.00). Staff turnover can mean that there is continual movement between jobs and a drop in service levels while a new person is getting up-to-speed. If the person doesn't live in the community, there can be a disconnect with actual local needs. One community activist stated: 'People operating on the front-line of service delivery usually have a good handle on what's needed and how to ensure resources are targeted.' The question of whether a government service should be tasked with providing educational disadvantage services versus funding non-governmental organisations like Foroige or Barnardos is a political hot potato.[38] My sense is that the killer arguments in support of non-government agencies is the key role played by volunteers. In the sports arena we see the hugely important role that, for example, the GAA plays in so many communities across Ireland. Where I grew up in Cabra, Naomh Fionnbarra has been in place for over 70 years. The club does brilliant work with children and across the entire community (older folks etc.) and has become a core part of the social infrastructure. In contrast, when community activation becomes *formal*, for example, a Drugs Task Force is established (with governance, management routines and so on), one respondent suggested that this can diminish enthusiasm and reduce power. Formality may create the illusion of progress ('That's done now') while actually putting a brake on it. Allied to the debate on methodology/structure, there's a ton of confusion in the sector about the players. In relation to community and voluntary organisations, just answering the question 'what's in place at the moment?' hasn't been easy. If the education system is labyrinthine, mapping it was a walk in the park compared to trying to understand the voluntary and not-for-profit sectors. There are so many local services (voluntary, statutory, some a combination of both) that it's hard to know where to start. Oftentimes, there are a number of agencies with very similar or overlapping missions, a duplication of resources that runs counter to the stated government policy to eliminate quangos.[39] Figuring out the optimum infrastructure within communities to tackle educational disadvantage is a centrally important issue to be resolved.

Community Regeneration

During the Celtic Tiger years, several of the poorest communities around the country had a makeover. By far the most expensive, but arguably the easiest thing to do, is physical regeneration. Communities which have poor housing stock are generally supportive of regeneration, provided they have a say in the planning and design. What's not to like here? I've visited some of the new housing in Ballymun and the inner city where the standard of design is generally fantastic. After each visit to a regeneration area, you take away a renewed sense of hope. And, while it's hardly a scientific measure, Ballymun seems much less in the news than it was historically when a host of negative stories emanated from the area. Arguably, new architecture in Ballymun has brought forward a newfound sense of hope, a foundation that can be built on in tackling educational disadvantage. That's if, and it's a *big* if, we can figure out exactly what to do once those new houses are built. The central concern with regeneration is that you simply move from high-rise to low-rise deprivation. Side by side with the new housing stock, communities need investment in social regeneration, driven with an intensity of approach to really make a difference. Regeneration on its own is like building computer hardware.

Outwardly, the machine looks good, but the software needs to be installed to make it work. In the case of educational disadvantage, the community software needs to be re-programmed to communicate the 'why' and the 'how' to be successful. We need to install the support mechanisms to ensure that a better tomorrow isn't just an empty promise.

Using Community Resources: No School is an Island

The Department of Education/Combat Poverty Report on Educational Disadvantage argued:

> While the school is still seen as having a crucial role to play, it is now recognised that the educational system has to work with other institutions and agencies, both statutory and voluntary.[40]

While schools could become a centre of learning at the heart of each community, the reality is that many schools are closed and dark from the early afternoon onwards. Better utilisation of school buildings would potentially allow the development of community learning initiatives (already in place in some areas). Personal skill development programmes for parents can bring about a boost in confidence and self-esteem. It's a social outlet for adults who can subsequently become partners in their children's learning journey.

Mixing the Tribes

Up to this point the core idea under discussion has been the treatment of educational disadvantage where it resides. Of course, a more radical possibility exists, for example, to mix the tribes. Recognising the potential positive impact of having working class and middle class communities living side by side, the idea was mooted to designate 20 per cent all new developments as social and affordable housing. Licenses would only be issued to property developers on the basis that units constructed would be for mixed use – 80 per cent of people would purchase apartments in the normal way; the remaining 20 per cent would be allocated the exact same living space through local authority housing lists.[41] It was to be a new experiment, a place where the middle and working classes could co-mingle. The philosophical aim-point was to move towards an integrated society. Outwardly the argument to do this was housing equality. The unspoken (because it was politically incorrect) view was that middle class values (e.g. a core belief in the power of education and lower levels of social problems generally), would trickle down, and positively influence everyone in a development. It never happened. Anticipating that potential purchasers wouldn't welcome this (and therefore wouldn't buy the commercial apartments), property developers came up with an ingenious solution. They 'bought out' the social housing obligation, paying huge sums of money to the local authorities to spend as they saw fit. The message: We are happy to give you money to 'fix' the other tribe, as long as you keep them separate. The good thing about ghettoes is that they have a boundary. You can see them. You can police them. Best of all, you can avoid them. Rudyard Kipling described this as 'never the twain shall meet.'[42]

The local authority, flush with this new money, could spend it remediating the very social problems that the mixed housing system was designed to overcome. So, how exactly did this radical new experiment in Irish housing policy get thrown overboard? The answer is, quietly! As they say in Hollywood 'and so, it continues...'. It must rank as the shortest social housing experiment in human history, now consigned to the dustbin of promising ideas – perhaps deemed overly idealistic.[43] One respondent argued: 'Lower middle class civil servants, who make those type of decisions, are close to the line. They don't want to agree to implement anything that might remove the advantage that their own children enjoy.' Perhaps that view is overly simplistic (others, with a deeper understanding of what actually happened, can decide). I can't see any Irish Government – in the near-term future – seeking to actively mix the working class and the middle class. My guess is that we are likely to continue with a 'two-tribe' society for the foreseeable future. While we would never actually use this coarse language, we seem more than happy to continue with this coarse policy. Realistically, if mixing the tribes isn't an option, we need to find a way to intervene in disadvantaged areas, to put education centre stage. The missing link is a well-thought-out community development model that actually delivers equality. The RAPID infrastructure was outlined in some detail to make a single (but critically important) point: we now have significant experience in community interventions which can be built on to tackle educational disadvantage in a focused way. We don't have to start with a blank page.

STRAND #3: THE SCHOOL AGENDA

Pre-School

While there is some pushback against the idea of hot housing children for success at a very young age, we saw earlier that playschool is a very different concept than a crèche or a child-minding service. The research evidence suggests that starting on the educational ladder as soon as possible makes perfect sense. And, it's not all po-faced; learning can be seriously good fun.[44] But we can't do this unless the teachers are appropriately trained, which is patently not the case at the moment across the pre-school sector.

Teacher Profiles in Primary Schools[45]

At primary level, a centrally important question is where do our school teachers come from? In disadvantaged areas, students need people 'like us' standing at the top of the class. For many years, Ann Heelan, Director, of AHEAD, has highlighted the inflexibility of the entrance requirements for teacher education. She argues that the current policy does not serve the needs of students with disabilities; the same point applies across the board. We need more teachers from working class backgrounds. People who 'sound like us' and who can tell their own stories, thus becoming role models for the children. The exact opposite is a teacher who exhibits social distance. We know that children don't relate well to teachers who 'look down on them' or act in a superior fashion. When I encountered this first, I thought it might be a case of *projection* (essentially children projecting an inner sense-of-inferiority on to the teachers). But, the feedback was very clear on this point. Students are well able to differentiate between teachers who make them feel inferior and those who don't (if projection was the core issue at play all teachers would receive the same label). Of course, this issue is not wholly related to the social class background of the teacher. However, the starting point has to be recruiting teachers from a broader gene pool.[46]

Higher Turnover of DEIS Teachers Damages Education

We also know that teachers in DEIS schools have a higher turnover rate that teachers in mainstream schools. In one DEIS evaluation report, principals expressed concern around the difficulty in attracting trained and experienced teachers and the ongoing challenge of retaining staff. Why might this be the case? For some, it's dealing with the students:

> I'd been giving one lad a hard time about never doing
> homework. One morning he waltzed into class an
> hour late and I asked him where he'd been. He said,
> 'I was finishing my homework.'

Depending on your viewpoint, that response is either cheeky or brilliant. Part of the working class culture is less *social filtering,* being more open and honest. It suits some teachers, but not everyone. Indeed, the core role of teaching is a good fit for some people but not for everyone who joins the profession. Key questions are whether the *right people* are entering the profession and, should those teaching in DEIS schools receive additional training, for example, conflict resolution skills? Teachers impact all of our lives, every single person in society, in a way that no other profession does. That's why the selection of teachers and the quality of teaching is fundamentally important. In my role as an Executive Coach,

I've had the opportunity to work alongside many successful people. A huge percentage highlight particular teachers as being the most important or influential people in their lives. While teachers play an enormously important role, under the current 'high points' system the custodians of the future are selected from a very narrow band. Teachers are the engines of the education business, that is, the most important part that needs the most attention. While some people suggested paying a premium to teachers in DEIS schools, my instinct is that this might raise as many problems as it resolves. Would we pay doctors more for working in A&E, pay some Gardaí more for policing tough areas and so on? While DEIS teachers need to be incentivised, I don't believe that additional payment is the answer.

Professional Development and Support

Teaching in disadvantaged schools requires high levels of professional development. The DEIS evaluation report found that teachers in DEIS schools didn't feel fully equipped upon leaving college to teach in those schools, that is, their training wasn't extensive enough. Day-to-day teaching practice can seem somewhat removed from theories addressed in college. Current Bachelor of Education qualifications don't adequately prepare a teacher for the professional challenges of the DEIS environment. Teachers working in a DEIS setting require specialist training to interact with children who need more nurturing and encouragement. Teachers dealing with emotional, vulnerable and troubled children require a deeper understanding of how to shape, lead and support, in some instances working alongside child psychologists. Additional elective modules to the Bachelor of Education Programme which provide the graduate with a differentiated qualification with direct application for working in DEIS schools (coupled with ongoing professional development and support) would help to attract and retain the very best teachers in this specialised area.

Measuring Performance

A key question raised is who monitors the teachers? In Ireland, most teaching work is done without supervision. In contrast, in

Estonia and Sweden, the parents of children can join the class at any time and watch what's happening. The underpinning philosophy is, 'We've nothing to hide, come and see what we are doing.' Try suggesting that at the next INTO conference! My suggestion would be to have a fast car and a driver on standby outside the hotel; you'll probably need a quick exit. Currently, the classroom is considered an inner sanctum and it's impossible to see what happens there. The (then) Minister for Education Mary Hanifin, herself a former teacher, made an effort to tackle the issue of underperformance and suitability:

> Many of the young people we spoke to across the schools indicated that their teachers did not listen to them, were not interested in them or would 'put them down', which certainly contributed to negative feelings about teachers, school and learning. Some students felt that they were neglected by their teachers because of their low academic ability which in turn contributed to feelings of rebellion articulated through misbehaviour or poor attendance.[47]

Tackling Underperformance in Teaching

The starting point is to recognise that not everyone is suitable for teaching. One person told the following story:

> There was one principal working in a DEIS school who really shouldn't have been in that job. But there was nothing anyone could do. It's a horrible thing to say, but the single best thing that ever happened educationally in that area was when that man died and someone with a real interest took over the school.

It's some indictment of the existing system that we have to 'pray for someone's demise' to tackle underperformance. There's no suggestion here that a teacher should be 'dragged around to the back of the school and shot' at the first misdemeanor! But what level of underperformance is acceptable? Dr. Paul Downers offered an example of this and detailed the consequences. Where a teacher publicly humiliates a student, the child can become a target for other children. Like sharks smelling blood in the water, children pick up on weakness and victim status. We need to ensure that all teachers have the appetite and the ability to work with children, including the tools and the support to deal with children exhibiting difficult behaviour. In parallel, we need an effective mechanism to remove teachers who simply can't cope and are working in the wrong job. Somehow, somewhere along the line, a percentage of people who enter the teaching profession with idealism get turned into labour lawyers who know more about their contract than high educational outcomes. We need to provide the correct supports to teachers so that they can fulfil their obligations to the next generation of learners. But, alongside teachers rights, we need to be clear on teachers responsibilities. We need to establish a floor of teaching practice below which no one is allowed to fall. While the core responsibility to address this falls squarely at the management table, the trade unions can't continue to support burned-out or cynical teachers at the expense of a whole generation of students. Paul Downes expresses this colourfully to emerging classes of primary school teachers in St. Patrick's:

> Ask yourself, do you love this job or hate it? If the answer is that you 'hate it', then go and do something productive with your life. Don't make both yourself and the kids miserable.

The new 'Fitness to Practice' system in place is certainly a start but it's too soon to determine if will work in practice. For the sake of the next generation of learners, it has to be made to work really well.

Improving Expectations Across Whole Schools

When children from poorer families attend a school where there are lots of other poor students, they can become mired in lowered expectations. Some teachers are not attracted to working there. Some families with more ambition for their children send them further afield to better schools. It can plant the seeds of a negative, downwards spiral with the danger that a whole school can become sub-par. One senior academic stated: 'Given that some schools are physically so dark and dreary and the culture is so anti-children, the question isn't why do some kids leave school early, but why they stay for so long?' One child had remarked to a researcher that there was 'no sunlight in the school' – a perfect metaphor for the culture there.[48] Working with principals and teachers around setting high expectations, developing a broader understanding of ability, understanding the implications of processes such as 'streaming' and so on are key topics. We know that only 12 per cent of students from DEIS schools currently go to college. But no measurement system is perfect and this number doesn't tell us that the existing supports are not working. To prove this scientifically, we'd have to align 'matched disadvantaged schools' and withhold supports in some of them over time, to monitor what happens. But children are not white rats in a laboratory and this method of social science research is unethical. So, while it's difficult to prove the exact impact of DEIS schools, it's the best system we have for tackling education disadvantage. We now need to make it work.

Interrogating the Current Curriculum Design

One author[49] posed the provocative question: 'What's the point of school?' Is it to regurgitate information at exam time? Or is it to nurture curiosity and teach people to think for themselves? 'The ability to think critically and creatively, innovate and adapt to change, to work independently and in a team, and to be a reflective learner are prerequisites for life.'[50] Assuming that we want the education system to produce something more than the skill of 'exam passing', we need to recognise that the current curriculum is not designed to deliver this. The Irish education system, particularly at second level, has morphed into an academic model. The focus is on preparing students to successfully pass two exams, the Intermediate Certificate and the Leaving Certificate. While the Leaving Certificate, originally established as a university entrance exam, has undergone many syllabus changes over the years, no fundamental structural changes have taken place. According to one critical respondent, 'It's been a tinkering around the edges.' The overall point is that an examination system measures performance, but not ability. While students who achieve high outcomes undoubtedly have ability, it doesn't follow that those who score poorly lack ability. There are many different ways to measure intelligence; the ability to pass examinations is one of them. The central thrust of this argument is that the current model which dominates our education system design is not 'fit for purpose'. It's too narrow in conception and needs to be radically overhauled. We need to re-set the goalposts, creating a learning environment where all students can flourish. Consider the following:[51]

> Don't establish the boundaries
> First the squares, triangles, boxes
> Of preconceived possibility
> And then pour life into them
> Trimming off left-over edges
> Ending potential

Education is not just about qualifications. It's not about the establishment of a well-oiled certification system like some form of degree factory. It's about allowing children (and students of every age) to develop their potential and to feel successful. Realistically, education also has a social engineering component in the sense of creating active and responsible citizens. We're not training people in order to give them a piece of paper; we are trying to equip them for life. The current system simply has too many fallers and doesn't prepare those who survive to become self-directed learners.

An Initial 'Rejection' of Self-Directed Learning

The Leaving Certificate Redesign journey suggested will not provide an easy ride for students. To illustrate this point let me relate a short story. A couple of years ago, I secured the contract to teach a group of professionals (technology sector company) on 'how to manage people'. Deciding to conduct a small experiment, I put a huge amount of time into developing the background materials and put together really comprehensive workbooks, a sort of '10 Commandments' around managing people. The workbooks were given to participants with the following instructions: (a) decide what you want to achieve as a learning outcome, and (b) structure the workshop, that is, use the time as you see fit. For two days, I sat outside the training room in a hotel lobby area. The groups could come and consult with me as they wished; otherwise there were on their own. I almost had to quell a mini-riot. The group initially went bananas. Having launched the experiment, I had to stay with it, but it was decidedly uncomfortable (both for them and for me) until they settled into a pattern of actually doing the work. Of course there's a big market for spoon-fed, disempowered learning where the expertise of the teacher (or consultant) is passed to students. That's exactly what this group had expected. They turned up on day one with an expectation of being trained, perhaps even entertained. Trainees have become sophisticated consumers; the MTV generation won't accept 'death by PowerPoint' and want to be engaged with multi-media content and great jokes! I'd 'broken a norm' with this unconventional approach. Trying to change any training system is neither easy nor popular, at least in the short-term. But I've become convinced by many similar experiences since that time that self-directed learning produces superior learning outcomes (in the meantime, I've learned how to introduce it better and I'm still working on the jokes).

Understanding Why Students Disengage

All of the evidence suggests that the process of disengagement involves a gradual withdrawal from school-sponsored events. Young people become increasingly alienated from other students who are doing well (by the standards of the school) and bond with other potential failures. As a result, there's seldom a single decision to leave school; rather, young people who become disengaged are likely to 'mitch' more frequently, leaving and returning several times in a process that Kelly describes as 'fading-out.'[52]Continuity in curriculum between primary and second level education is also associated with dropout rates. Students who find Irish, English and Maths about the same in first year of secondary (vis a vis sixth class of primary school) had the lowest dropout rates. Fidelma Healy Eames explains the process:

> Unfortunately, the opportunity, the hope and enthu-siasm they frequently feel at moving to post-primary level is quickly quashed. The pace of instruction and curriculum delivery and the lack of consistent home support means they lose pace very quickly with their peers. These students are not adequately coached and supported from the outset when they enter school. As a result, they experience under-achieve-ment and failure from an early age.[53]

A Continuing Religious Dominance in Irish Schools

Sean Campbell suggested that, historically, Ireland 'punched above our weight' in educational terms because of the involvement of the religious orders in education. Given the volume of scandals that beset the Catholic Church (and other religions) in recent years, it's not an argument that gets much traction.[54] But there are some legacy issues which still impact the education system. For example, while the religious schools are owned by the Church,[55] they are funded by the State. The taxpayer pays teaching salaries along with day-to-day running costs. It's arguably a civil rights is-sue that people who are non-denominational have to get children Baptised in order to get them registered in a local Catholic school. The charade around First Confession, Holy Communion and Con-firmation, where families that don't practice religious beliefs par-ticipate around the time of these ceremonies, seems like a complete sham and is hardly a good moral education for the children (I'm saying that having gone through this myself three times with my own kids). While 86.8 per cent of people described themselves as Roman Catholic in the 2006 Census,[56] many children are not from Catholic homes, that is, many of the homes that declare themselves as Catholic are non-practicing: 'The classical sociological theory of secularisation – that as society becomes modern, it becomes more secular – fits the experience of Western Europe.'[57] At the present time, the overwhelming majority of schools fall under Catholic control. If the local school is Catholic, there may be very few alternatives for children. In theory, children can opt out of Religious Education at their parents' request, but schools may be unwilling or unable to accede to this (arguably, breaking international law around freedom of conscience).[58] Even if the parents wanted to do this, my guess is that many children wouldn't welcome the extra attention. Children are normally trying to opt in to the group, not ostracise themselves on a point of principle. A central question is what's the appropriate degree of separation between church and state?[59] While we wrestle with that overall topic, my personal view is that religious instruction soaks up far too much of the current timetable.

Parental Involvement

Some schools don't seem to realise the importance of involving parents in the children's education. Educational researchers Anne Henderson and Nancy Berla summarised a large number of studies conducted in the USA. They showed where parents are involved in children's education, children do better in school and the schools they attend are better:

> The evidence is beyond dispute. When schools work together with families to support learning, children tend to succeed not just in school but throughout life.[60]

In some cases, school initiatives to involve parents have limited success and are quickly abandoned. In others, parental involvement is not seen as a partnership but more of a service to the school (for example, painting the external railings). In Ireland, while parental involvement is encouraged, the 'how' is not specified, that is, it's decided by individual principals and boards of management. The general consensus across the people I've spoken with is that a 'partnership model' is seldom developed. Many schools treat parents as if they were a *pain* (interference) or a *problem* (indifference):[61]

> While complying with the national policy of parental
> involvement, the school can involve only their 'good'
> parents who comply with school norms and can 'be
> trusted not to rock the boat'.[62]

In relation to volunteering generally, Professor Putnam argues:[63]

> Generally speaking...volunteering and philanthropy
> are complements, not substitutes. Some of us give
> lots of both, while others give little of either.

While the USA experience may be different, Irish schools that
don't involve parents cut off a source of funding and other support.
But, more than this, they definitely cut off opportunities to partner
with parents in the educational mission during the 80 per cent of
the time the children are not in school.

The Impact of Resources: What if...?

Throughout the educational disadvantage debate, the issue of adequate resources continually resurfaces. Ann Mc Cluskey[64] framed
this as follows:

> As Principal, I can document that the only undimin-
> ished resources available to us since 2008 are the
> idealism of the teachers and the receptiveness of the
> pupils to learning and new ideas.

She went on to highlight that the cuts during the longest recession
in the history of the state, have not been spread evenly, specifically
citing an 85 per cent reduction in resources to encourage Traveller
education:

> While much media attention has been given to the
> 'squeezed middle', disadvantaged areas could be de-
> scribed as the 'crushed bottom.'

Our general discussion on educational disadvantage has to be seen
against a backdrop of pervasive expenditure cuts. Cutbacks may
have very little immediate impact on access (some of the interven-

tions suggested later are around encouraging a child in pre-school today to go to college 15 years from now). And, no one supports 'fat' in terms of resource duplication or excessive expenditure. But at some point, cuts injure muscle or even remove bone. At what point is a service so denuded of resources that it ceases to function in anything but name? If we are serious about tackling educational advantage, it needs more than platitudes or ad hoc support for high-profile initiatives. It needs more than the 'kindness of strangers' in the form of philanthropic contributions from corporations or generous individuals. While all of these may be important sub-components, the system has to be resourced to operate on a stand-alone basis. I can think about going to Spain as much as I want. But at some point I have to grab my wallet and buy an airline ticket. So too with tackling education disadvantage. Wouldn't it be just great if there was a real-life example of an entire community and school system being given sufficient resources to prove that this investment works? Hey, wait a minute; we have an example of this.

DDDA Initiative

The Dublin Dockland Development Authority conducted an educational experiment which ran for over 10 years in a defined geographical space. While the DDDA is sometimes derided for being part of the Celtic Tiger excess, problems with the purchase of the Bottle Glass Site in Ringsend have overshadowed some of the excellent work completed. In many ways this provides an almost perfect educational 'experiment.'

- *The area was disadvantaged and educational underperformance was well documented.*
- *Significant resources were invested to counteract this.*
- *There was a high level of community involvement (parents, schools etc.).*
- *It led to measurable improvements across a number of indicators.*

To give some idea of the breadth of this intervention, consider the following list of educational activities funded by the DDDA in a single year.[65]

Project/Activity	Budget[66]	# of Schools
Psychological Assessments	€20,000	20
Drama Programme	€140,000	15
Incentive Behaviour and Attitude Programme	€30,000	20
Literacy Programme	€10,000	4
Circle Time Programme	€120,000	16
Twinning with EU Schools (French Programme)	€80,000	6
Therapeutic Crisis Intervention Management	€5,000	3
Life Centre Special Projects	€5,000	1
Schools Music Programme	€25,000	17
Caught on Camera (Photography)	€25,000	12
Emotional Intelligence	€125,000	8
Schools Festival (Dragon Boat Racing)	€20,000	5
School Bands	€10,000	1
Sound School Programme	€30,000	4
PE and Healthy Eating	€100,000	8
African IT Programme	€60,000	5
ERSI Schools Database	€50,000	24
School Principal's Forum	€25,000	24
Dockland's School Yearbook	€65,000	24
In-Schools Project	€15,000	3
Family Learning Through Coaching	€50,000	7
Third Level Scholarships	€120,000	6
Schools Counseling Programme	€10,000	3
Total Budget	€1,140,000	
Average spend per school	€47,500	
Average spend per pupil	€316[67]	

Methodology Problems

The projects chosen were selected through a combination of 'top down' (DDDA chosen) and 'bottom up' (schools made specific re-

quests). At the time there were some dissenting voices. Some people suggested that the DDDA showed favoritism to particular schools. In a small number of cases, people were annoyed that particular projects they'd suggested were not funded. There was supposedly little transparency in the selection criteria and some personality clashes occurred between DDDA Executives and members of the local community (including the local educational leaders). Overall, there was a degree of cynicism, the core argument being that the DDDA were more interested in spin than education. My own sense, in working in partnership with the DDDA (when I worked in NCI, they funded some projects), was that there were actually too many initiatives underway and resources were spread thinly over too wide an area to have a deep impact. However, while it's impossible to keep everyone happy, the fundamental objectives of the programme were above reproach. Unfortunately, this initiative didn't have rigorous before and after measurements across all areas, so we have to exercise some caution in extrapolating the findings. [68] But, it does allow us to draw some inferences.

Tentative Outcomes

In 1997, 35 per cent of Docklands children dropped out of school before the age of 12. By 2005, that number had fallen to 13 per cent. The percentage dropping out of school by age 16 declined from 65 per cent (1997) to 30 per cent (2005). In 1997, 10 per cent of Dockland's children sat the Leaving Certificate. By 2005 that number had risen to 60 per cent. In relation to third level attendance, the needle moved from 1 per cent (1997) to 10 per cent in 2005. These achievements, made in a period of just over eight years, are quite remarkable. In essence, the docklands schools became advantaged because of the value added by the DDDA Education Programme. If we wanted a 'case study' to show what can be done, this is it. Let the skeptics be silent.

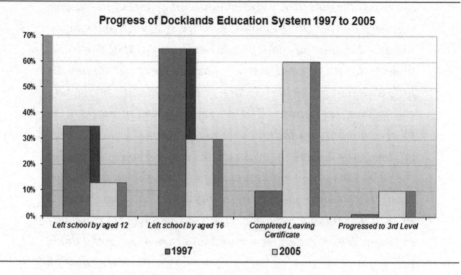

Progress of Docklands Education System 1997 to 2005

■1997   □2005

Educational Disadvantage: Who Owns It?

Dr. Aideen Quilty in UCD posed the following question: 'Who owns the problem of access?' At a political level, is educational disadvantage an education or a social issue? We know that politicians change every couple of years. We also know that some Ministers for Education are particularly attracted to the cause of educational disadvantage, others less so. So, the issue receives a lot of attention every couple of years and then, slips onto the back burner. Across the civil service, we've seen that several departments are connected with this issue. Because the ownership of educational disadvantage is diffused, the risk is that it becomes an *orphan issue* and gets neglected. At an institutional level, the same basic confused ownership point applies. As a single example, within UCD there's a School of Education, an Adult Education Department, a Centre for Teaching and Learning, Community Training interventions (which fall under the heading of social justice), the Access Department itself and the College Foundation (fundraising arm). Each of these impact the access agenda in some or all of what they do. Yet, there isn't a single agreed approach to educational disadvantage, albeit UCD have recently set up a widening participation group to progress this.[69]

Political Level

Most Ministers want to be associated with *new* political initiatives – that's the policy trend in Ireland. Politically, there's little mileage in supporting a previous initiative (even one that's working reasonably well). There's no photo opportunity in visiting a disadvantaged school and announcing, 'All's well. Let's keep things as they are.' So, over time, the continual introduction of new initiatives leads to a hotchpotch where numerous (sometimes overlapping) initiatives are put in place. A plethora of innovations is the result: each college has a unique access system; each DEIS school runs customised initiatives: each community adds its own individual twist. The 'I' of Innovation blocks the 'I' of Implementation. In numerous dealings with Government departments, both as a management consultant and while directly employed in the education sector, what clearly emerged was an inherent conservatism, a 'keep things the way they are', a disdain for anything deemed radical. The unspoken culture is as follows: Tweaking is OK; changing isn't. The focus becomes 'Minding the Minister' (avoiding any embarrassment) as much as breakthrough thinking. What happens is that the continual announcement and launch of minor initiatives provides the outward illusion of progress without any real gain. To move the needle forward, you need a sustained, impactful attack on the key roadblocks to educational achievement. Perhaps you are familiar with the saying, 'Eventually, every great idea degenerates into donkey work.' We now need to complete the 'donkey work' part of this equation and forgo the continual announcement of 'great ideas' (many of which we already know).

STRAND #4: THE PERSONAL AGENDA

The Fear of Failure

When I worked at the National College of Ireland (NCI), without doubt the happiest event in the academic calendar was Graduation Day. People almost danced up to the podium to receive certificates, diplomas, degrees and post-graduate honours. While

the awards were different, the emotions were similar. Gradu-
ates were proud that they'd made the journey; their families were
proud and relieved! Nothing great can be achieved without effort.
We all know the line that the only place that success comes before
work is in the dictionary. The graduates had earned their moment
in the sun. But if education is such a great idea, why don't even
more people get involved? At an individual level, there's no simple
answer to this. Sometimes it's conflicting responsibilities ('three
kids, all in nappies'). Sometimes it's financial ('I don't have the
spondulicks'). Sometimes it's a lack of commitment; about 90 per
cent of people have the capability to complete a degree but only
60 per cent do it (success in college is more about stickability than
capability). But an enormous mental impediment is that people
won't go into the ring because of a fear of failure – particularly if
their earlier experience of school was negative. That 'tape' is often
still playing inside their head on a continuous loop. Poor writing
skills or spelling (sometimes undiagnosed dyslexia) or inadequate
maths training gets misinterpreted into a neat (but incorrect) slo-
gan: 'I'm stupid.' People carry that slogan for life and it continually
damages their self-confidence.

Alongside all of the obvious practical barriers, for example,
family commitments, childcare, transport and so on, self-limit-
ing beliefs pose a considerable barrier to continued learning or
a return to education for mature students. One writer,[70] using
the term essentialism, described this as people convincing them-
selves that they aren't capable of certain things. It can manifest
itself in such self-defeating comments as: 'I'm no good at that,'
'I'm not that sort of person' or 'That's not the way I'm built.' These
views set unnecessary boundaries to progress. Mature learners
returning to education often have to overcome 'internal demons,'
for example, a lack of confidence about their ability which can
have a 30, 40 or even 50-year history, an emotional scar that's
never fully healed.

Bringing Universities *into* the Community

One specific finding from the research is that 'Access Students don't travel' and prefer to stay close to home. Depending on where they live (they seldom live beside leafy colleges), access students often have to get 'two buses' to college and this can pose a barrier to attendance. In trying to understand why this might pose a barrier, the reasons put forward were diverse. Some access students prefer to psychologically stay close to home (there's an anxiety about moving into less well-known areas and they have to battle self-doubt, at least initially). In a phrase I hadn't encountered before, Dr Aideen Quilty described this as the 'geography of belonging.' This aversion to travelling can certainly be frustrating for those trying to establish access initiatives. While some students simply can't afford the expense of travel, it seems deeper than this.

Progressions Initiative

In NCI we set up a programme called Progressions, designed to help people from disadvantaged areas secure a role in financial services. There was a strong classroom element running in parallel with work experience in participating companies. Having invested a lot of personal energy (as part of a team that set this up), it was somewhat annoying when some of the candidates wouldn't travel to jobs that were awkward to get to. Ambitious middle class people, some of whom would go to the dark side of the moon for the right opportunity, find this confusing. Here we see a group of people who outwardly want to secure employment and then, almost inexplicably, shoot themselves in the foot by not availing of the opportunity offered. Why might this be the case? From speaking directly to participants, there's a mixture of factors at play. Some people, dependent on the welfare state for so long, can develop an expectation of 'being minded,' with the college expected to take on a sort of parental role and remove the pain of personal effort (what sociologists describe as 'learned helplessness'). In other cases, the refusal to travel masked a deeper fear of the 'new doors' being opened. People knew how to behave and survive in their existing world. While it wasn't always perfect, it was known. Now, they were being offered an opportunity to move into a new, exciting, but somewhat scary place, without the supports that many of us take for granted. They were worried about their accent. They were concerned about the dress code. They questioned if they were 'biting off more than they could chew.' And so on. Some of this was conscious and could be articulated; sometimes it just seemed to produce a generalised anxiety, without any particular label. On the question of displacement, non-traditional third level students often return home to families who can ask, 'how did you get on?' but may have zero experience of the process. Students breaking the mould of educational disadvantage face this journey alone. These complicated factors can be communicated as a reluctance to travel! If it doesn't sound too patronising, I think that the secret is what might be labelled 'small steps.' You get people to step a little outside of their comfort zone. You load the dice (to make this initial effort successful). Then click onto the next forward step.

Working *with* Local Communities

In relation to providing third level education in disadvantaged communities, one simple idea is to bring the college *into the community*. If people are scared of a college campus, the journey can be reversed, that is, the college is brought to the people. For example, in one UCD outreach programme, teaching is done in a 'kitchen in Clondalkin' with a UCD pop-up banner prominently displayed in the background. Dr. Aideen Quilty, someone enormously committed to the access agenda, describes this as follows:

> Participants get a students card with the UCD logo. Somehow it becomes real and translates into 'I'm a legitimate student here.'

It's labour-intensive, but it works. Historically, many universities used disadvantaged communities as social science laboratories, studying people to understand how different classes thought and behaved. In conjures up a picture of a middle class researcher darting into these communities, completing the research, then getting out as fast as possible (hoping that their car wasn't damaged or stolen during the process). We now collectively owe a debt to these same communities – it's payback time from the third level sector.

Throughout the book, I've tried to use positive examples to illustrate the arguments made. It's all too easy to cite negative examples and make yourself look clever by making someone else look stupid. But, where mistakes are made, lessons can be learned. In Ballymun, Dublin City University has an outreach building located in the redeveloped area close to Shangan Gardens. The idea was soundly based, that is, encouraging local people to use a local DCU facility rather than having to attend the main campus on Glasnevin Avenue, about a mile distant (while a mile may not seem far, attendance on a university campus is mentally a 'thousand miles distant' for some early school leavers). So far, so good. But the actual location of the outreach centre is problematic. It sits in one section of a community divided by a main road. People from the *other side* tend not to cross over. At night, the area is dark and anti-social problems deter people from attending. The net effect is that this facility is under-used. A lot of money is spent (ongoing) repairing plate glass windows in the building. A better solution was to develop a central facility in the heart of the community, where all members could attend. This was well known to people working on the ground but according to one respondent, they were 'not consulted.' I've become a fan of Dublin City University and very much admire the efforts made to tackle educational disadvantage, sustained over many years. In this specific case, it might represent a small misstep. This vignette highlights the importance for all third level colleges to work in partnership with local communities, a fundamentally different concept to supplying services to them.

STRAND #5: POSITIVE THIRD LEVEL COLLEGE EXPERIENCE

Should Students Pay College Fees?

There's been a lot of debate around the return of college fees in recent years, a move that was supported by the OECD review of Irish Higher Education in 2004. Why? Because, higher education is currently heavily dependent on public resources. In 2009, the then Minister for Education and Science, Batt O'Keefe, argued that the abolition of fees had not achieved greater equity of access to Higher Education for under-represented groups. He argued that this issue would be better progressed by direct funding of access programmes and through student grants. In more recent times, the National Strategy for Higher Education to 2030[71] stated:

> The only realistic option to support growth in partic-ipation is to require students or graduates to directly share in the cost of their education, reflecting the considerable private returns that they can expect to enjoy. A direct student contribution, based on a com-bination of upfront fees and an income-contingent loan scheme, is recommended as an essential ele-ment of future funding arrangements for the system.

We've seen throughout that, over recent years, Ireland has wit-nessed significant improvements in the numbers of people attend-ing college, including students from under-represented groups. To the layperson, it's therefore difficult to argue that the abolition of fees had no positive impact (albeit the 'cause and effect' argument is much more nuanced). A key concern is that a reintroduction of fees would be perceived as a lack of capacity in the public purse, that is, economics (rather than a failed social policy) might be seen as the culprit!

Oops! Learning From Mistakes

This argument is complex. The water charges debate, which has become a hot political topic, offers a useful analogy. The core rationale for the introduction of water charges, based on the initial communication, was to 'conserve water'.[72] Water meters were installed to measure consumption and would operate on the 'user pays' principle (use more water, pay higher charges). Surplus funds generated would help to upgrade the overall water system (reducing leakages and improving drinkability) to ensure that everyone had access to a safe, clean and continuous water supply. Having a single water authority (Irish Water) was said to be more efficient than having water managed by 26 different local authorities. Then what happened? These arguments became hopelessly mired in controversy. An alternative view took hold. This was a new tax being imposed as a way to increase revenue to the Government. It was a sop to the European Union who'd suggested that Ireland needed to broaden its tax base. The conspiracy theorists believed that this was Phase 1 in a two-part dance; Phase 2 would be the sale of Irish Water through privatisation (similar to what happened to the water system in the UK). The ideas around water conservation, improved service quality and the rationalisation of the industry became lost in a political storm. In the court of public opinion, the government arguments were essentially dismissed as bullshit.

The question of college fees has the exact same potential for confusion. For 'Joe or Joan Average', the re-introduction of college fees would almost certainly be seen as an additional tax. There's a strong belief in Ireland around 'what we have, we hold' and people don't like paying new taxes.[73] For a small number of high rollers, the fees might be inconsequential. For middle-income earners, particularly those on the borderline of qualifying for a grant to cover fees, the re-introduction of college fees would be a significant additional cost. Those from lower socio-economic groups would probably qualify for a grant. So, in theory at least, this shouldn't impact progression rates from disadvantaged groups. However, it could erect a psychological barrier. If potential students came to believe that 'the piece of paper is useless' (that is, there are no jobs for people with degrees) or that 'I will be saddled at 21 years of age with €50,000 of debt', it would be easy to lose an entire generation of learners. While the balance of advantages is to reintroduce college fees (more on this later) there's some genius required in the detail of exactly how this would be done. The expansion in state subvention of third level education can be seen in two ways: (1) as a genuine effort to improve how the education systems functioned and to allow more disadvantaged students to maximise their potential, or (2) treatment of the electorate as consumers whose votes can be bought with gimmicks and tricks.[74] There's an enormous political dimension to this question. Rory O'Sullivan argues:

> In any society, public policy is skewed towards benefitting the dominant group as the development of public policy is an act of power. Consequently, the less dominant benefit least and are excluded. In Ireland, as in most advanced economies, public policy and public services are designed for the most influential rather than everyone.

One thing is certain. The fees issue needs careful handling.

Declining Funding for Third Level Institutions

Third level colleges have been arguing that funding has been in decline over recent years. At third level, there's anecdotal evidence that this squeeze is having a disproportionate impact on access programmes. It raises three important questions. Firstly, how well does the recurrent funding model reflect the actual costs to institutions of access programmes? Put crudely, do colleges 'make a profit' on access, break-even or lose money vis a vis the funding allocated by the HEA (there may not be a single *answer* to this question across all colleges)? Secondly, is 'access money' ringfenced for access initiatives or does it get diverted, that is, mixed in with the general overhead costs of running a third level institution? Thirdly, would higher levels of funding for access produce superior outcomes?

Access Funding

Core access funding in 2013 was €29 million. This money pays for staff to run foundation programmes along with the programme elements detailed earlier.[75] When the Strategic Innovation Fund (SIF) was in play, a range of themes were supported, for example, outreach, modular access programmes, work-based learning, reform of the HEAR/DARE schemes and so on. The interim evaluation of SIF by Dr. Gordon Davies produced some salient findings: (1) It assisted in developing institutional capacity for collaboration on Access and Lifelong Learning, (2) SIF Access and Lifelong projects collectively advanced the access agenda across higher education, and (3) large regional collaborations between third level institutions have been successful, encouraging learning from best practice and, just as importantly, avoiding duplication of effort. However, because some of the historical funding was 'separate' (under SIF), it may have inadvertently communicated that access was a project, that is, something that needed to be funded separately. A centrally important point made throughout is that access activities need to be embraced as a core college activity and become mainstreamed.

'Rate My Driving' (of the Access Agenda)

Some colleges are not just supportive of the access agenda, they lead in this area. Some play 'catch up' but are broadly committed. Others pay lip service and use access as a way to chase funding (from the HEA and philanthropists). While the HEA needs to recognise and celebrate best practice, there's also a need to be courageous and tackle poor performance to prevent access from limping along or falling off the radar altogether. In order to do this, the HEA has recently introduced Performance Compacts (participation, access and lifelong learning is one of seven categories). When the performance-funding framework is implemented, up to 10 per cent of the total core grant available will be performance-related. Is this working? Unfortunately, it's too early to tell. It remains to be seen how this new system will work in practice. For example, how well has the joint setting of targets worked? Has the contradiction between 'realistic and ambitious', targets been navigated?[76] The change in the HEA's role (from 'Funder' to 'Regulator') offers a more powerful influence on how the third level system tackles access. In practice, this 'regulator/evaluator' role is not universally welcomed. It has become part of a broader debate across the third level sector about what's often described as 'creeping managerialism.'[77] On paper, the emerging HEA role offers a mechanism to drive best practices from the centre.

My personal experience in working with the HEA is very positive and the access question is centre-stage. Yet there are severe resource contradictions. The National Access Office employs less than 10 staff, a level of resourcing that seems ludicrous for a group tasked with tackling this agenda. In addition, in recent years this group has suffered from 'mission creep' with huge involvement in labour activation. For example, while helping Quantity Surveyors to retrain as Web Designers might be a noble cause, it does nothing to tackle disadvantage. While the agendas overlap, the idea that both topics can be driven from an initial poor resource base makes little sense. Current resourcing is a recipe for mediocre progress, regardless of the talent and commitment of the people involved.

Internal Resistance to Access

There are pockets of excellence across the third level system. Staff who are über dedicated, who've managed to overcome roadblocks – money, resources and a lack of institution attention. But some feel that the only place there should be an access sign is *Access Restricted* to preferential parking. University missions often seek to develop new knowledge through research, an aspiration that shouldn't be mutually exclusive from great teaching practices. The reality is that some academics find it hard to connect with a non-traditional cohort of students, a tribe they've never encountered. In some quarters, unfortunately, there's a residue of elitism. While constructing this book, one academic remarked, 'They'd let anyone in here now.' Confronting internal bias within the third level sector needs to remain on our collective 'to do' list. While great strides have been made, we're not quite there yet. An attempt to summarise the central features, which influence a student's educational journey, is detailed in the following graphic:

Access to Education: Key Factors which help to predict if a person will ...
a. Successfully complete 2nd Level. b. Go to further/higher education. c. Return to education as a mature student

1. Family ———— High value placed on education within the family unit

| **Reasonable Expectations** about kids completing education | **Family Interests** Learning, reading materials, curious minds | **Good Routines** Discipline around studying, bed times | **Financial Means** Pay for books, tuition costs, educational trips | **Family Stability** Housing, employment, health, stable membership |

2. Community ———— Circle of Influence supports the idea of college attendance

| **Peer Group** Peers value educational achievement | **Role Models** People who've made the journey (in the family & the community) | **Community Values** Educational is rated highly. Local Leadership: strong, positive community influences e.g. active GAA, soccer or sports clubs | **Resources** Community Centre & Leadership Training | **Provision** Range of Further/ Higher programmes run 'locally' (adults and children) |

3. Schools ———— Clear philosophy & supports: Student experience of school system generally positive

| **Committed** friendly staff & great teaching practices | **Aspirations** High % of students expected to go to College | **Interesting Curriculum** Students see relevance of topics | **Small Wins** High % of students 'feel good' about their performance | **Early Identification** & intervention with those who struggle e.g. poor attendance | **Career Guidance** Help students navigate the system and set personal goals | **Links** Strong links and Liaison with parents, community and state agencies |

4. Personal ———— Personal goals becoming clearer... individual can overcome self-limiting doubts

| **Awareness** "I know how the system works and how to progress" | **Clear Prize** "Education would improve my life" e.g get a great job | **Self-Belief** "I could successfully make it through college" | **Self-Sufficient** "I can get a grant or part-time job and survive financially" | **Accessibility** Close-by or accessible opportunities exist e.g. blended learning | **Disability** "I can overcome some physical or mental condition which makes life more difficult" |

5. College ———— Positive 3rd Level Experience...college has an underpinning 'success for all' belief

| **Philosophy** "No student left behind" (Vs. survival of the fittest) | **Student Integration** "I know how this place works and I fit in here" | **Committed Staff** Great teaching & learning practices - practiced by all | **Resources** Sufficient budgets, people and executive attention paid to Access | **Best Practice** 'Joined-up' thinking on Access e.g. strong links with secondary schools & communities | **Support** Recognition of differences & difficulties for some students, e.g. finance, counselling |

6. Workplace ———— Employers encourage ...continuing education and upskilling of all staff

| **Philosophy** Continually invest in Human Talent. Encouragement of lifelong learning | **Openess** Diagnosis of current skill levels e.g. literacy | **Co-Operation** Links with external education providers -public and private | **Resources** Sufficient budgets and training facilities. Range of options (starter to more advanced) | **Jigsaw** 'Joined-up' thinking e.g. rewards for skills acquisition |

Education Changes Lives:

Sara Gwiazda

Medical Doctor, Trinity College

My family moved to Ireland from Poland just in time for me to start secondary school. This made the educational transition easier as everyone was in the same boat, wondering what things would be like in the new school and not really knowing anyone else. While I already understood English, it was rusty as we hadn't been speaking it on a daily basis. Shaky, but good enough.

Being foreign made me different which wasn't ideal. Like most teenagers, I didn't want to stand out from the crowd. There was definitely some bullying. Nothing too dramatic, more name-calling and not being accepted into some of the 'cool' social circles. A commitment to school work and to making good grades was also a source of bullying from some quarters. I did have a small group of friends in school but we never really became what you might describe as 'close'. In a weird way, the social isolation helped me focus energy inwards and work on my own goals rather than being distracted. It may even have helped to build some resilience. In an environment where I couldn't rely on peer support or encouragement, I became self-dependent (I wouldn't recommend it as a success strategy). Looking back now, it was a lonely time. It's never easy to integrate into a new culture and become part of an established clique. I suspect it's pretty similar for many non-Irish students.

I always had huge support from my parents. They were firm believers that you can do anything you want if you put your mind to it. When I realized that I wanted to become a doctor, it seemed achievable and all of the family got behind this. Their positive attitude was backed up by a great school. The teachers at the Donaghies Community School made every effort to help me get the best results and were always available for any extra help or advice needed. They genuinely wanted all of us to succeed and this was a hugely positive factor in being able to achieve the Leaving Certificate results required.

Coming from a disadvantaged area impacted my college studies, at least to some extent. Many of the medical students had doctors in the family who were able to provide insights and lend a helping hand throughout college. I'm the first doctor in our family, so had to learn the stuff from the baseline upwards. It's a subtle point, but most of the people studying medicine came from families where it was taken for granted that they would go to college and continue into one of the professions. In my family, my mother was the first person to get a college degree and to break the cycle of educational underachievement.

The overall formula seems to be as follows: supportive parents, committed teachers willing to give you the information and a mindset that you CAN succeed, regardless of background. This wasn't an easy climb (not for me anyway) but I was delighted to complete the program and continue this new family tradition of educational success. I hope that this short story encourages you to stay with your own educational journey. Don't give up!

Chapter 7

Practical Solutions: How Can We Change the Paradigm?[1]

But when you can no longer dream, no longer see possibilities
No longer see alternatives. When you can only see limitation
Only despair and negation. Then you are in the way
You are also the problem, the exhausted obstruct[2]

Before we consider the individual recommendations, it's worthwhile to briefly reflect on what we are trying to do.

Q: How will we eradicate educational disadvantage?

A: Educational disadvantage is multidimensional. It impacts the lives of children, families and communities. It also features across every single level of the education system. There's no single magic bullet solution.

Q: OK, it's complex. But how do we decide which issues to progress?

A: Historically, views on educational disadvantage were more art than science. Everyone had opinions on what worked and what didn't. That's changed. We can now select initiatives which deliver a disproportionate impact based on proven outcomes.[3] The recommendations detailed are a 'debate starter'. I'm not making a claim that this is the definitive list. But I am strongly making the point that we need an agreed list of exactly what needs to happen.

Q: Are some 'elements' more important? Should we start with the schools?

A: Schools are certainly part of a solution. But like the song, 'The knee bone's connected to the thigh bone', we can't fix any one part of the system in isolation. These recommendations are an integrated package. It's not a menu of options where particular elements can be chosen a la carte. Partial fixes don't work. Like a cancer that hasn't been fully removed, educational disadvantage can easily return. It needs to be eradicated. Piecemeal interventions and short-term initiatives don't work (assuming that we are serious about tackling this).

Q: It's clear how each recommendation will work?

A: Yes and no. Yes, in the sense that the individual recommendations are clear. In areas where I don't have expertise or which need more analysis, the recommendations made are directional. More detailed work is needed to flesh out how the implementation stage (the 'how') should be constructed.

Q: What would the Philosophy/Vision element look like?

A: The following will provide a working draft for the 'implementation group' (see later recommendation) to consider....

Target Setting

The floor of educational attainment is Level 4 of the National Framework of Qualifications. Every Irish citizen should meet this as a minimum. We will set targets for each 'level' of the education system, for example, the per cent of the population who should hold qualifications from level 4 through to 10.

No-One Left Behind: The starting position = each person lost to education is a system failure.
Later = Too Late. The importance of addressing educational disadvantage in early years is captured in the tagline 'later is too

late.' We need to front-load our educational investment in those all-important early years.

Success Gets Rewarded (not punished): *Existing metrics punish success, creating a fear that schools will lose resources. If they don't make a breakthrough, the extra resources remain. If they do break the educational disadvantage cycle, resources are pulled. We will design a system where success gets rewarded and failure gets actively managed.*

Measure the Score: *We need scorecards in place to track performance. We measure outcomes and move quickly to 'fix' elements, which are off-track. Scorecards will include several new measures, for example, retention rates rather than just entry into college.*

Value for Money: *Every part of the system has to provide value for money to the taxpayer. That requires a clear mission for each organisation and zero overlaps or duplication. We focus on the 'p' of performance, and show a disdain for the 'p' of politics between competing entities.*

Future Investment: *We've seen the numbers. Education is an investment for the future. For every €1 invested in educational disadvantage, the return to the exchequer is multiplied. We cannot fund an economy class education system and expect business class outcomes. Our philosophy is backed by investment.*

Q: What's the thinking behind developing 'Best Practice' models?

A: A best-practice model sets minimum standards, for example, a *floor* below which no part in the system (for example, an individual school) is allowed to fall. It also details the 'Rolls Royce' standards, for example, aspirations/aim points to shoot towards. While the North Star can never be reached, it has guided sailors for thousands of years. Best-practice checklists play a similar role and offer guide points for each key strand in the fight against educational disadvantage. Checklists work well in the airline industry (for pilots), in medicine (for doctors) and so on. In exactly the same way, we can determine the 'vital signs' around educational disadvantage. The checklists offer a self-evaluation tool and a guide to external auditors. The current hotchpotch system, that is, *pockets of excellence* in some areas and *black holes of nothing* in others is not sustainable.

Q: The recommendations made are all 'new' ideas?

A: Absolutely not. Like educational disadvantage itself, some of these ideas have been around for quite some time. Marie Antoinette said, 'There's nothing new, except what has been forgotten'. Several ideas have already been piloted, that is, tried and tested, providing us with a good understanding of what works and what doesn't. Some ideas are more experimental. I'm less concerned about whether an idea is new or old; the more important criteria is right or wrong.

Q: What's so important about this particular 'list' of recommendations?

A: To construct this set of recommendations, three issues have been addressed: (a) Understanding the present consensus, the points of agreement around what's important. For example, there's a strong consensus that focusing on early years offers a high return on educational investment. My suggestion is to concentrate the early years efforts in disadvantaged communities. (b) Consider some radical alternatives, not for the sake of being controversial, but to question the existing hegemony, for example, abandoning the teaching of Irish as a compulsory subject. (c) Figure out a way to actually make this stuff happen. It's not so much that we 'don't know what to do', more that we don't know how to put it into practice. There's an *implementation* rather than an *intellectual* deficit.[4] This list of recommendations is important because it tackles educational disadvantage in a holistic way, a review of the entire system rather than the individual elements.

STRAND #1: INTERVENING WITH FAMILIES

1.1 Mainstream Early Learning with Families in Disadvantaged Areas

We know that parenting has an enormously important impact on children.

> The physical, social, emotional and cognitive development a child gains in early childhood draws the blueprint for their adult life, directly influencing their future mental and physical health and well-being.[5]

A positive start reduces the need for later remedial actions that are typically more intensive and costly.[6] Resourcing child development offers an enormous return on investment; however, the economic benefits are often overlooked or discounted as the long-term effects are not immediately apparent or measurable within the lifetime of a government.[7] The recommendation here is to select a small number (perhaps 1 or 2) methods of working with families in disadvantaged areas and roll these out nationwide. Here's one example:

Early Learning Initiative

The Early Learning Initiative has been underway at the National College of Ireland for some years. The initiative, launched by Professor Joyce O'Connor, is funded by a small group of philanthropists.[8] Selected women from the local community (disadvantaged area) are fully trained in early childhood learning practices and become Home Visitors.[9] Local families then volunteer to be part of the programme. One child is selected in each family along with one parent (normally the mother). The Home Visitors work with these families on a scheduled basis and role model early childhood learning practices – reading, playing educational games and so on. The families chosen don't have a third level background so this is their first exposure to college. There's no stigma; parents self-select to work with the college. The families are also encouraged to come to events in NCI. Throughout the programme, which lasts for 18 months, the child's development is carefully monitored. It costs €3,000 per year for each participating family (arguably, it costs less because the Home Visitor's own family also benefits).[10] There are also spillover benefits into the wider community with some local mothers shadowing the programme on an informal basis. A centrally important design feature is the fact that it's run by local women. It's not middle class people helicoptered into the community, telling locals what to do. The learning happens in the home, where people have been invited inside. Does it work? The Early Learning Initiative at NCI has been subject to intensive scrutiny on several levels and has proven to be extremely effective. For example, in numeracy, the Dockland's children's outcomes are starting to mirror those in middle class schools.[11] A national roll-out of this (or a similar programme) would begin to break the cycle of educational disadvantage from the moment of birth.

1.2 Increase the Investment in Early Years Education

We need to raise spending to 0.8 per cent of GDP to match the OECD average spending on early years, with a view to moving this to 1 per cent of GDP over a defined timeframe which is recognised internationally as best practice.[12] However, this extra spending would not be spread 'across the board' to all children but concentrated in areas of disadvantage (in line with the recommendation above). As detailed earlier, we only need to fix this once.

STRAND #2: BUILDING POWERFUL COMMUNITIES

Under this heading, the goal is to increase 'social capital' across disadvantaged communities. In his brilliant book *Bowling Alone*, Robert Putnam explores the decline in social capital in small communities in the USA since the 1950s. It has a number of consequences. When social capital is high, children do better in school, neighborhoods are safer, people prosper, are happier and healthier. A deficit in social capital leads to more suicides, depression, crime and a range of other social problems. While increasing social capital is not a simple task, the goal is to form new associations that get people actively involved. As long ago as 1924, Mary Parker Follett defined power as 'the ability to make things happen.' Therefore the goal under this heading is to reinstate agency at the community level to combat apathy and defeatism. If it takes a 'village to rear a child', we need that village to be functioning well – with a particular focus on education. The specific recommendations follow...

2.1 Construct a Community Diagnostic Model

We need a diagnostic framework that can be applied across all disadvantaged communities. The objective here is to (a) evaluate the educational needs in each community, and (b) take a 'Polaroid Snapshot' of the current services in place and measure the gaps. To develop this model we should review earlier community development approaches, for example, the RAPID system to see what worked and what didn't. The particular focus of this initiative would be around diagnosing the educational needs and barriers within each disadvantaged community. This isn't the Third Secret of Fatima. For example, where childcare is a barrier, community volunteers could take care of children while the parent studied.[13]

2.2 Standardise the Interventions/Approach

We need to agree a standard set of interventions, essentially a suite of programmes that have been 'field tested' (where there are good existing models of practice we can adopt them). There's too much innovation in the sector, too many customised initiatives, too many arguments that 'this group' is unique. We need to select a range of off-the-shelf solutions that can be applied across all communities. Each community would be able to access a number of standard education offerings. From a content perspective, Liz Waters suggests[14] that these should include foundation courses (personal development and basic education), community leadership training, third Level qualification courses and employment related education like the ECDL (European Computer Driving License). In terms of delivery, Dr. Josephine Bleach is a passionate believer that community action research works best – annual plans devised by locals, which are then implemented. It's the Japanese Kaisan method – small percentage improvements each year – applied to community development. The investment would support local people doing something positive in their own community, rather than outside professionals bouncing in and out.

2.3 Simplify the Providers

In 2015, the consulting company Mazars completed a report on homelessness. The report found that more than 75 organisations had received €95.9 million funding in the previous year. Based on an average of 5,000 people who were without homes at that time, this equates to the State spending circa €20,000 per homeless person (it would have been cheaper to give each person a house and for the government to pay their mortgage). If the money that these agencies raised voluntarily is added into the mix, the total income for that sector rises to almost a quarter of a billion euro.[15] In short, there are too many organisations chasing the same problem and too few long-term solutions. It's critical to simplify the supports available to communities. The current system is a complex structure that's difficult to understand and almost impossible to navigate. More importantly, it's ineffective.

For example, in the North Wall Area, a relatively small community of around 1,800 people, one report noted that there are 19 community agencies offering a variety of services.[16] Organisations contributing funding into this community include: Department of Children and Youth Affairs, Department of Education and Skills, Department of Environment, Community and Local Government, Department of Justice and Equality, Dublin City Council, Dublin North Inner City Drugs Task Force, FÁS (now Solas) including CE Community Employment schemes, HSE (Health Service Executive), Pobal, External Philanthropic Funding, Probation and Welfare Service and CDVEC (City of Dublin Vocational Educational Committee). Apart from the waste created by overlap, when so many groups operate within a single community, there's often political tension and poor cooperation. To go forward, there's a need to rationalise existing structures, expanding the role of the 'best providers' with proven ability and disbanding organizations which are not performing or have become redundant. For example, in the area of youth work we have a couple of powerful models with a proven track record that could be installed across every disadvantaged community in Ireland (for example, Foroige). A Community Development Taskforce would be tasked with managing this transition/simplification over the next two to three years and would then disband.

Using 'Not-For-Profit' Organisations

There's a growing sophistication in the not-for-profit sector in terms of programme design and evidence-based initiatives. Sean Campbell, the CEO of Foroige,[17] argued that:

> Atlantic Philanthropies and the One Foundation[18] professionalised this sector. They imposed a rigor around donations that made all of us better at what we do. They gave the support, but we had to show that it was working and not just pouring money down a black hole.

This raises a difficult policy issue. Should government funding enhance public sector provision or support independent providers? In essence, should the Government outsource their statutory responsibility? Understandably, the views on this differed depending on whether the respondent was a public sector employee or worked in the voluntary sector. Those in the voluntary sector had a strong view that services to this cohort of children/learners can't be provided during a normal workday. Dr. Kevin O'Higgins offered one example:

> Students sometimes panic on Sunday evening trying to write an essay that has to be submitted on Monday. That's when you have to be there. The needs don't always fall into a neat 9-5, Monday-Friday circle.

But it's more than just flexibility around the timing and delivery of services. Voluntary workers in the not-for-profit sector often have a *crusading spirit.*

2.4 Activate Community Volunteers

An article in *The Irish Times* ('Volunteers who restored Kilmainham Gaol to get their moment in the sun') showcased the work completed by hundreds of people who'd given their time, without payment, to restore a building which had not been in use since 1924. The group of volunteers who restored Kilmainham Gaol essentially bonded around the shared vision of preserving a key element of Irelands' history. The intriguing part of the Kilmainham story is the amount of time that was given voluntarily to this six year-long project. We often decry the black economy where people work but don't pay tax. This initiative is a perfect example of the white economy, where people volunteer their time freely in the service of a worthy cause. Volunteering represents an enormous potential opportunity right across the country. Dr. Áine Gray stated:

> We need to get people in the community involved
> in education. Some people have time on their hands
> and, if partnered one-to-one with children, could re-
> ally help, especially in the primary school years.

In similar vein, Larry Mc Givern from St. Vincent de Paul argued:

> Without any extra money being available, we could
> expand literacy classes using volunteers. External
> volunteers could offer grinds. If children fall behind
> early on and aren't encouraged both at home and
> at school, they tend to fall between the cracks. It
> sounds utopian, but volunteers could fix this.

Consider the following vignette:

Common Purpose

A couple of years ago, a 'Common Purpose' group was formed in Cork with participants split across public, private and voluntary sectors. One of the members of the group raised the question of what could be done to improve education participation and lots of people (with a diversity of skills) were drawn to that topic. Betty O'Callaghan, a member of the group, picks up the thread:

> The overriding thing I recall is that all were willing to participate in a voluntary capacity in the education process to show, tell, read, mentor, run interventions, extracurricular activities and there was great excitement. Then the discussion turned to the nuts and bolts ... garda clearance, insurance, demarcation, aligning with the curriculum, the evidence base for interventions, pushing teachers to become facilitators, lack of structure, upsetting schedules. The result was deflation....

Of course, these people would need initial support and baseline training, but this could be a movement that builds on its own success. There are obvious child protection issues to be managed (for example, speeding up the Garda Vetting system and developing safe practices) but these hurdles should not blind us to the possibility of making a hugely positive intervention in children's lives. Existing volunteering could be extended across adult learning, for example, on numeracy and literacy. The potential resources that exist under this heading are enormous. Retired people, second and third level students and people who are unemployed represent an untapped social movement waiting for a noble cause.

While some individual charities use a volunteer model (in fundraising, staffing retail stores etc.), only a tiny fraction of the overall population are involved. Why is this the case? Firstly, there's often an inbuilt conservatism about using 'non-professionals', perhaps based on a fear that they wouldn't be up to the mark. Sometimes it's straightforward job protectionism from the professionals involved. And there are real fears around child protection which would have to be dealt with by strong protocols, that is,volunteer adults would not work alone with children. While these are real hurdles, consider the following: If we could activate 5 per cent of the Irish population, this would provide an army of 250,000 volunteers. Even if each volunteer could only provide two hours each week, this is the equivalent of an additional 12,500 'extra' people to focus on community development and education across disadvantaged areas. But it needs organisation to make it happen.

2.5 Progress Community Leadership Training

Having strong leaders in each community produces a ripple effect. At the time of writing, former TAP student Gary Gannon, a Dublin City Counsellor, was a candidate in the General Elections (North Inner City Ward). Another TAP student, Lynn Ruane, former President of the Trinity Students Union, was elected to the Senate. Communities need to produce strong leaders like Gary and Lynn. Historically, the religious orders filled this role. To some extent, this tradition continues with Sr. Stanislaus offering a voice on behalf of the homeless (Peter McVerry SJ and Brother Kevin play a similar role). Merchants Quay Dug Treatment has a religious underpinning and, in the AA, part of the 12-step programme is the ability to draw on a 'higher power'. For many years, religion provided a backdrop for social activism, for example, St Vincent De Paul Society is the largest voluntary social body operating in Ireland.

In Ireland today, while the formal religious culture has declined, we haven't developed a secular community culture to replace this. Let me make one point crystal clear. I'm no apologist for the terrible wrongs committed in religious-run institutions. However, many disadvantaged communities now face a leadership vacuum. Sometimes social entrepreneurs fill this gap. We also have to admire the tremendous work completed by sports organisations, for example, boxing, martial arts, dancing, soccer, GAA and so on. In a sense 'Strong Community' can become the new religion, that is, it offers the potential to provide a real sense of meaning in people's lives. To support this we need to provide both structured and informal leadership development opportunities to people from a young age – helping them to make a difference to the places where they live. While some existing programmes are already underway, this should become a systematic endeavour across the community sector.

2.6 Establish Lifelong Learning Centres

Each community should have a Lifelong Learning Centre that's open at night and at weekends. This might be the local school, given over to community development purposes or the local library, a place for community activists to meet. These centres should be run by local volunteers. A slightly black humour (but funny) joke underscores the lack of community facilities in many disadvantaged areas:

> A report on the news stated that a million euro was discovered in [named disadvantaged area] at 06:15 this morning, hidden behind the local library. A local spokesperson said that the community was shocked. They didn't know they had a library.

2.7 Tackle Literacy and Numeracy

The ability to read and write is critical to success at school, yet one in ten children in Ireland leaves primary school unable to write properly, a figure that rises to one in three in disadvantaged areas. Despite this obvious problem, Ireland has no national-level literacy policy.[19] We need to launch a national campaign and use the existing infrastructure (NALA or others) to address this issue. We need to make the issues of literacy and numeracy discussible for people who didn't get an opportunity to complete this baseline education first time around and for schoolchildren currently struggling. There's a huge opportunity to involve volunteers in this endeavor right across the country.

2.8 Community Development Recognition Ceremonies

The underpinning philosophy is clear; people shouldn't be abandoned. With suitable supports, most people can continue to grow and develop and become productive members of society. The pushback is that this may seem like a constant mantra of community organisations looking for additional funding support. The ring-wingers will argue, 'The problem with socialism, is that you soon run out of other people's money to give away.' But, as we've seen earlier, there are enormous economic savings to be made in moving people off welfare supports, reducing the need for regular serious health interventions and so on. This isn't 'do-gooder-ism'; it's enlightened self-interest.

> Inequality is not just bad for an unlucky few; it affects the whole of society by undermining economic growth and destroying social cohesion. We know that more equal societies are safer, happier and healthier places to live for everyone – even those at the top.[20]

To reinforce this point, there should be annual competitions within each community to highlight individuals who've really delivered within the local community. We need to recognise and reinforce *extra-ordinary* commitment.[21]

2.9 Establish Community Development Foundations

The goal here is that local communities should lead this pioneering effort by operating the programmes described above. To do this they have to be able to raise money both from the government, from the private sector and through fundraising efforts from their own sources. The creation of Community Foundations – with appropriate fund raising models and governance – would be an additional step towards reinstating agency in local communities.

Strand #3: Changing the School System

3.1 Standardise the Early Years Curriculum

The early years education system detailed earlier should operate a standard curriculum. The early years curriculum framework (Aistear), should be implemented in all early years settings. The staff should be trained to a minimum Level 5 Teaching qualification. We should set a timeframe for this to happen, for example, over the next five years, after which no one who doesn't hold this level of qualification should be allowed to work as an early years teacher.

3.2 Abandon Compulsory Irish[22]

Irish is a compulsory subject requirement at all school levels. It begins to be taught from the moment that a child enters school and is compulsory until the age of 16. Teaching of Irish takes up a huge chunk of time during primary and secondary school. Abandoning compulsory Irish is not a new idea. It was a rallying cry in the 1961 general elections over 50 years ago and is a low-key argument that resurfaces from time to time. The arguments in favour of the existing arrangements are (a) it's part of our national heritage, (b) the language makes Ireland distinctive/unique, and (c) the beauty of the spoken/written language. The core argument against compulsory Irish is that this is a failed experiment. Very few people use the language on a day-to-day basis. In relation to educational disadvantage, children can't identify with a language that's not spoken at home or in the street. Because it's compulsory (and children cannot see the benefits) it plays a particularly strong part in the disconnection between children and schooling.

Currently, students cannot gain entry into teaching colleges unless they pass Irish in the Leaving Certificate, effectively ruling out people who may be brilliant teachers but can't overcome this particular hurdle. We need the teachers standing at the top of the class to be a diverse group, representing all parts of society. Of course, those who wish to do so can have their children educated in a Gaelscoil, send them to the Gaeltacht or speak Irish at home. I believe that Irish, taught on an elective basis, would become more of a *living* language. The notion of compulsory Irish is intertwined with our history as an oppressed country and the efforts to establish a separate identity from the United Kingdom. The efforts made to date are certainly understandable when framed against this historical backdrop, but it's time to move on. In the USA over 300 million people don't have their own language but still communicate a strong national identity. Likewise, I doubt that the Swiss feel any less Swiss because they speak German, French or Italian.[23]

3.3 Rebalance the Teaching of Religion

There should be a radical reduction in the number of hours devoted to the teaching of religion. Too much of an already short year is spent working on religion, arguably a subject that should not even be taught in schools if we believe in the separation of church and state. A suggestion made by some respondents was to completely abandon the teaching of religion and to use this extra time to teach baseline subjects (reading, maths, computing and so on). My sense is that religion should be maintained as a subject area for two reasons. Firstly, the teaching of ethics, philosophy, logic and diversity has a place in everyone's life. For example, in the Educate Together schools (75 schools, or almost 2 per cent of the total number) religious instruction has four strands: Moral and Spiritual; Equality and Justice; Belief Systems; Ethics and Environment. None of these are faith formation to a particular religion. Secondly, in relation to education disadvantage, the subject of religion is not resented in the same way that compulsory Irish is. Brian Mooney, Editor of 'Education Matters' and *Irish Times* Education Columnist argues:

> In a world where religious intolerance and hatred between sects within the Islamic faith reaping havoc throughout the middle-east, it has never been more important to ensure that our children understand the phenomenon of religion within human society and its expression in various belief systems and codes of morality.[24]

There is a place for moral education in school and the teaching of comparative religions to promote diversity and understanding. But if a parent wants to instruct a child in a *particular* religion, this should be done at home. Faith formation could either be taught in separate Catholic schools (private schools which do not receive any state subvention) or at Sunday Schools set up by parents. The teaching of a single religious theology has no place in a secular society. In London, the School of Life offers a secular alternative to church-led schools. This offers a possible way forward as each new school comes on stream. But why would we wait for this issue to be resolved by stealth, which might take about 200 years? We need to show a bit more impatience and tackle this issue now.

3.4 Make Transition Year Compulsory

Transition Year is undervalued.[25] In some schools it's not currently offered at all; in others, students can decide to skip this completely. It's seen by some parents as a doss year with the fear that students will 'take their foot off the gas' of studying, reinforcing the view of our education system as a method solely designed to produce high points. Dr Kevin O'Higgins argues that we should value education for its own sake, as an absolute necessity for a healthy society and not just a means to an end, that is, to secure employment. Transition Year allows an opportunity to teach leadership, team working and entrepreneurship with very little additional investment. It should follow a standard curriculum and be mandatory across the secondary school system.

3.5 Re-Imagine the Leaving Certificate

The focus in the Leaving Certificate should be to teach children to 'ask the right questions' not 'give the right answers' to a list of pre-formed questions. We need an entirely new Leaving Certificate which includes project work, more social justice and less rote learning. We also need more art. Dr. Paul Downes argues that art has a huge role to play in education as it offers creativity, individual expression and innovation. While this applies to all students, it has a particular impact on students from disadvantaged areas:

> Aesthetic objectives, not merely social ones, are obviously important. That said, art is especially useful in transcending conventional social barriers. Moreover, social capital is often a valuable by-product of cultural activities whose main purpose is purely artistic.[26]

One DEIS school, Colaiste Eoin in Finglas, had a problem with bullying (it's probably more accurate to state that all schools have a problem with bullying, but some decide to tackle it). With the help of the Principal, Paula O'Brien, and the teaching staff (but, largely, under their own steam) students made a 'Rap' video with the message that bullying 'isn't cool' and how students can unite against it. In similar vein, when I worked in NCI we set up a 'Graffiti Wall' where artists helped local children to understand that particular medium. The level of energy generated in both of these projects was incredible. There are probably a million similar examples across the country. I'm not naïve enough to think that school can be *fun* all of the time. But, neither does it have to be boring all of the time. A specialist educational team would complete the re-design of the Leaving Certificate. I don't have the expertise to make specific recommendations about its final shape, but there are plenty of people who have that competence. We're not lacking expertise; we are lacking the guts to admit that the current system is broken and the will to fix it. This is a centrally important recommendation that would affect all (not just disadvantaged) children. The rationale has been touched on earlier, but, given the importance of this particular issue, it's worthwhile to reinforce the key points.

Understanding Intelligence

Some people have a leaning towards logic/mathematics. Others excel in the verbal/linguistic space. But what if your intelligence lies elsewhere? The exam system has not kept pace with our evolving understanding of intelligence. How do you measure caring or social conscience? Within my own family, one nephew struggled at school with dyslexia. It was an impediment to learning from the outset and school was tough going. My sister (his grandmother), predicted: 'He's a great kid. It'll be a happy day when he finally leaves school and goes to work.' And so it came to pass. He's now a successful locksmith, loves his job, works hard and earns good money. Was he a failure in the education system or did the education system fail him? As soon as he left school he thrived. The academic bias in the current system doesn't suit all types of intel-

213

ligence. I'm not sure how many of the U2 band went to university but their songwriting and performance is genius.

The Limitations of IQ

Professor Áine Hyland suggested that in the Aran Islands 100 years ago being able to cope with the weather, being self-sufficient, having the wisdom to understand when the sea offered safe conditions and so on were the signs of intelligence. Different cultures have always valued different things. Intellectual learning was something that the upper classes were interested in – easy to understand when servants took care of all the day-to-day needs. Intelligence Quotient tests were originally designed[27] to identify students who'd find it difficult to cope in university where large classes of up to 100 students studied together. The concept of IQ therefore started out with good intent, designed to measure the intelligence of middle class white males. But more than 100 years later we find that the central design feature of our entire education system is based on this incredibly narrow idea of measuring one particular type of intelligence. It's way past time for change.

Hiring Skills

Many years ago I devised a simple three-question formula for making hiring decisions. We would try to ascertain (1) CAN this person do the job, do they have the requisite skills and abilities required to complete the role? (2) WILL this person do the job, what's their motivation, does this job 'make sense' from a career perspective? (3) will they FIT in, how will they integrate socially? A reliance on an IQ measurement would only address the first question and perhaps only part of that. Making a judgment on IQ alone is like assessing the roadworthiness of a car by checking the tyre pressure. Yes, it's an important measure, but it's narrow and limited.

College Transitions

The transition from secondary to higher education puts a particular strain on students to adjust to a more independent method of learning. The rote/dependency learning approach fostered in schools is problematic for many students who go on to third level (not just disadvantaged students). Many experience 'academic culture shock' as they move from a regurgitation to an experimental learning system. It's a big shift and it happens at a difficult life stage, causing too many students to drop out. Diarmaid Ferriter, an academic in UCD, observed:[28] 'The transition from second to third-level education is far from painless. For some it can be exceptionally difficult...' Some students experience the freedom of college as a 'freedom to do nothing', staying in bed (parents often don't understand or can't police their lecture schedule), playing pool all day in the students' union or skipping lectures and drinking. A potential solution here might be to change the first year in college to make it more like the final year in secondary school. But this just takes an existing broken system and extends it outwards for another year. A better solution is to re-imagine the role that the Leaving Certificate plays in the education and formation of our children, and change the way we teach students from the moment they enter the secondary school cycle.[29]

Changing WHAT We Teach

W.B. Yeats said: 'Education is not the filling of a pail but the lighting of a fire.' The role of educationalists is to empower children and allow them to explore. It sometimes seems like pedagogy is a word that's learned in teaching college and then abandoned as soon as teachers get inside the school gates. The Socratic method of teaching is over 2,000 years old, but can still be usefully employed to embed learning. And, a Chinese saying captures the truism that leaning is embedded by doing: 'I hear and forget; I see and remember; I do and understand'. Side by side with overhauling the methodology ('how' we teach) we also need to change the 'what'. Earlier this year a segment ran on the Ryan Tubridy Show on RTÉ radio on Pythagoras' Theorem. Do you remember it? The square of the of the hypotenuse (the side opposite the right angle) is equal to the sum of the squares of the other two sides. The question was as follows: Who (that is, people in what occupation) ever uses this? When the listeners rang in, one caller suggested that painters could potentially use it to decide the angle of a ladder and therefore the length of the ladder needed. Most of the painters I know seem to have managed okay without this incredible insight! In fact, zero practical examples were offered. But, hey, let's keep teaching it anyway because it's part of the curriculum (as if the curriculum was some form of untouchable education bible). At the time of writing, there is an emerging discussion around making PE an official subject in the Leaving Certificate, allowing children with physical intelligence to shine and offering a potential solution to the growing problem of obesity. If this comes to pass, it's a perfect example of a positive systems change. In a similar vein, we need to overhaul the rest of the curriculum.

3.6 Empowering Teachers: A Revolution in Purpose

In addition to the fundamental overhaul of the curriculum and teaching methodology, we need a revolution in teacher engagement. In terms of formation training, there's a requirement for modules on inclusion and diversity, helping teachers to recognise different types of intelligence and developing pedagogy to suit the needs of particular learners, using problem-based learning, incorporating technology and so on. But, beyond *method*, teachers need to become infused with an underpinning philosophy around children's potential. Áine Hyland describes this as follows:

> We need to convince teachers that the central question is: 'In what way is this child intelligent?' To unlock potential, the starting assumption is that each child has a unique intelligence.

This underpinning belief is more important than methodology or resources. For example, where a child goes to a 'special resource' teacher, does that inadvertently remove the ownership from the main teacher? Children being withdrawn to work with special teachers can erode classroom time, making it difficult to work with the entire class for a good period of uninterrupted time. While the big debate with teachers is normally about resources (class sizes and so on), we need to move the dial and begin to speak about purpose. The teachers unions can provide leadership on this topic:

> No just society will allow its weakest members to be ignored or its state systems such as education to disregard or pay insufficient attention to the fact that many children start school with major disadvantages. 'Society' implies a sharing based on need, a real sense of inclusion.[30]

While it's difficult to argue with the sentiment expressed, the actions of the INTO (and all the teachers unions) have to match the rhetoric.

3.7 Improving Teaching through Continuous Professional Development

Similar to all professions, teachers need to be involved in structured continuous profession development. Over the years, I've been fortunate to meet many inspirational teachers, people committed to students who *go the extra mile*, for example, buying art supplies from their own salary for the children to use. Áine Hyland related a story about a school where the former President Mary McAleese was visiting. One of the teachers was beautifully 'turned out' in a new suit and Áine complemented her. The reply: 'I couldn't let my kids down on their big day.' The class had become *her* children. The encouragement and development of all teachers is centrally important. In additional to their baseline formation training, a system of structured continuous profession development needs to be established. A National Framework for the CPD of the teaching profession should be developed by the Teacher Training Colleges with agreement from the teachers unions on how this will work in practice. As part of this, a new programme, 'Coaching for Teachers', should be offered to those working in disadvantaged schools, a recognition of the additional difficulties of this role. In the private sector, executive coaching has become a growth industry for a variety of reasons and has proven it's worth.[31] Up to two personal coaching sessions per year should be offered to teachers working in disadvantaged schools – a system delivered by external coaches who are not aligned with the Department of Education.

3.8 Improve Teacher Retention

Working in DEIS schools can be tough. In putting this book together I met several teachers who are actively committed to working in this space. But not everyone has this calling. Specific efforts need to be made to retain talented teachers in DEIS schools. There are a couple of possibilities under this heading: (a) free third level post-graduate education offered to DEIS teachers (in areas relevant to their role) to encourage longevity in the role, and (b) introduce rotational roles for teachers in DEIS Schools. Earlier we looked at the various support roles in place to deal with children in disadvantaged areas. A common solution within industry to the issue of potential burnout is to rotate people between roles. Rotating teachers through a variety of roles (on a voluntary basis) would help to ease the burnout potential of working in DEIS schools and promote length of service.

3.9 Modify the Teaching Gene Pool

In Ireland, because of the very high 'entry barriers' we attract very talented people into teaching but we select them from a narrow pool. The Good News is that we have high quality teachers; the Bad News is that teachers typically come from the same demographic. You can't become a primary school teacher unless you secure 500 million points in the Leaving Certificate (a tiny exaggeration to make the point). So we end up with a group of teachers who are brilliant academically, but drawn from a narrow stream. The irony here is that, for many years, teachers' groups resisted access initiatives and didn't support students from disadvantaged backgrounds 'gaining entry' into the profession on a reduced points basis. Yes, pull up that drawbridge and lock it tight! We need to specifically change the entry requirements for teachers by developing a special entry route into teaching for students from disadvantaged areas (because of the critical importance of teachers in tackling educational disadvantage – my sense is that this needs to be something 'over and above' the existing HEAR mechanism).

3.10 Establish a National Teaching Competition

Every year we look at the Rose of Tralee festival to see who's written the best poem about their Irish roots or can play the tin whistle. The style and glitz that accompanies these nights seems like a bit of harmless fun. But let's get serious for a moment. We need to laud people who provide a *real service* to the country. While the ability to complete an Irish dance routine is neat, the ability to teach the next generation is powerful. We should establish a national teaching awards competition – to select the 'best of the best' – extraordinary examples of teaching excellence that teachers can aspire to. The competition should be run by the Department of Education, as a means of offering a public 'thank you' to those members of the profession who set the bar high. The competition should be televised to bring 'great teaching practices' to as wide an audience as possible.[32]

3.11 Fire Underperforming Teachers

I've also met some teachers who seem to be completely demotivated (it might be sheer coincidence that these were predominantly male). We've probably all met teachers who've burned out. People who feel *stuck* in a job. While we should do everything possible to encourage and support great teachers, side by side with this we need to systematically identify and, where needed, remove the deadwood from the profession. The *today* needs of teachers doesn't trump the *future* performance of students. The emerging Fitness to Practice procedures must have teeth and be made to work. For too long the teaching unions have supported underperforming colleagues, elevating their needs above the educational requirements of hundreds of children in their care over a lifetime of teaching.

3.12 Involve Parents Directly in Classroom Teaching

Under a programme called 'Teach For America' in the USA, children from disadvantaged areas get additional tuition for free. The programme is over-subscribed with volunteers. We need to establish an equivalent ('Teach For Ireland') where students in disadvantaged areas are given additional tuition with a specific emphasis on literacy and numeracy. The primary target for volunteers are parents of children attending the school, supplemented with volunteers. The classroom is a 'sacred space' in the sense that it's the place where young minds are growing and developing. But it should not be a *protected space* where the only person who can deliver education is the formal teacher. The education of future generations is a collective societal responsibility, not the sole responsibility of a single cadre of professionals.[33]

3.13 Ensure All Schools are Inclusive

We need to overhaul the admissions procedures to ensure diversity across all schools. For many years, students who presented with a disability were excluded from the education system. Thankfully, that's changed and as shown earlier large numbers of people now successfully overcome disabilities and fulfil their educational promise. Lindquist captured the underpinning philosophy:[34]

> The challenge now is to formulate requirements of a 'school for all'. All children and young people of the world ... have the right to education. It is not our education systems that have a right to certain types of children. It is the school system of a country that must be adjusted to meet the needs of all children.

To make inclusiveness a reality, the admissions policies of all schools have to be transparent and no school should be allowed to select students based on academic ability alone. There are significant current disparities between schools in terms of the proportions of vulnerable and at risk students and this is unacceptable when pursued as a deliberate policy of exclusivity:

> Above and beyond an individual's own social background, the social mix of the school is a strong influence on exam success within second level education

and on the likelihood of progressing to post-school education and training.[35]

The Minister for Education should make inclusive enrolment policy a legal obligation on all schools.

3.14 Ensure that DEIS Schools are Properly Led: Multi-School Principals

In a key report on educational disadvantage submitted to the Department of Education,[36] a central recommendation was to establish the post of Deputy Principal as a full-time administrative position in disadvantaged schools which employ more than 20 teachers, and to appoint a full-time Administrative Principal to the most highly disadvantaged primary schools with four or more teachers. It's hard to argue with the sentiment that these schools need the proper resources to manage what can be a difficult remit. But I'd like to add a rider. Leadership is a commodity in large demand but in short supply. Across the educational sector (at all levels), we see a range of small institutions, all with a requirement to be 'powerfully led'. Rather than adding additional roles/posts to *each* school, we should experiment with a new structural configuration where leadership is consolidated across a number of schools. In practice, this would mean that the crème de la crème principals would look after more than one school (this point applies to primary level, secondary level and further education colleges).

3.15 Retention of Traveller Children

The initial goal is that 100 per cent of all Traveller children transfer from primary to secondary schools. To support this we need a better way to manage the transition from primary to secondary. Thereafter, we have to ensure that all Traveller children complete the Junior Certificate. There are two possibilities here to support this transition: (a) use other students and set up a 'buddy system' in the first year of secondary school, or (b) some teachers should 'cross the divide' (from primary to secondary school) for the first year. The current boundary between primary and secondary school is artificial and not designed to meet the needs of these students.[37]

3.16 Development of Afterschool/Homework Clubs

Children living in emergency housing or overcrowded settings often have no physical space to complete homework. All DEIS schools need to provide Afterschool/Homework Clubs, a secure space where children can complete their homework before they leave school each day and where the learning can continue in a high quality environment.

3.17 Put Adequate Resources in Place to Deal with Troubled Children

Let's start with the easy bits. Firstly, we know that a small percentage of children coming to school will be troubled due to a variety of causes. Secondly, we know that without adequate resources these children can have a disproportionate negative impact on a school. The Business Case for intervening in this area is stark. According to Fergus Finlay, CEO of Barnardos, the cost of failure when a child comes to the attention of social services can be as high as €200,000 per annum. In the small number of cases where that same child needs secure care, that cost rises to €500,000 per annum.[38] Preventative family support, which can change this paradigm, costs circa €3,000 per annum. So Ireland Inc. is faced with a choice. We can proactively make this investment up front or spend the money in remediation when the train has already derailed. Of course, not all families are saveable. A small percentage will choose the path of criminality or will have major physical/mental health problems and their children may be lost to the education system (I've already made the point that 100 per cent 'market share' isn't available). Recognizing that, we have to design the system so that the overwhelming majority of children can safely navigate their educational journey. There are a couple of sub-recommendations under this heading.

3.17.1 *Additional Psychological Support Services in DEIS Schools*[39]

One report suggested:

Expansion of the National Educational Psychological Service (NEPS) and the establishment of a panel of clinical psychologists are urgently required to support the growing number of children exhibiting emotional and behavioural problems.[40]

Having an educational/developmental psychologist assigned to specific DEIS schools, someone who could develop a relationship with the children and help steer them through turbulent personal journeys would be a huge asset. This system would be more beneficial than having an 'external psychologist' who has no ongoing contact with the child and where they meet for a single session – to essentially 'write a report' on their behaviour. Marie O'Neill spoke about the time it can take to get a psychologists report completed.

We had a child with severe learning difficulties start school in September. We needed a report to see what teaching approaches or learning aids could be employed to help her. Fifteen months later it was sitting on my desk. In the meantime, we did the best we could.

3.17.2 Set Up Behaviour Support Classrooms

Schools should develop their capacity in approaches aimed at coping with challenging behaviour, including anger management, conflict resolution, cognitive behaviour therapy and restorative practices. Schools that cater for students who regularly challenge acceptable levels of discipline should have a Behaviour Support Classroom. Students with serious and persistent disruptive behaviour can be placed here, allowing them an opportunity to modify behaviour in line with socially acceptable norms while teaching and learning continue in the regular classroom.[41]

3.17.3 Appoint Additional Speech and Language Therapists for DEIS Schools

In 2014, over 3,000 children were waiting more than 12 months for speech and language therapy, with a further 1,940 waiting for more than a year to complete an initial assessment.[42] A lost year is a large chunk of a child's life, ground that can't always be recovered. I'm not close enough to these services to make a specific recommendation regarding the level of speech therapy required in DEIS schools (others can determine the optimum numbers).

3.17.4 Formalise the Terms and Conditions of Home School Liaison Officers

This area needs to be regularised in two ways. Firstly by ensuring proper training: Here's one teacher's experience:

> When I worked as a Home-School Liasion officer, we didn't receive any extra training. All of a sudden I was plunged into an alien world of addiction and mental health problems. It was scary because we simply didn't know what to do.

Secondly, by putting a formal pension arrangement in place with the Department of Health for people who complete this role. This is a key element of the 'infrastructure' to tackle educational underperformance, and can't continue to be managed on an ad hoc basis as it is at the moment.

3.17.5 Assign Mentors

We should partner selected children with an external mentor. Many former alcoholics speak about the power of mentors and the non-conditional support they receive. While there are probation officers and juvenile liaison staff, it's hard for kids not to see these as being 'on the side of the system.' As an experiment (Pilot Project) we should assign mentors (with clear roles and groundrules) to work with troubled children, adding an extra layer of support into the lives of children who are struggling to cope in the education system.

3.18 Re-Skill Career Guidance Teachers in DEIS Schools

There are two elements to this recommendation. Firstly, we need to support career guidance teachers to complete their role in an expert fashion. By implication, if career guidance teachers have been in the teaching profession all of their working life, it can be difficult to offer fact-based career advice to students (for example, many of the available jobs in the technology sector didn't even exist 15 years ago). There's enormous potential here for external volunteers to work with children who are expressing specific career interests to provide insights into particular professions. Secondly, selected career guidance teachers working in DEIS schools should up-skill as counsellors, with the proviso that they are properly trained, that is, this is not 'amateur night' covered by a weekend-long course in psychotherapy. While not everyone will wish to return to education to complete another full degree programme, it should be possible to develop a 'conversion programme' within a shorter timeframe. This is an overt recognition that the issues faced by career guidance teachers in DEIS schools often fall well outside the 'career guidance' space. If that's their daily reality (which it is) we have to equip teachers to deal with these much broader requirements.

3.19 Provision of Hot Food in DEIS Schools

Every DEIS school should be able to provide hot and healthy food to schoolchildren, with a target of breaking even on the food with equipment and labour costs supplied by the government – the cost of this being partly offset with savings in other areas.[43] Fergus Finlay argues: 'There's no good reason why, in 2016, any child should be hungry going to school.' A sub-possibility here is that volunteers in the community could provide this labour.

3.20 Identify the Specific Requirements for Children with Disabilities

There's huge scope to improve the education system for children with disabilities, for example, people on the autism spectrum who can make a real contribution. Robert Ward made the point that there's good evidence to indicate that there are certain roles where people who have this condition have advantages over 'neurotypicals'. The software company SAP (and several others) have hiring policies which target people with autism for specific roles where their attention to detail can be a huge asset. The suggestion here is that every mainstream school should have a specialist Autism Spectrum Disorder (ASD) unit, staffed with teachers and SNAs specifically trained in this area. At the moment even schools that have an ASD unit staff it with a regular primary school teacher without the requisite specialist skills. In line with the mantra of 'nobody left behind', many more children with disabilities can make a contribution if they are given the right support early on.

3.21 Map the Education System Electronically

The education system is complex and people find it hard to navigate. The starting point is to understand how the system works. Producing a physical 'map' of the educational system would go a long way towards meeting this need – and I've made an initial effort to construct this (see following page).[44] A final version of this map would be electronic, that is, it would contain 'drop down' menus of information about how each 'station' on the map works. The final version of this map would be made available in all schools and places of education (for example, community centres) and staff would receive appropriate training in its use.

3.22 A Single Website to Make Course Information Easily Available

In 2009, the website, http://www.bluebrick.ie, was launched by the Institutes of Technology to assist those looking for more information about part-time study options in higher education. The following year (2010), the HEA Mid-Term Review reported that almost 40,000 people had accessed the site. The situation is becoming ever more complex. The number of part-time, short duration, distance and e-learning programmes has more than quadrupled in the Institutes of Technology since 2008. Of course, this is only a partial solution in the sense that it doesn't provide a full picture of all the available programmes on offer countrywide across the third level Sector. The goal here is simple. To produce a single, easy to navigate website which contains all college courses.

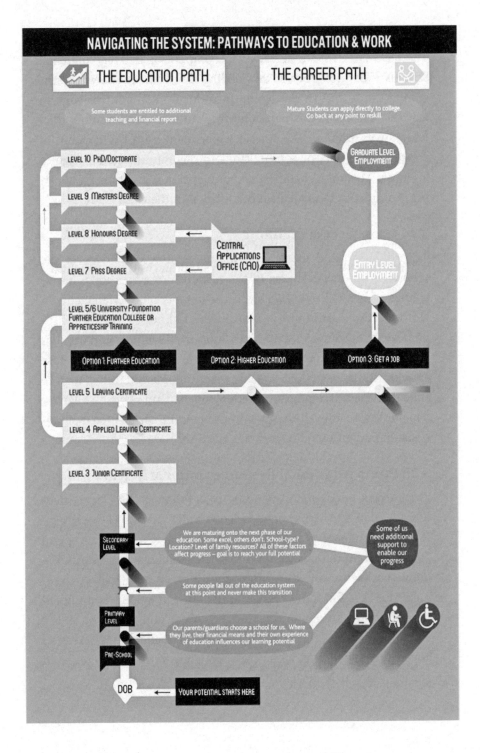

3.23 Introduce Competitions Between Schools

There is a large role to be played by competition between matched schools. The introduction of Spelling Bees, talent shows, Maths competitions and so on, would introduce a competitive edge to learning and make the high-achieving students heroes rather than targets for bullying. We should experiment with the concept of regional inter-school competitions to give an additional edge to learning. Most of us believe that competition is great on the sporting ground, but many balk about using it in the classroom. Why?

3.24 Cross School Planning

Co-ordination and integration of the existing initiatives in the schools is an essential part of the response to educational disadvantage. This will only happen if the key people – Management, Home School Community Coordinator, School Completion Programme Coordinator, Learning Support Teachers and regular Teachers – have time to meet and plan interventions. I'm not close enough to this to make a specific recommendation, other than to state that the existing 'co-ordination' mechanism needs to be overhauled. We do this all the time in the commercial sector in situations that are often quite complex to coordinate.

3.25 Pump Additional Resources into Early Years

The current educational spending is as follows: The Department of Education and Skills spend twice as much on third level education (per student) as they do on primary education. They spend 70 per cent more on third level than on secondary education. We know that 'better off' students go to college and that's likely to remain the case for some years. So, the current system is designed to support the students who stay the course and these are, in the main, middle class.[45] As a policy, we need a realignment of overall government spending, with proportionately more money targeted at early years, primary and secondary education.

3.26 Multi-Year Planning

Central government funding for DEIS schools should be increased and safeguarded to reflect the actual funding requirements in these schools. It should not be subject to populist political trends or competing local electoral interests during annual budgeting. We need a central, ring-fenced funding stream, which is easy to access and which is managed by the Department of Education and Skills.

3.27 Stop Subsidising Fee Paying Second Level Schools

It's difficult not to come to the conclusion that fee-paying schools are 'a gathering of the advantaged.' Herding wealthy children into a small number of schools, essentially removes this cohort from public schools, with the consequent loss of a positive trickle down impact of high aspirations. As teachers are paid directly by the State, private schools don't pay the fully loaded costs of running their institutions. Professor Pat Clancy makes the point that private schools forego the capital grant from the DES but charge tuition fees to parents, which greatly exceeds this amount. The net effect is that they have more money and can offer superior facilities. In effect, parents get private education at a bargain basement price. And this privilege shows in the results: 'Despite accounting for just 7 per cent of secondary schools in the country, fee paying schools account for more than two thirds of the top ranked boys schools and half of the top ranked girls schools in Ireland.'[46] It's a clear demonstration that the investment of sufficient resources (coupled with high aspirations) produces solid results. Unless, of course, you are still clinging to the idea that all the smart kids in Ireland live in Blackrock! Within our education system we want to give both parents and students choice. Freedom of choice is an important political freedom, perhaps every bit as important as equality. But, it's difficult to see these schools as offering choice. This is the continuation of a system of educational discrimination in which the state colludes.[47] Stokes argues that 'the Irish school system reflects, reproduces and indeed reinforces the inequalities inherent in Irish society.'[48]

Economic Arguments

There are several economic arguments at play here. According to Dr. Bill Toner, the State doesn't pay all teachers in fee-paying schools, but operates on a ratio of 1:23 (one teacher to 23 students) versus a ratio of 1:19 in the non fee-paying sector. For example, in one fee-paying Jesuit College, there are 70 teachers of which only 46 are paid for by the State. Further, there are substantial costs involved in the maintenance of school buildings and it's rare for the State to give any money towards this in fee-paying schools.[49] Bill Toner estimated that stopping payments to fee-paying schools (if the schools subsequently had to be taken over by the State), would cost the exchequer about €150 million a year in lost parent and donor contributions. If the schools didn't close they might become even more elitist. For example, in Great Britain fees of upwards of £30,000 per year are paid for a small minority of children. He also pushed back against the 'couple of scholarship students' in fee-paying schools argument.

Belvedere College has 88 such students in 2016, close to 10 per cent of their cohort. While the closure of fee-paying schools might bring about a level playing field, he argues that it would be 'a leveling down' and questioned if the Irish taxpayer will ever fork out enough tax to pay for really good schools. Interestingly, Dr. Toner is on record for publicly stating that he wasn't convinced that the Jesuits (or other religious orders) should be running fee-paying schools – as a priority apostolate – but he staunchly defended the right of parents to spend their money on their children's education as they see fit. However, my central argument against fee-paying schools is the negative impact on *equality* rather than *economics* per se. I accept the point that if middle class parents didn't send their children to fee-paying schools and a range of new primary and secondary schools had to be built, the financial impact for the state would be negative. For the record, I've huge personal respect for Bill Toner stretching over many years. I was a student in NCI when he was a brilliant lecturer there and when he subsequently led the college with distinction. But on this specific point, we will have to agree to differ. Philosophically, I can't see how we can underfund educational disadvantage while, at the same time, prop up a system of private schools. In this instance, already advantaged children get access to additional resources and the state is effectively reinforcing inequality. While this is not the most pressing of the recommendations made, it's an important philosophical point and it should be a medium-term goal to phase this out. [50]

STRAND #4: WORKING WITH INDIVIDUALS

We have shown earlier that a person's baseline confidence and their *perception* of the difficulty of third level, can become barriers to success. This strand of recommendations looks at some tactics to overcome these self-limiting beliefs. The core intent here is to market college attendance to students in disadvantaged areas. Conceptualising this as a marketing problem allows us to deploy a range of tools to 'sell the benefits of college' to students, some of whom will be reluctant buyers. We saw a simple example of this earlier ('The Million Euro Decision'). The general point is that the benefits of going to college need to be made memorable and easily understandable.

4.1 Develop a 'Go to College' Marketing Plan[51]

We need to develop a professional marketing plan to help sell the concept of further and higher education. This will include all normal marketing media, for example, social media, website and other promotional materials to be used across radio, print and TV. According to Robert Ward, a centrally important point is to get to this target market early, that is, at the start of the secondary cycle (by fifth and sixth year we are already talking to the converted, persuading them to go to college A over college B). This marketing plan would have a number of separate components, perhaps something along the following lines.

DVD Production

Produce two DVDs illustrating and reinforcing the rationale for going to college, one for primary schools and one for secondary schools to be shown to all schoolchildren on an annual basis. A 'Facilitators Guide' will accompany the DVDs with suggestions on how they should be introduced and the subsequent discussions facilitated.

National Spokesperson

Appoint a National Spokesperson(s) on Access, a well-known media or sports personality who will lead on this topic for the next three years. National county GAA players or sport stars like Conor McGregor or Katie Taylor would have huge clout.

Media Awareness

Full-blown media programme (print and radio) to ensure that this topic is regularly rehearsed and systematically targets the five key educational disadvantaged audiences.

Professional Website

A powerful website with separate sections for each targeted group and other key stakeholders (for example, career guidance teachers).

Books on Access

Develop new books to be used in schools. Include key stories: 'How college changed my life.' Both positive stories and regrets from a range of high profile individuals.

Reality TV about College Life

Choose a student in each of the five categories to illustrate the reality of going to college. Follow them through a full academic year. A 'day in the life' of a student.

Art Competition

Multimedia art competition around what it means to go to college. Adjudicated by age category.

In Community

Design and roll out training on Access (train the trainers) giving community leaders support materials, for example, powerful graphics to help local people understand and make the choice of going to college.

Develop a Simple Mnemonic, for example, ACE it!

Appetite: Do you have an appetite to do something great? Going to college will allow you to maximise your talent to become the very best that you can be. **Confidence**: It's more than money. Going to college will improve your personal confidence, in social and work settings. Now, that's 'priceless'. **Earnings**: Education is the single best predictor of earnings. Whether you decide to become a barman or a barrister, going to college will allow you secure an interesting job. At some future point you can become fully independent from the 'Mother Ship'. What's not to like about that!

Develop Common Questions and Answers

Anticipate the most commonly asked questions and develop a standard set of answers...

- **Argument**: If you go to college, you can't get a job. My friend's brother did a degree in Engineering and he's unemployed. What's the point?

- **Answer**: The rate of graduate unemployment is currently 2 per cent versus 9 per cent in the general community. You are four times more likely to be out of work as a non-graduate than as a graduate.

- **Argument**: I know someone who did a degree in Arts, focusing on French Literature. Where would you use that stuff?

- **Answer**: Going to college equips you with a depth of understanding of particular subjects. But more importantly, it teaches you to research topics and communicate your analysis to others. Learning how to capture and synthesize information are key skills which you will use over and over again in the jobs market.

- **Argument**: It's 'who you know', not what you know. If you don't have connections you won't be able to get a job. Simple as!

- **Answer**: Going to college offers three advantages. Firstly, you have a great interview story to tell an employer. Secondly, you maximise your skills and self-confidence. Thirdly, you start to build your own network of contacts, making you better connected. Family connections are definitely a bonus. But it's not the only game in town.

Reaching Young People Through Sports Clubs

Work with key sporting organisations, for example, GAA or FAI, and target young people where they congregate with the 'go to college' message. The very origins of the GAA lie within the educational sphere (Michael Cusack, the founder of the GAA, was a schoolteacher). The ideals of the GAA encourage a level playing field for all, regardless of postcode or social standing and the GAA is the lifeblood of many communities. This special relationship offers a powerful way of engaging with some of the most isolated young people in society. *Message:* Off the pitch young people face enormous challenges from poverty, social disadvantage and lack of access to educational opportunity. Video and other materials would be developed and played to groups of young people after training (or at other times deemed suitable by the club). The materials would feature GAA stars and other personalities. Young people are used to viewing slick presentations, so production values would need to be TV quality. Potential positioning: 'Education Gets You in the Game.' We would profile people who have careers in sport. For example, Barry Cahill (Dublin) combined playing with founding a successful sportswear business. People need to pursue education to reach their goal. *Message:* There are lots of careers in sport, provided you have an education.

4.2 Annual National College Awareness Week[52]

Part of this week would entail bringing DEIS students (from first year in secondary school onwards) to physically visit one or more college campuses. It would also involve getting these students to think about future jobs and map this out using a variety of interesting media (for example, art or music). Where possible, role models from the local community would also be invited to speak to the students and to tell their story, encouraging others to take that path.

4.3 Teachers Describe 'My Personal Journey'

Teachers have a disproportional impact on students. Relating their personal story would give students in disadvantaged areas a link with someone they know who'd been to college. It would also be someone who knows them and who believes they have the potential to travel the same path. This is a 'low cost' reinforcement mechanism designed to communicate (a) you are smart, and (b) you should consider post-secondary education.

The Importance of Belief: Conversations Change Lives

Ellen Roach, an Executive Recruitment Specialist, runs the Search Practice which is part of PwC's advisory services. Like myself, Ellen is from Cabra. As a teenager, she was heavily involved in the Mater Dei Youth Club where she met Fr. Ivan Tonge. Those of us who grew up in that era mostly remember Ivan's mop of fuzzy hair. He certainly didn't fit the stereotype (at that time) of an austere priest. One day Ellen, Ivan and others were working on a community project and he said: 'You'd be good at that Ellen. That's something you should study at college.' Prior to that moment, she hadn't even thought about going to college. While Ellen is not given to exaggeration, she believes that single conversation (with the underpinning belief 'you will be going to college') changed her life. Contrast that with some alternative conversations that happen within schools. One respondent suggested that it's all too easy for teachers to get into a sort of 'groupthink' about particular children. They say: 'We know where he will end up' and it becomes a self-fulfilling prophecy. Of course they don't say this it public; but staffroom conversations are full of it. Tom Crean takes up this point: 'No 7-year-old has already decided to become a criminal.' Perhaps if a teacher doesn't fundamentally believe in the idea that there's hope for every single child, then they are working in the wrong profession.

STRAND #5: EMBED ACCESS ACROSS THE THIRD LEVEL SECTOR

Two introductory points are worth making: Firstly, for some people the recommendations in this section will have a *corporatist overtone*, that is, a movement away from the idea of a university as a 'Republic of Scholars' towards an organisation that satisfies the needs of various stakeholders and is beholden to the evaluative power of the state.[53] In this particular case, I feel that the general benefit to society, that is, a radical improvement in getting more disadvantaged students into college is a worthwhile outcome – the gain is worth the loss of *some* local autonomy. Secondly, access should not be tokenism, diving into a working class area, picking up a handful of bright students and making them a success. Access is about designing a system that allows people from every townland and village, from every county council estate and corporation flat, from every walk of society the chance to explore and exploit their potential.

5.1 Recognition of Prior Learning

The development of a national plan for the recognition of prior learning (RPL) has been discussed since 'God was a boy'. Under this heading, individual skills would be recognised and transferrable, that is, it would allow exemptions from topics already studied or where people can demonstrate the baseline skills. To work, it needs to be simple and non-bureaucratic. While there's a 2015 requirement for all EU countries to have a national RPL policy in place, there's little sign of this actually happening. Part of the problem is unclear ownership (QQI, the agency who were expected to develop this policy, stated publicly that it was not their responsibility). As RPL is a critical enabler for older learners to access higher education, we need action to progress this, rather than territorial disputes. This one needs to be resolved by the DES and QQI.[54]

5.2 Standardise Entry Rules

The rules around college entry are complex. Each college decides its own entry requirements. Many have special entry routes, which are determined locally. Example: One IOT takes account of issues like long-term unemployment history, low family tradition of progress into higher education and difficult family circumstances which prevented a student from reaching their 'full potential' (these factors are determined at interview). While the ideal is to 'make access easier' for students, the development of local rules on admission could actually promote elitism in individual colleges. Of course, it's possible to find out the rules by speaking with college admissions staff or checking individual websites, but it's difficult to offer general guidelines to students who (rightly so) find this area extremely confusing. College entry requirements (sometime referred to as 'Matriculation Requirements') were historically set by each university and are different across the educational system. For example, within the National Universities of Ireland umbrella group (University College Cork, Maynooth University, NUI Galway, University College Dublin) there is a requirement for a four honours/two passes minimum in the Leaving Certificate, including a subject requirement for a foreign language. Why? Why not just take the best six subjects? Some of the IOTs decided to 'opt out' of both the HEAR and DARE entry schemes as a sort of protest about lack of resources. Several years later, they are still outside the system. The entry requirements should be standardised for all third level colleges. The goal is to have a sector-wide admissions approach which can be communicated to all potential students.

5.3 Mainstreaming Access: Annual Presidents Meeting

Higher Education Institutions are now required to have access plans embedded in their wider institutional plans. In some cases, there are some excellent examples where university presidents have led transformative approaches to access and this has become a central pillar in the college strategy. Yet in other institutions, the perception remains that access is a peripheral activity. Strategic and operational plans can state anything; real policy is dictated by on-the-ground behaviour. Access needs to be led by the college leaders and kept centre stage through continuous reinforcement. As part of this there should be a full-day annual meeting of all third level college leaders, devoted specifically to the topic of improving access.

5.4 College Access Practices: Develop a Best Practice Checklist

The current System across the third level sector is as follows. All 26 higher education Institutions develop institution wide approaches to access and submit these. On the plus side, the plans show the diversity of programmes currently underway and the richness of local innovation. However, it's almost impossible to determine how the existing system works within each organisation, for example, how many people are employed in the Access Office, how funding is allocated internally and so on.[55] The core idea here is to develop a standard institution-wide access plan. At the moment there's too much diversity in the plans produced and too little learning between the colleges. As with some of the areas reviewed earlier, the focus needs to shift from *innovation* to *implementation*. To progress this, a checklist of 'best practices' should be developed and each college self-audit against this. *Goal:* Establish a 'floor of practice' across the sector. No individual college will be allowed to do less than this. While some smaller colleges have less resources, it's useful to have aspirational targets to aim towards. A self-evaluation approach will help to identify what's working well and highlight gaps in practice. The ultimate goal is to replicate the best practice examples nationwide. Performance against this checklist would be the main agenda item for the college presidents meeting. A draft checklist is detailed in Appendix B.

5.5 Each Access Department to be Led by a Highly Competent Leader

Third level colleges are tasked with delivering on the goal of widening participation in line with the National Access Plan. While this system has been in place since 2004, the on-the-ground response has been piecemeal.[56] Why? One argument is that colleges are primarily populated by middle class academics that don't always identify with this agenda and there may be a grain of truth in this (middle class bias will not be eradicated overnight). Other respondents argued that access students consume disproportional resources and are resented because of this (albeit the current HEA funding model explicitly addresses this point). My sense is that the actual problem is a bit more mundane. Within each college, access has to compete with a range of other agenda items and doesn't always get executive attention. In some colleges the person running the Access Department has clout and influence, for example, an ability to highlight the social justice arguments alongside the business case, demonstrating how access initiatives feed into college fundraising and so on. In other colleges, the Access Department clout is weaker because of the poor leadership of the person running this section. Putting access 'centre stage' requires a strong institutional commitment. Every Access Department needs to be led by a person with a level of influence on par with other department heads across the college. This person should hold similar level educational qualifications (if not, they are often held in less esteem by their academic peers) and be paid at a broadly equivalent rate. Tackling educational disadvantage is a tough battle; we need to use our best troops!

5.6 College Recognition: The Access Oscars

The HEA should recognise and reward excellent performance on access. An annual competition between all third level colleges should be established to determine who's making the most progress. I've attended enough awards nights to know how seriously they are taken. Suitable criteria would need to be developed (the best practice checklist would guide this), with allowances made for institutional size and resources. As part of the evaluation, 'audit teams' from across the sector would review on-the-ground practices and decide who should be nominated. In addition to the small personal prize, a substantial monetary reward to be reinvested in access initiatives should be made to those colleges who exhibit the best practices in this area. While the exact methodology needs to be developed (for example, the national level competition might mirror similar 'in-house' competitions) it will likely include awards for:

- Institutions (ranked by size of student population)

- Individuals (outstanding individual student access stories)

- Practitioners (Access Officers going the extra mile for students)

- Academics (those who personify the 'best of the best')

5.7 All Colleges Should Provide Foundation Courses

The provision of access/foundation courses and the progression routes into third level isn't clear. Some colleges provide these; some don't. Most foundation courses are not formally linked to the NFQ. As far back as 2007, the HEA advised that access courses should be positioned at level 5 or 6 on the NFQ and that they should be delivered by the further education, in collaboration with the higher education, sector. Third level colleges argued for their continued positioning within the sector, due to the unique potential to familiarise prospective students with higher education from the inside. While this is still an open debate, there's little doubt that foundation programmes help to prepare students and there are good examples at both further education and higher education levels.[57] All third level colleges should either directly run Foundation Courses (pitched at level 6 on the NFQ) or have direct links to further education colleges to secure students who come from this stream.

5.8 Staying In: Improving College Completion Rates

Getting students into college is challenge number one. Keeping them there follows immediately afterwards. Encouraging someone to attend college if they can't successfully make it through the system is arguably unethical. Would they be better off if they hadn't gone in the first place? The big concern is that 'going and failing' can damage a student's confidence – perhaps knocking them out of the education system for life. We've already looked at some of the statistics and seen the high percentage of students who don't complete programmes. We know that a disproportionate number of working class students fall out of the system because they enter college with lower points (high points being the single biggest determinant of college success). But we've also seen that where proper supports are put into place, the success rates for foundation/access students can be on par or even better than mainstream students. There's been some really good work completed in this area with several colleges producing guides on 'how to survive'. But, in essence, this is treating the symptoms rather than the causes of the problem. In order to lower the dropout rate we have to ask if students are being forced into too narrow study bands and into making choices based on poor information? Arguably, it would be better if colleges could operate a 'general' first year and specific study choices were subsequently made. As part of the suggested review, the UCD initiative (Horizons) where students could 'Pick 'n' Mix' courses (similar to how the college systems works in many parts of the USA) should be looked at in detail. I'm aware of the logistical implications of this recommendation, and that's why I'm suggesting a formal review of this option rather than something definitive.

5.9 Introduce Service Learning: Focus on DEIS Schools[58]

Service learning is a powerful idea that should be installed across the third level sector to provide students with exposure to work and to teach the values of community service. Yet, it's not an easy idea to implement. Appropriate placements have to be found for each student to ply their trade. For example, a student studying accountancy might work in a not-for-profit local organisation, helping to ensure that the financial control system is 'fit for purpose'. Secondly, students moving outside of the college need to be mentored. You can't just tell a 19 year old, 'Here's the address of the place you've to go to. See you in three months. Good Luck!' Physical visits to the site and ongoing telephone/on-line support needs to be in place. So, the academic work involves more coaching and less teaching. Thirdly, the work completed within the community setting needs to be evaluated, something that can't be done by having everyone sit a standard exam. Overall, the idea of service learning poses quite a challenge to third level institutions. Rather than seeing this as a sort-of sheep-dip where all students follow the same process and are spat out at the other end with a qualification, this is customised learning.[59] It's certainly not a new idea. The School of Education at NUI Galway already offers an elective service learning module as part of its teacher education programme (homework and general support is provided to secondary school students from disadvantaged and ethnic minority backgrounds). Likewise, DIT have had elements of service learning in place for many years. A philosophical question posed is whether we want to elevate student's academic achievements over their responsibilities to others in the community? If the goal is to promote a deeper understanding and respect for others, especially people who are *different* in terms of background, service learning offers a perfect vehicle.[60] But in some colleges, the pressure to perform academically squeezes out the time and energy students have to contribute to others. Introducing service learning across the third level sector is a powerful stand-alone idea. But it could be doubly useful when married with the idea of promoting access if students became 'third level ambassadors' to the DEIS schools. In addition to the teaching offered to the children, it provides another vehicle to bring college into disadvantaged communities and demystify what happens there.

5.10 Adequate Financial Support: Tackle Existing Grant Anomalies

Encouraging students from disadvantaged areas to go to college will require tackling several anomalies in the provision of student grants. Example: Students completing foundation courses are ineligible for the financial supports normally available to higher education participants, for example, the Student Assistance Fund or the Fund for Students with Disabilities. From a policy perspective, this doesn't make any sense (the 'grants' area is complex and would require a separate book to detail how the current systems operate). Financial and other support systems for individual students are critically important in helping them make their educational journey. At the moment, the level of support given to individual students is actually in decline. Recent changes include reduced mileage allowances, lowering of the grant amount, lowering of qualifying income levels, removal of book allowance, removal of maintenance portion of the grant from those on the Back to Education Allowance and a host of other changes – the numbers all heading 'south'. By promoting the goal of access while, at the same time, reducing funding support for the most vulnerable students government actions are contradictory. A full review of the current funding system to identify key remedial elements and to establish a new 'floor of funding' needs to be conducted. As part of this review (which should include all key stakeholders), the entitlements of ethnic minority students needs to be clearly established. The recommendation here is that an expert team from the third level sector and the HEA be established to review this area. They should work to a short timeframe, possibly three months, to (a) identify the exact barriers to access in the current grants system, (b) develop a listing of recommendations to overcome them and (c) do a cost savings analysis. For example, a lot of administration time is taken up in processing. Sligo IOT estimated that the Student Assistance Fund can take up to two hours per student. As part of the review of the funding programmes, we need to simplify how such programmes work.[61]

5.11 The HEA Should 'Renew Its Vows' to Access

For many years, both the Department of Education and the HEA, followed a policy of allowing autonomy to third level institutions to 'act as they consider best' (preface to the 2008-2013 National Plan for Equity of Access). In more recent times, the new compacts with third level colleges changed the nature of the relationship and it has become more evaluative. Perhaps we can look forward to a time when colleges will not need a separate Access Department – the policy will be so mainstreamed that we won't even think of it as a separate activity. Until access becomes deeply embedded across all third level colleges, I suggest the following:

1. Audit access progress[62]: This is supposed to form part of the annual evaluation of each third level institution (and impact funding through the new compact system). But given the ex-

isting staffing complement in the National Access Office, is it possible to properly evaluate this?

2. Establish an annual practitioner forum: HEA should convene an annual forum of access practitioners. The purpose of this forum will be to review progress, share best practice and provide input into the Continuous Professional Development of this group. The goal here is to ensure that emerging ideas can spread like a positive virus across the sector (I'm in violent agreement with the HEA on this specific point).

3. Develop an access website: Identify a single person to 'own and edit' a central access website. This person should work directly for the HEA. The website will be used to showcase best practice, celebrate success and keep this topic 'front and centre' on the agenda for all third level institutions.

4. Reinforce third level access networks: A significant level of networking currently happens across the third level sector where a range of active networks are already in place.[63] Some individual colleges progress this agenda strongly, for example, DIT working with AHEAD on needs assessments for staff (DIT have been very collegiate in opening up seminars to academics from other institutions). The access networks should be actively coordinated and promoted by the HEA.

5.12 Expand the Teaching and Learning Brief[64]

We need to expand the brief of the teaching and learning functions in the third level colleges to include Continuous Professional Development in the area of access/lifelong learning for all academic staff. The national access office should promote equality training for all staff in higher-education institutions with a specific emphasis on addressing any 'anti-access bias' in the system. We can learn from the experiences of other countries in this. Professor Angela Thody (international expert of access) warned:[65] 'Excellence can't be used as a proxy for exclusion.'

5.13 Run Integrated Graduation Ceremonies

Many colleges have segmented graduation ceremonies where people being awarded Bachelor's Degrees, Masters etc. are conferred at the same time. In some of the large third level institutions, this is simply a logistics issue; with so many people graduating, the ceremonies have to be coordinated. However, foundation level awards are sometimes made at separate ceremonies, which can be interpreted as 'You're not as important.' To allow community level students aspire to continue their education journey, award ceremonies for access students should be fully integrated. At the present time, some lecturers working in the access area have to personally become 'event managers', negotiating rooms and space for community level learners to graduate – almost as if a favour was being bestowed. No more. This should be part of the normal graduation system and be fully integrated in all colleges.

5.14 Properly Resourced National Access Office

The HEA role in progressing access needs to be significantly strengthened. The current level of resourcing is ludicrous for a group tasked with tackling this agenda. The sense is of a central group, which gets things started, and then (because of inadequate resourcing) delegates this to the colleges/networks. The significant involvement in labour activation, for example, Springboard is an attempt to drive two separate agendas from an initial poor resource base and makes little sense. The current system is a recipe for mediocre progress. There is a need to strengthen the capacity of this office by adding several additional roles. It might be possible to fill some of these roles with people on secondment from the colleges/universities making the barriers between the HEA and the third level sector porous, further sharing and strengthening best practice. The new roles might include:

1. Marketing Director: With specific experience of the third level sector. To run the range of national access marketing initiatives/programmes detailed earlier.

2. Implementation Manager: Benchmark/ideas sharing. Disseminate best practices across the sector through an active com-

munications programme; build and lead a network of highly skilled practitioners. Keep the website and other information up to date. At the present time the 'ownership' of the Qualifax website is unclear (undermining a great opportunity to have a single source of information available on college courses).

3. Best Practice Auditor: Completing on the ground audits vis a vis the best practice checklist. The earlier suggestions entail using funding as a lever for change, encouraging best practices locally and withholding funding from colleges who ignore this agenda. This system needs to be audited locally (with a focus on positive reinforcement).

STRAND #6: LIFELONG LEARNING: PROMOTING EDUCATION IN THE WORKPLACE

6.1 Market College to Adult Learners

At 5.5 per cent, participation rates for adult learners in Ireland are less than half of the EU average of 11.4 per cent.[66] In targeting this audience, we would use a similar approach as suggested earlier for all access students but the messaging would be customised to appeal to this specific cohort. Perhaps, something along the following lines...

Education is Different

Re-entering the education system may seem like a daunting prospect, but it should be a pleasant surprise, very different to some people's earlier experience of school. You'll meet teachers who want to teach and students who want to be in class. There's no conscripts, only volunteers! A range of supports (induction, peer mentors, small group tutorials) are in place to make the journey easier. Fundamentally, adult education is designed for success. You will be welcomed to college as an adult, your opinions respected and your experiences will shape what happens in the classroom. There's no downside (other than missing a couple of episodes of *Game of Thrones* and you can always guilt someone into buying you the boxed set for Christmas). Get yourself back in the game.

Encourage Your Kids

When our teenage son was doing the Leaving Certificate someone commented, 'There must be a lot of tension in the house.' I replied, 'Yes, his mother and myself are really worried about it!' It's hard to get the 'importance of education message' across to teenagers. You've probably tried all of the usual techniques ('You're grounded'; 'Gimme that phone'; 'That girl is never to call to this house again'). Going back to college gives you an additional weapon in the struggle to survive teenagers! Lead by example and offer a role model to those around you who are also studying. It's a win/win.

Choose the Right Programme

There are a range of subsidiary questions. What course should I undertake? What topics would provide the best opportunities in the 'smart economy'? Can I get credits for stuff I've already done? Is there financial support to help pay the fees? The career guidance/admissions staff at your local college can answer these and any other questions you may have.

What's the Prize?

A better job. Higher pay. The opportunity to work overseas or become your own boss. A wider network of contacts. Personal fulfillment. The list goes on. At the heart of this argument are two central beliefs: (1) you are the CEO of your own life – 'If it has to be, it has to be me!' (2) We can all maximize our potential. Why settle for good when you can be great? The challenge is to discover what you can be great at. You'll be pleasantly surprised at the warm response you'll get from your selected third level college. For some people, avoiding education is the equivalent of scoring a career own goal. You can't live in yesterday's time capsule forever. There's a world of great topics out there.

6.2 Making College More Accessible Through Blended Learning

Sometimes potential students are physically distant from college and can't come on a scheduled basis. A policy commitment to the provision of more part-time and distance/e-learning provision addresses this. Yet here again practices lag behind policy. Some colleges have excellent provision in this space; others have nothing to offer. In recent years a significant level of open-source learning materials have become available, for example, Massive Open Online Courses (MOOC) run by internationally reputable higher education institutions. This has a potential impact in terms of the way Irish education institutions design and deliver courses with huge potential savings in time/money. At the moment on-line learning is progressed in multiple ways by a number of colleges working separately. Across the third level sector each institution (and some clusters of institutions) pursue different initiatives. Having a single approach would add significant value in terms of course design and technology utilisation, agreed methods on how such programmes are accredited to ensure that students gain currency (educational credits) and so on. What's required here is a sector-wide approach to open learning, distance learning and blended learning. While the expertise lies within the third level sector, this process should be centrally facilitated by the HEA.

6.3 Working with Employers: National Skills Upgrade Scheme

A recent suggestion from one of the third level unions was to impose an annual 1 per cent corporation tax to fund third level colleges. The argument was that the same corporations benefit from the outputs of colleges; on the *consumer pays* principle they should help to fund the sector. Regardless of the merits of this particular suggestion, what's clear is that employers have a huge role to play in encouraging older learners to get back into the education ring. Many already do this, running in-house development programmes and funding employees who wish to return to college. The question addressed here is whether we could expand what currently happens to a much wider group? Could we extend this outwards and if so, how? There is huge potential here around the further/ higher education sector working in partnership with employers to re-skill the workforce. There are many examples of this happening in practice. Over 30 years ago I worked with academics in DIT to 'upskill' craftsmen to technicians. Today, there's a huge amount of work underway in this space under the umbrella of Skillnets. The goal here is to develop a national plan to work with employers (for example, partnering with IBEC, Small Firms Association) to ensure that the education needs of adults in the workplace can be met.

Education Changes Lives:
Tom McCabe
Lifelong Learning

When we were growing up, I suppose we were disadvantaged, certainly compared to my kids today. It's all relative. Looking back, Ireland was a third world country in the 1950s. Poor accommodation. Outside toilets. Cheap lino on the floor. Oil cookers and coal fires. We'd put my father's old coats on the bed to keep warm in the winter. It would be many years before I even heard about central heating. My Da came from a long line of farm labourers and was a builder's labourer for much of his life. While he ended up as a supervisor in the County Council, most of his days were spent building houses in Whitehall.

We were skint. My Ma worked as a domestic with the toffs of Swords, doing housekeeping. Da had a few pigs at the back of the house in Main Street where we were renting. He also grew flowers and my Ma would sell these in the Dublin Flower Market, travelling in on the bus during the summer. As a sideline, he did nixers, extensions to houses and various renovations. Sometimes I was drafted in to help, but was probably more in the way than anything else. They certainly worked hard for their few bob.

I grew up working various jobs from early on. General dogsbody in a grocery shop, washing bottles and helping to fill them with stout for sale. Then a messenger boy delivering groceries on a bicycle that was probably bigger than me with a huge carrier box up front. Later, as a teen, I graduated to lounge boy. Money earned went to pay for school fees, buying a uniform for secondary school and into my Ma's purse. I did an exam for the De La Salle in Skerries, the nearest boys secondary school (there was nothing in Swords then). It seems hard to credit now, but at that time the population of Swords was less than 2,000 (at the last census it was 67,000+).

I was the only person to do the Leaving Cert in my entire family circle. As a result, very few of my cousins even talked to me as they considered me an upstart. Following the Leaving Certificate, I was accepted in Bolton Street College (Mechanical Engineering Technician). After that it was time to get a real job and I started working as a junior draughtsman. Eventually, in Technicon in Swords, I managed to get an apprenticeship and became a Jig and Tool Design Draughtsman.

Mid-twenties and now married, I went back to night school. I did two years in the College of Industrial Relations (now NCI) with Father John Brady SJ and the great teaching crew there. A few years later I did two years of a BBS in the NIHE Dublin (now DCU) but dropped out, because I hated accounting (still do). When I went to work with General Electric, the HR team encouraged me to complete an MSc. in Management Practice at the Irish Management Institute and that was really developmental. However, despite the variety of training, I secretly felt a tiny bit jealous (maybe even a bit inferior) to the engineers who'd gone to college directly after school and finished their degrees. So I dived back in again and completed a Doctorate in Business Administration in the UK. In my early fifties at the time, it was tough to hold down a full time demanding job (Managing Director of a Pharmaceutical multinational) and to keep the family going. I don't know how Mary didn't murder me with all of the time I spent away. Between travelling for work and swotting, I was an absentee dad. We celebrated our fortieth anni-

versary a few weeks ago so, somehow, we pulled through and the kids are still talking to me.

Embarking on a personal educational journey, however modest, is never easy. There's always a good reason 'not to' do it. The timing isn't right, the cost is too high, the kids are too small and so on. But, the biggest obstacle is that little voice inside your head that keeps saying, 'hey, maybe I won't be able for it'!

Education is transformative. Over the years I've seen so many people develop their potential and become the very best they can be. Hopefully I've encouraged some of them – as I was encouraged myself – to see it through. I told them that if I could make it through the system, anyone can, and that's not false modesty. Education has certainly changed my life for the better. We even have that central heating installed now.

Chapter 8

Making It Happen: Getting Money and Movement

Q: How might the Action List be agreed and how would we get movement?

A: To get movement on educational disadvantage, we have to start a national debate. The simplest and quickest way to do this would be to gather a group of key stakeholders – people who are knowledgeable and passionate about this area, including those with 'skin in the game' (politicians, community leaders, educationalists etc). We would bring this expert group to a single location. Then we might 'lock the doors' and tell them that, like the election of the Pope, they can only re-emerge when key decisions have been made. Making the exact same point, Pat Hoey from Limerick University argued: 'I would get "everyone" in a room in order to review all activity and come up a "Grand Masterplan" of joined up thinking as to how all the pieces of system should fit together.' The task would be to (a) agree the philosophy/vision of what we are trying to do, and (b) agree best practice approaches to address educational disadvantage across every part of the system (families, communities, schools, colleges etc.). That room might have to be kept locked for a week or so and we'd work through a lot of frozen pizzas in an intensive debate. But it could be done. Quickly.

Q: Is there an alternative?

A: Of course, there's always the age old alternative. The recommendations produced in this book could be placed in a library for a future researcher to discover. He or she could then develop an 'amended list'. That's the worst-case scenario. I really hope it doesn't happen.

Q: What would stop that from happening?

A: Well, we should start with strong political leadership. Tackling educational disadvantage requires strong political leadership, a clear grasp of what a better tomorrow would look like and a willingness to fight for this. Sometimes what passes for political debate in Ireland is whether 'Party A' will/won't allow 'Independent B' to be part of a grand coalition. If leadership is defined as 'the ability to bring about positive change,'[1] sometimes you'd weep at the lack of forward movement. While it's obviously a critical personal issue for politicians, getting re-elected doesn't count as forward movement for the nation. During the leaders' debates prior to the most recent general election (I watched all of them), there was almost zero mention of a better future. The debates became mired in policy minutiae, for example, parsing the difference between a €72,000 and an €80,000 cut off point for the Universal Social Charge on a family with two children. Of course, these are important questions, but they hardly represent political leadership.[2]

Q: So, this is a 'Political Problem? Politicians should 'fix this'?

A: No, it's not just a political problem. When it comes to tackling educational disadvantage, it's actually difficult not to feel some sympathy for politicians. We've seen earlier that educational disadvantage is (a) hard to diagnose, (b) often falls below the radar and (c) the fixes are not immediately apparent. A fundamental problem is that we haven't make the ask crystal clear. The core policy task is to develop an 'integrated plan' to tackle educational disadvantage. This book is a 'first-pass' attempt to construct this.

DEVELOPING AN INTEGRATED PLAN TO ELIMINATE EDUCATIONAL DISADVANTAGE[3]

Educational disadvantage is not wholly owned by the Department of Education and Skills. It's currently 'co-owned' by the Department of Children and Youth Affairs, specifically by TUSLA (the

Child and Family agency) under their heading of Educational Welfare Services.[4] According to their website:

> The statutory and school support services of the Child and Family Agency's Educational Welfare Services work together collaboratively and cohesively with schools and other relevant services to secure better educational outcomes for children and young people.

We've seen earlier that a number of other Government departments are also involved in funding pieces of this jigsaw. But without a central owner educational disadvantage is tackled on a piecemeal, reactive basis. In contrast, the establishment of the DEIS schools initiative was a structured attempt to tackle disadvantage. While this isn't perfect, it has definitely had a positive impact and demonstrates what can be done when a systematic approach is taken. Assigning a central owner for an integrated plan would be a key first step.

Pass the Parcel

In one submission to the Department of Education on Educational Disadvantage,[5] the point was made that five other departments (Social and Family Affairs; Enterprise, Trade and Employment; Community, Rural and Gaeltacht Affairs; Health and Children; Justice, Equality and Law Reform) are all involved in the provision of education services. *Result:* There's endless confusion and overlap around *who owns what? who's paying for what?* and *who's measuring what?* According to Dr Paul Downes: 'It's like playing "pass the parcel". How did this scenario come about? The full history would require an extensive review; here's the short version. In the absence of an overall vision, policy initiatives develop on a piecemeal basis. We end up with numerous ingredients but no overall recipe and there's no one in charge of the kitchen. And, add this into the mix. Sometimes there's a jealous guarding of money. Where a department secures money/resources for a project, they don't want next year's budget to be lower. When it comes to budgets, government departments generally follow a 'less = less' principle. No one wants to manage a smaller portfolio, regardless of whether this makes sense for the ultimate clients. So we just keep on, keeping on, like the lyrics of a badly written country and western song. This confusion around the ownership of education disadvantage tells part of the story. It becomes entangled with the lack of vision around what we are trying to achieve. Arguably, if this is not too cynical, a lot of Irish politics is non-ideological. One respondent, asked to comment on a key player in the education sector, replied, 'He's remarkably unencumbered by vision.' The vision to eradicate educational disadvantage is missing. A systematic, sustained, multi-dimensional and multi-year attack is missing. The entire topic is left to the mercy of occasional advocates. And then we ask, 'how come more progress isn't being made?'

A Smothering Conservatism

The combined policy and agency confusion described results in a patchwork of funding mechanisms, each with its own governance requirements. It's a huge time-soak, quadrupling the work for people on the front line trying to run services. But this is about something deeper than just money or cutbacks or even bureaucracy. It's really about a fundamental appetite to wade into the messiness of this complex debate. Here's how one respondent described their dealings with the Department of Education and Skills:

> When the recession hit, all government departments came under pressure. At that time, there were a number of cross-agency initiatives underway, Drugs Task Forces and so on. The Department of Education were represented on many of these. I'd describe their general view of the world as follows. 'We are in the business of managing schools and nothing outside of schools.' When the recession hit, the door opened an inch and they bolted out like lightening from every single committee and external involvement.

Perhaps the Department of Education and Skills would argue that this is real politics, that is, 'cutting their cloth to suit the measure.' At several points in this book, the Department of Education and Skills have come under fire. Over the years I've had the opportunity to meet a couple of Secretaries of the Department along with a range of officials holding a variety of positions. Almost without exception, the people met were talented and committed to education. But, somehow, the sum of the whole seems to be less than the individual parts. There's a collective conservatism that blocks forward progress. When we require clear and decisive leadership to overcome roadblocks, we get conservatism and 'kicking to touch.' We've seen earlier that politicians often operate to a different (shorter-term) rhythm. Few have the luxury that I've had to take a 'deep dive' into this subject. In relation to educational disadvantage, we need the real policy makers (the permanent public servants) to take educational disadvantage out of the unsolvable file, to place it centre stage and keep it there over a sustained period, ideally, for a decade or more.

The Political Skill Required to Overcome Vested Interests

In addition to the political *will*, there needs to be enormous political *skill* in moving this agenda forward. There are huge vested interests involved. Particular government departments hold sway over the allocation of resources, teachers unions will defend territory like female lions protecting their cubs and so on. So the changes required would need a George Mitchell-type facilitation to bring the parties forward. According to one respondent, the core of the problem in the Irish education system is the plague of over-consultation:

> We have somehow come to believe that everyone's opinion matters equally and that nothing can be done without consensus. In reality, the interest groups in education are very powerful and there's often a stalemate in terms of reform.

The current debacle around the (relatively minor) reforms in the Junior Certificate support this view. While no one would argue against the teachers unions having a central role in shaping the system, they shouldn't have a veto which can stymie progress. The design of the Irish educational system overrides the needs of any single lobby group. Supporting the view that 'change is difficult', Fergus Finlay offered the following vignette:

> We put a proposition to Jan O'Sullivan, the most recent Minister for Education, that primary school should be 'free' for all children. That's free books, free transport and the provision of simple school meals. Along with this we suggested restoring the capitation rates to 2009/2010 levels. The combined cost was €103 million.[6] Set against the overall Department of Education and Skills budget of €8 billion that represents 1.28 per cent of the budget. What happened? Absolutely nothing.

While this level of expenditure should be 'petty cash' for the department, it can seem impossible to get movement within the system, even with the support of a *progressive* Minister. The solution is to elevate the issue of educational disadvantage and provide it with a separate infrastructure and funding stream until it becomes embedded across the system.

Establish an Education Disadvantage Committee

The political parties need to be jointly tasked with working together on the eradication of educational disadvantage.[7] This topic – and some of the specific suggestions made in this book – have potential to become political footballs, where the future success of children could become secondary to the immediate political gains offered by adopting a popular stance. The establishment of a cross-party Education Disadvantage Committee to secure implementation of the key recommendations would be a major step in the right direction. Of course there's a role for balance and positivity. There's much to celebrate in the Irish educational system. The personal care and attention given to students in so many schools is a case in point. But a recognition of what's working well is very different from accepting how things are at the moment. For too long we have tiptoed around educational disadvantage. It's time to place this in the spotlight.

Funding the Programme

Many of the recommendations made to tackle educational dis-advantage are 'cost increasing' in the short-term which raises the obvious question, 'Where will the additional money come from?'[8] During the most recent elections in Ireland, a number of left learn-ing political groups put forward the following argument:[9] The top 1 per cent of people own 75 per cent (or 85 per cent or 95 per cent, it's hard to keep up) of the wealth in Ireland. The simplest solution to raising money for social causes is to 'take this from them' (in the form of penal taxation) and redistribute this enormous wealth to everyone else. In one bold step, we can level the playing field! It's certainly an interesting idea. Just a pity that it's never been done. Anywhere. And, where some version of this has been tried, those same 'selfish rich people' tend to up sticks and move somewhere where the rates of taxation are less penal.

If that particular strategy is not going to work, here's another idea. Perhaps we could change the rules on inheritance. If this was completely abolished, all wealth would automatically go to the state. Try selling that idea to the farmers and their first-born! No, I don't think that would work either. Perhaps a more realistic method to raise revenue is to look at the corporate sector, where the actual rates of taxation (not the 'headline rate of 12.5 per cent) can be extremely low through manipulation of transfer pricing and a range of other financial measures. For sure, there has to be a widespread perception that the taxation system is fair. A percep-tion of fairness seems at least as important as the relative amounts paid. Coming back to our central focus, the core problem remains that we need to set realistic investment targets to tackle education disadvantage. So what is a realistic target? Paul Downes and Ann Louise Gilligan suggest that 'we need to revisit the percentage of Gross National Product assigned to education from the National

Budget and raise it by 1 per cent.'[10] As a single example, annual investment in third level access initiatives is currently €29 million or about 2 per cent of the overall spend across the sector. Access could become a much more significant component if we increased this to circa 5 per cent or €50 million per annum. **Bottom Line:** Access is not something that magically *happens*. We need to make it happen by making the requisite investment and demonstrating our commitment.[11] One possible method is through the reintroduction of college fees.

Reintroduce College Fees

We could secure the additional money for investment through the reintroduction of college fees and re-investing this money directly into educational disadvantage. While this would be a controversial measure, it has merit. Like the smoking ban or the tax on plastic bags, we've seen that Ireland can introduce controversial and sometimes unpopular measures and make them stick. The movement away from third level fees was a bold experiment, but one that didn't work in terms of achieving its stated aims of improving access for disadvantaged groups. That policy now needs to be reversed despite the fact that it will be politically unpopular and will undoubtedly be challenged by the self-employed, farming lobby groups and so on.[12] The arguments are as follows.

Underpinning Philosophy = Consumers Pay

The cost of education should be shared by the students who benefit from this. While the actual cost of individual programmes needs to be determined,[13] as a broad guide going to college costs €10,000 per year. 'High cost' programs, for example the study of medicine, actually cost more to complete. While some colleges may be more efficient than others, perhaps even able to offer lower fees, in general the fees would be set at a particular 'bar height'. The core idea is that the cost of education should be borne by the students who receive the service. In addition to the fairness argument (those who consume services should pay for this), paying for education should encourage students to demand more from the education system. They won't accept poor quality teaching or lecture cancellations without explanation and will generally be more demanding in terms of achieving value for money.[14]

Introduce a Loan System to Cover Fees

Students who can't fund the annual fees would be given a Government loan to complete their education. While the exact operation of this needs to be decided,[15] it might work along the lines of the Australian Higher Education Contribution Scheme (HECS), which is income-contingent, that is, student loans become repayable when their income goes above a certain threshold. The loans made could include living expenses (maintenance) for the students while they are in college, which would also be repaid. Technically, a student who received a loan for a four-year degree @ €10,000 per annum plus a maintenance grant of, say, €5,000 per annum, would need a loan of €60,000 to fully cover her/his costs. Stay with me on this.

Strong Communication of the Fees Rationale

We have seen that the removal of college fees didn't, in practice, impact the percentage of access students attending third level. However, the reintroduction of college fees might put people off the idea of attending college. On first glance, this may seem like a logical fallacy. If removing fees didn't spur more access students to attend college, why would re-instating fees damage this? The answer is that the perception that college is becoming more expensive (and the publicity which would inevitably surround the reintroduction of fees), might erect a mental barrier and negatively impact the attendance of less well off students. The overall communication would need to be carefully devised to ensure that this is not an unintended consequence. Let's agree one centrally important point: Generating additional income while lowering the participation rates for less well off students would be a brutal, negative outcome. That is not the intent.

Introduce a New 'Means Test'

In cases where a student's family had an income below a certain threshold, grants would be made to cover college fees/pay maintenance costs up to 100 per cent on a sliding scale. These grants would be based on a newly devised means test. This test should have two elements, taking account of both the accumulated wealth of families alongside a focus on income.[16] In focusing solely on income, the current means test ignores accumulated wealth. While income can be manipulated (by moving assets and liabilities in particular tax years), wealth is more permanent. An income test alongside a 'capital' (wealth) test seems a much fairer system to determine ability to pay. The reality is that the self-employed, farmers etc. are currently in a much better position to manipulate the current maintenance grants application system than a PAYE worker. By taking account of overall family wealth, new thresholds would be set and more wealthy families would have to fund third level education (alternatively, the students themselves have the option to take out repayable loans).

'Ringfence' the Additional Income to be Spent on Access Initiatives

This is a central point. The additional revenue generated by this measure would be 'ringfenced' and re-invested across a range of access initiatives, such as the earlier listing of recommendations made (or a modified listing). So what additional income would this produce? To calculate this, we need to make some assumptions. For the sake of argument, let's keeps the math simple:

- Current numbers of students in third level = 220,531. Let's 'round this down' to 200,000.

- Estimated number of students who would receive 'free fees' grants: 25 per cent (lower than the current 40 per cent because of the suggested changes to the means test).

- Therefore, the number of students who would pay college fees (75 per cent of 200,000) = 150,000.

- The fees generated @ an average rate of €10,000 per student = €10,000 x 150,000 = €1.5 billion annually.

- The per cent of students who would 'default' on the repayment of student's loans. Estimate = 5 per cent based on international comparisons.

- The annual cost of the collection mechanism to administer this system. Estimate = 7.5 per cent.

- The net revenue annual inflow to the exchequer = €1.5 billion less 12.5 per cent (5 per cent+7.5 per cent) = €1,312,500 (one billion, three hundred and twelve million).

Bottom Line: That's a lot of money to be reinvested in tackling educational disadvantage.

Philanthropic Contributions: Making Access a Noble Cause

In the USA, philanthropy is hardwired into the culture. In Ireland, we have Chuck Feeney and a handful of others. People who've made a lot of money are generally successful in holding on to large parts of it. But we could encourage more philanthropy (big and small amounts) if we had a compelling idea, rather than chasing the same small group of high net worth individuals with a hotchpotch of ideas from different colleges.

National Level

A small specialist team comprised of key individuals from the third level foundations (fundraising arms of the universities and colleges) should construct a national 'Breaking the Cycle' philanthropy programme and this money would be ringfenced to target the disadvantaged schools and communities. The educational disadvantage message is complex and 'hard to sell' without clear messaging. We need a *big* idea, a 20-year vision that's clear and credible.

Local Level

College alumni and people with close personal links to particular geographic areas could also be targeted for support. Some colleges have already made significant progress in this. However, others struggle and don't have the in-house expertise to maximise this opportunity. A pro-forma fundraising plan based around Access could be led by the HEA for third Level educational institutions who do not have existing expertise in this space. The money raised to be used 'locally' on tackling education disadvantage initiatives.

CONCLUSIONS

> If you are planning for a year, sow rice: if you are planning for a decade, plant trees: if you are planning for a lifetime, educate people – *Chinese Proverb*

We have seen throughout that educational deprivation results in fractured lives, broken families and the expensive waste of human potential. Solving the puzzle of education disadvantage can provide lasting improvements. It can overcome persistent, intergenerational social problems and deliver huge savings in public spending. Based on the evidence from many successful (and unsuccessful) initiatives, we know how to intervene and produce dramatic results.[17] This can be done.

Despite the enormous prize, efforts to defeat educational disadvantage continue to be dogged by institutional and financial obstacles. There's a sort of invisible bias in favour of the status quo. When John Kotter, Professor of Leadership at Harvard Business School argued that *complacency* and a low *sense of urgency* are the central impediments to progress, he might have been describing the Irish educational system.[18] However, while it's relatively easy to state the problem, the leadership requirement is to determine the route forward. The are four central steps needed to make progress.

1. Shared Vision

Our education system should be built around the philosophy of 'cherishing all the children of the nation equally.' 100 years on, in a year when we celebrate the foundation of the state, people are still drawn to the powerful idea of creating a level playing pitch for all Irish citizens. Our goal is to narrow the gap between rhetoric and reality, ensuring that fewer people will be left behind. In the absence of this overarching vision, we are educationally bankrupt.

2. Student Driven

With 1 million full-time students in Ireland,[19] our core task is as follows: 'To maximise their potential.' The central design issue revolves around teaching students how to learn, equipping them with skills for life, not for passing exams. The key delivery issue occurs within each educational institution where the needs of students should be at least on par with the teachers in a positive partnership.

3. Delivering Changes

We need to break-out of the historical bargaining pattern around making changes that's become a recipe for incrementalism. Charles Stewart Parnell said, 'No man shall have the right to fix the boundary to the march of a Nation.' In a similar vein, no group should have the right to veto changes to the education system. Putting an end to the *education apartheid* that currently exists requires overhauling both the current education and community development processes. This isn't tweaking the wing-mirror on the car; it's a fundamental redesign of the engine that powers the social and economic future of the country.

4. Better Tomorrow

Making this happen, will require a large-scale investment. We need to put our wallet behind our vision, knowing that the payback (detailed earlier) will be a huge multiple of the investments made. Between 2016 and 2021, €27 billion is earmarked for capital projects in Ireland.[20] Should we build bridges to span railway lines or build human capital for the future at a tiny fraction of the cost? As part of this, we need to sign up for a multi-year programme, seeing beyond the life of a single political administration. Educational disadvantage doesn't exist because that's the way things are: 'Inequality is perpetuated and entrenched because of political decisions made at every level of Government. It doesn't have to be this way.'[21]

I began writing this book with a vague sense of unease that not enough was being done to tackle education disadvantage and in the hope of discovering how we might move the needle forward. As the individual layers of discrimination have became clearer, I now feel a growing sense of outrage. While we continually construct policy documents and commence a million debates, this injustice continues. It continues away from any media spotlight. When a single life is lost in a traffic accident, that tragedy becomes front-page news. Yet we sit on our hands while 9,000 children each year silently fall out of the education system before even completing second level education. Many of these lives are blighted because of our inaction. Larry McGivern observed:

> I've met quite a few young people who didn't finish school. If the numbers in this small area are indicative of what's happening in the rest of the country, we're facing a lost generation who'll drift along in varying states of depression. There's not a lot to live for when the only future you have is to become totally dependant on the state.

Unless we intervene, now, educational disadvantage will continue to destroy individual lives and act as an anchor on social progress. Perhaps Lech Walensa, the former electrician who later became President of Poland, said it best:[22]

> The world market for words is saturated. It's time for action.

Education Changes Lives:

Beverley Maughan

Mature Student, Dublin City University

I still remember my first day at St Joseph's school in Ballymun. The school bag was thrown at the teacher and I kicked her in the leg while clinging tightly to my Mother. Some start! The teacher was so lovely, I'd soon settled in. The sins of four-year-olds tend to be forgiven. In second class the world turned upside-down when we ended up with the worst teacher in the school. He had a drink problem and permanently stank of alcohol. As seven-year-olds, we thought it was funny. Looking back now, we didn't make much progress.

In fourth class the boys started to get a bit rough. When one of them pulled an earring out of my ear, my Mother went mental and sent my sister (two years older) and myself to Our Lady of Victories on the Ballymun road. I cried my heart out. The teacher was about 100 years old (or so I thought). For some strange reason, the fact that she brought a flask of tea with her every day somehow made her seem even older. We had a 'stand-off' relationship; she didn't like me and I was afraid of her. My strongest memory of that time is feeling stupid and I thought that school was very hard. When we moved to fifth class, we got a new teacher. Strict but warm, she helped me with maths and spelling. When we did tests, I'd score 2 out of 10, way below the rest of the girls. It was the first time I realised how much I'd fallen behind. Something clicked, I started to get serious and the marks improved. We had an altar in the class. I loved it and had something similar at home in my bedroom. I wanted to be a nun and my Mam used to say 'Yea, where there's none wanted.'

First year in Secondary School ended with a great result (I've still got a copy of that school report). But when I moved across to the Senior Comprehensive, things started to go downhill again. One person in the class messed all the time; everyone messed a lot. The Irish teacher continuously spoke in Irish and we didn't understand a single word she said. In terms of encouragement, I remember getting called to the Career Guidance office for a chat. It took about three minutes. What would I like to do when I leave? That was it, a few weeks before we left the school. Despite everything, I sat the Leaving Certificate and managed to pass almost all subjects (securing 3 honours). But, I'd failed maths and was upset and I certainly felt a failure. Soon after, I went to work in a Fish Factory in Finglas. Never really settling into any job (I had about 30 jobs altogether), I bounced around between shops and factories.

When your self-esteem is low, you make poor personal choices. I ended up in an abusive relationship that lasted for a number of years. When we emigrated, the abuse got worse and I decided to leave with our son and come home. I'll skip the gory details but it was an unpleasant patch and my confidence hit rock bottom.

Back in Ireland, I ended up on a Community Employment scheme. Encouraged to do further training, I started legal studies, mainly to sort out my own situation. Subsequently, I completed a Family Law programme in NCI. All along I'd been dealing with the Law Centre in Ballymun. Frank Murphy, who worked there, suggested that I should apply for a law degree in DCU. I thought it would be too difficult. Frank said 'You're doing it already' (i.e. representing myself in court on the family case). No-one was more surprised than me when I secured a place on the course and a whole new world started to open up.

But, things are not straightforward, not in my life anyway. After completing two years, I became ill and deferred for a year. Then, just after I returned to studying, my folks got cancer. They chose to stay at home and I had to defer again. Eventually, in 2016, I successfully completed the course. DCU had been supportive throughout this long journey. It seemed like I'd travelled a million miles from where I started.

Thankfully, today I'm in a much better place. My personal circumstances have improved dramatically and I'm really happy now. I have a burning passion to effect changes in how the law treats victims of domestic violence. Overall, my life is better today than I could ever have imagined and education has played a key role in this. I'd love to see other kids from disadvantaged areas getting the encouragement and support that I received along the way. It might change their lives too.

Appendix A:

THE LIFETIME IMPACT OF MOVING FROM WELFARE TO PAID EMPLOYMENT[1]

The central theme of this book is as follows: there are enormous benefits to be captured if those who currently drop out of education at an early stage can be encouraged to stay on and complete a tertiary qualification. The financial and non-financial benefits for an individual learning skills which equip them to become gainfully employed are significant. We have earlier estimated the financial benefits of this as somewhere in the region of €1 million per person over a lifetime of employment.

State Benefits

However, as shown below, the financial benefits for the State are equally compelling.

Caveat

Undertaking a precise calculation of the financial benefits for the state is fraught with difficulties. We cannot be sure how the jobs secured by the now-qualified individuals will compare to those already in the workforce. We can't say what households these individuals will form and hence cannot be sure what tax they will pay. But, based on the principle that it's best to be approximately correct than precisely wrong, the estimates below were based on some fairly simple, conservative assumptions:

- Unskilled individuals receive Jobseeker's Allowance at the standard rate for 47 years until they become eligible for non-contributory old-age pension.

- They are eligible for a medical card throughout this period. A medical card would cost the state approximately the same as a Plan B VHI Scheme.

- If, instead, the individuals who were previously unemployed, secure a third level qualification and hence manage to secure jobs which deliver the same wage distribution as we observe among the working population, they will pay taxes instead of being in receipt of social welfare.

Lifetime Cost of Providing for an Unemployed Individual

The value of the payments and benefits made by the State to an unemployed individual is in excess of €500,000:

Jobseekers' Allowance	Age	Weekly Payment	# of Years
	19-24	€100	6
	25	€144	1
	26-66	€188	40
Medical Card		€1,500	47
Total Payments Made		€500,228	

Lifetime Taxes Paid by Employed Individual

When an individual is working, they pay tax and social insurance to the State. The table below assumes that current tax rates and wage distribution obtain into the future (we have not made any allowances for inflation). It estimates the State will receive over €640,000 including income tax, employer and employee PRSI and USC:

Salary (€)	Net Income (€)	Employee Deductions (€)	Employer PRSI (€)	Earning (per cent)
15,000	14,790	210	1,275	20.0
20,000	18,448	1,552	2,150	18.0
25,000	21,632	3,368	2,688	15.0
30,000	25,1578	4,843	3,225	9.8
35,000	28,442	6,558	3,763	6.5
40,000	30,967	9,033	4,300	5.5
45,000	33,492	11,508	4,8938	4.0
50,000	36,017	13,983	5,375	3.0
55,000	38,542	16,458	5,913	2.8
60,000	41,067	18,933	6,450	2.0
65,000	43,592	21,408	6,988	1.8
70,000	46,117	23,883	7,525	1.7
75,000	48,518	26,482	8,063	1.4
80,000	50,918	29,082	8,600	1.3
85,000	53,318	31,682	9,138	1.2
90,000	55,718	34,282	9,675	1.1
135,000	77,318	57,682	14,513	3.9
250,000	132,518	117,482	26,875	1.0
Total Employer and Employee Payments			€643,246	
Total Payments Made			€500,228	
Total Benefit to the State			€1,143,474	

Bottom Line: The total benefit to the State exceeds €1 million when an individual becomes productively employed (based on a combination of taxes paid and the 'non-payment' of benefits by the state).

Additional Net Income Received by Employed Individual

The individual also benefits significantly: whereas payments of €500,000 are received from the State when on social welfare, net salary in excess of €1.3 million is received when working. Thus, the individual benefits by more than €800,000 over their working life.

Employee Net Income	€1,333,138
Social Welfare Received	€500,228
Benefit to Individual	€832,910

Total Benefit of Individual Moving from Welfare to Employment

In aggregate, the benefit to the individual and the State is almost €2 million.

Benefit to Individual	€832,910
Benefit to State	€1,143,474
Total Benefit	€1,976,384

While undoubtedly this precise figure is incorrect, nevertheless, the financial benefits to society (the individual and the State) are of such magnitude that they cannot be ignored. Very few initiatives could ever produce such a significant return from a relatively modest investment. Education pays the bills!

Appendix B:

BEST PRACTICE ACCESS CHECKLIST FOR COLLEGES (WORKING DRAFT)[2]

Philosophy: Higher Education institutions have a moral along with an educational role. We need to *lead for good* and produce superior societal outcomes. Universal access to third level education is one such outcome. 'Intelligence, talent and creativity is distributed equally. We can't justify the fact that a swathe of people are excluded from the education system' – Mary Doyle, DOE.[3]

Our goals are:

- **(A) College Aspiration:** Improve the likelihood that all people will aspire to attend college with a particular focus on five access categories who are underrepresented in college: mature students; students with disabilities; students from the Traveller community; students from ethnic minority backgrounds and students coming from socio-economic deprived areas

- **(B) Successful Completion:** We encourage each student to become the very best they can be. Our teaching methods help students become independent learners. Our support systems ensure, as far as is possible, a positive college experience for every student. While there will always be exceptionally talented students, this is not a 'survival of the fittest' contest. Our target is that all entrants will complete their study programme of choice. While the focus in this document is on Access students, the practices listed will benefit *all* students.

STRAND #1: UNIVERSAL ACCESS TO THIRD LEVEL EDUCATION

Everyone is Encouraged to go to College

Clear Philosophy and Targets

◊ Twin elements known to all staff.

    a. 'Full Access' (encourage everyone to attend college, regardless of background) and

    b. 'No student left behind': We make it work.

◊ Clearly identified *needs* understood/documented for each access category

◊ Clear targets (recruitment and completion rates) set for each access category

◊ High Level 'Widening Participation' group in place to monitor progress and improve internal systems e.g. how to ease transition from second level'

◊ College President/senior team committed to this agenda

School Links: Demystify what happens in college

◊ Single point of contact for all primary and second level schools in catchment area: Particular focus on DEIS schools: Every disadvantaged school will have a nominated 'third level partner'. *'They know us; we know them.'* No competition for schools

◊ Solid links with Guidance Counsellors: Scheduled rota of meetings

◊ Spend time on-site with each school against an annual schedule/rota

◊ Encourage schools to visit the campus and involvement e.g. school plays, choirs used during all college ceremonies

◊ Programmes which capture young students' imagination e.g. Sport 4 Success or Robot Wars. Goal = ongoing linkages rather than 1-off initiatives

Networking with other Education Providers: Progression Routes

◊ Links with PLC providers and Further Education colleges as feeder streams

◊ Promote access and explain how progression routes work in practice

Community Links: Bringing Access 'Alive'

◊ Work with community representatives from disadvantaged areas/minority groups to promote access possibilities e.g Travellers

◊ Run community based programmes *bringing learning to the learners*

◊ Offerings for each group e.g. mature learners which meets their particular needs

◊ Staff work outside 9-5 hours to ensure that these links are actively in place

Workplace Links: Marketing Access to Workplace-based Learners

◊ Where possible run workplace-based programmes to encourage access

◊ Part-time provision meets the local needs and encourages participation

◊ Accreditation for Prior Learning (RPL). Make it known/easy for students to get credit for prior work and study experiences

Campus Environment is Open and Welcoming

◊ Workshops and activity classes for Potential Students e.g. Open Days allow students to assess the physical campus

◊ Highlight vibrant sports, social and recreations programmes (non academic)

◊ 'Taster' programmes allow potential students to experience college life e.g summer programmes and maths grinds for second level students

◊ Local Community use College meeting spaces for variety of purposes

Admissions Procedure is Non-Bureaucratic

◊ Clear website/social media routes to information provision
◊ Annual Prospectus of offerings
◊ Information made available in accessible formats for all groups e.g non sighted

Admissions Procedures

◊ Online application and registration available.
◊ Special entry initiatives for students from under-represented groups made clear
◊ 1 to 1 appointment available with Admissions Officer to discuss choices
◊ Positive Discrimination: per cent of places reserved for Access students in all courses

Relevant Provision

◊ Foundation programmes in place (1 year) for Access students

STRAND #2: PROVIDING A POWERFUL STUDENT EXPERIENCE

Brilliant Learning, Teaching and Assessment

Academic Methods:

◊ Learn-to-Learn modules for all students.
◊ Personalised feedback from tutor for all assignments
◊ Small tutorial class sizes with a focus on specialist topics e.g. essay and academic writing workshops, maths tutors offering 1 on 1 support etc.

◊ Use of innovative instructional strategies e.g. problem based learning (PBL) and enactments with an emphasis on practical application of learning

◊ Wide variety of assessment techniques to measure learning outcomes

◊ Work experience programmes supplement classroom learning

◊ Student teams work on real life projects

◊ 'Excellence Initiatives': Awards system recognises academic success

Service Learning

◊ Academic marks given to service learning projects. College students work with younger students from disadvantaged areas/DEIS schools

Student Voice

◊ Students Union: In place providing support and encouraging service improvement

◊ Appointment and training of Class Representatives

◊ Annual student feedback to full-time and associate faculty

Faculty Development

◊ Mandatory faculty professional development in teaching and learning

◊ Internal Teaching Fellowship competitions showcase the 'best of the best'

◊ PG Diploma in Teaching and Learning to be completed by all staff

Specialist Inputs

◊ Links with 'industry captains' and a range of external practitioners.

Technology Enhanced

◊ Use of technology to enhance learning (e.g. Moodle, Turnitin, Webinars etc.)

◊ Distance and blended strategies allow students overcome geographical hurdles

Onboarding

◊ Identify potential 'early fallers' and help them get settled

Progression Routes

◊ Internal students can move from Higher Cert to degree level
◊ Modular/flexible course structures. Clear rules on 'transfer' between courses

First Class Student Support

Professional Resourcing

◊ Professional Access staffing on par (in terms of quality personnel) with all areas of the college.
◊ Student support with Careers, Disability, Finance, Academic Coaching, Counselling, Medical
◊ Sufficient staffing in place to meet the needs of access students
◊ Access Professionals active in both internal and external Networks and embedded in all college academic committees

Peer Mentoring

◊ System in place with full training given to student mentors

Disability Support

◊ Full awareness and use of assistive technology for students with disabilities. All courses audited against the principles of Universal Design.
◊ Ability to complete diagnostic learning and disabilty assessments for students
◊ Specific supports in place (e.g. use of Facetime software for students in hospital)

Financial Support

◊ Comprehensive understanding of all available financial options for students to secure € support

Office Facilities

◊ The Access office is in a prominent position on campus and has adequate space for confidential meetings with students

Sport and Recreation

◊ Goal = foster a sense of belonging/healthy campus
◊ Social space for student use and Arts events to broaden student experience
◊ Student Residences: Refurbishment and Upgraded facilities including: internet access
◊ Strand #3: Developing Active and Responsible Citizens

Managing the College/Work Transition

◊ Career and Opportunities: Placement service for final year students
◊ Standard module to promote transferable and employability skills.

High Quality Graduates

◊ **Craft:** Graduates will have gained the practical knowledge and skills necessary to be master practitioners in their chosen area
◊ **Profession**: Graduates will have assimilated the values, ethos and professional standards of their chosen discipline
◊ **Business**: Will be able to succeed, lead, create, innovate and adapt to changing business environments
◊ **Community**: Demonstrate a commitment to social justice by becoming responsible and active citizens
◊ **Personal**: Graduates will be self-directed learners with the capacity to think critically and to pursue their own goals throughout life

Uplifting Graduation Events

◊ Ceremonies involving families celebrating the educational success

◊ Embed ceremonies with 'upbeat' Access student stories. Goal = the ceremony's should have a powerful emotional connection with students and their families

◊ Flat graduation structure (all disciplines and levels graduate together to promote diversity)

◊ Ceremonies made 'accessible' e.g. use of Latin and traditional forms kept to a minimum

◊ Students selected for special recognition awards

Continual Links with Students: Alumni Relations

◊ Comprehensive database of all former students – where they ended up working e.g. student profiles, data and first destination reports

◊ Alumni help to tell the 'story of college' to external audiences

◊ Alumni continue to work with the College (associate faculty, meeting with students to plan careers etc).

Q: How Would this 'Access Checklist' Work in Practice?

Realistic Proposal

Some of the colleges are very large while others are quite small in terms of student numbers. It's difficult to develop a single Checklist which would span this diversity of institutions. However, we are not being prescriptive with regards to the exact numbers of staff, reporting requirements or organisation structure. These are local management decisions. We are being prescriptive about certain baseline services being in place at all colleges.

Agreed Purpose

a. The checklist allows colleges to self-audit i.e. it's a self-improvement guide

b. It's a mechanism to share 'best practice' between third level providers

c. The checklist could be a mechanism to make reporting easier to the HEA i.e. it gives a 'common' data collection mechanism across all colleges.

Rating System

Each of the 'elements' would be rated, perhaps by giving each section a numerical ranking: **Stage 4: Yes** (fully achieved/in place) **Stage 3: Yes, but** (achieved to a significant extent, but not yet fully achieved) **Stage 2: No, but** (not achieved yet but development work in progress and **Stage 1: No** (not progressed yet). If each section was given a rating this would convert into an overall score for the college and identify where they need to improve.

Action Planning

The checklist would be designed with *space* for written descriptions. This would assist the Executive Team and the Access Officers in each College to understand progress being made under the various headings. This might be in the form of **(1)** 'What's going really well under this heading?' **(2)** 'What's not going really well?' **(3)** Are there initiatives which have not yet commenced? **(4)** What do we propose to do to progress the issues detailed?

Overcoming Resistance

There may be some resistance to this idea on the basis that the HEA may be seen as trying to *disempower* colleges with additional central control and this 'creeping manageralism' will stifle innovation and creativity. There are strongly held views around this topic (which is broader than Access). In practice, this trend towards centralisation is actually underway for some time e.g. the fact that the National Access office was established 10 years ago, currently requires each college to submit progress reports on access and so on. The suggestions here are a refinement of practices already in place. Orla Christle made the point that, quite apart from any legal issues, that the HEA couldn't (and shouldn't) *micro-manage* HEIs. If the overall framework of accountability and agreed best practice is in place, highly qualified and experienced staff in each institution should be able to deliver on this agenda, supported by HEA.

Endnotes

Chapter 1

1 The author Peter Townsend stated that he didn't want to 'give the impression of being some kind of intellectual imperialist, gobbling up areas of expertise believed previously to be remote from my interests and competence.' While I'm neither an education nor social policy expert, the broad nature of educational disadvantage doesn't require any particular background to address this. The wide range of people involved in this research highlights the breadth of knowledge needed to shine a light on this multi-dimensional topic.

2 McMahon, W. (2009) *Higher Learning, Greater Good: The Private and Social Benefits of Higher Education.* John Hopkins University Press, Baltimore. OECD (2008) 'Tertiary Education for the Knowledge Society'. OECD. Paris. See also McMahon, W. (2010) 'The External Benefits of Education'. University of Illinois.

3 The randomness of parentage can be likened to a lottery. Those born into wealthy families are said to have won the 'womb lotto'. However, those born into privilege may be more prone to assert that personal achievements, rather than factors beyond their control, garnered their success or wealth.

4 Meeting with the author, February 2016. Lynn was the former Trinity College Students Union President and was elected to the Irish Senate on April 28, 2016.

5 Every effort has been made to *fact check* the book to ensure that the arguments made are based on existing data (both supportive and contradictory).

6 Julie Bernard in DIT made the point that we can't assume that all foreign nationals are educationally disadvantaged. They bring diversity and key resilience skills, having already overcome many obstacles on their journey to Ireland.

7   The Access to Education topic is complex. Some expert readers will undoubtedly take umbrage that particular questions have received a light touch while others are ignored completely. Trying to find a balance between comprehensiveness and readability has been a central challenge.

8   The 1998 World Conference on Higher Education, run by UNESCO, reaffirmed Article 26 (1) of the Universal Declaration of Human Rights: 'Everyone has the right to education and ... higher education shall be equally accessible to all on the basis of merit.'

9   I've had the opportunity to work alongside numerous people in the Access space in the third level sector, a group that are all too well aware of the issues surrounding educational disadvantage. But, these are a small percentage of the overall numbers who work in the sector and a tiny fraction of the overall population.

10 Extract taken from 'An Elegy Written in a Country Churchyard', 1750.

11 It's difficult to discuss a sector (e.g. 'education' or 'community') as if this was a single entity. Similarly, when we highlight any group of professionals e.g. teachers or academics, we have to generalise. In reality these are not homogeneous groups and there are wide degrees of variation. Practices differ, even within individual institutions. It follows that while the points made are directionally correct, they may not be factually correct in every single case.

12 When we speak of ethnic minority groups being *disadvantaged* we have to recognise that this category is not homogeneous. Some of the 'new Irish' groups place an enormous focus on educational achievement.

13 Fees for post-primary education were removed in 1967. However, the term 'free' might be a bit of a misnomer. We investigate the monetary costs of education later in the book.

14 Throughput the text the term *college* is used to refer to a recognised third Level educational institution or university. Where 'community colleges' or other second level institutions of further education are highlighted, these are identified in the text. The DES 2013 report 'School Completers: What Next?', showed that 54 per cent of school leavers progress to HE. When later/mature entrants are added, participation is circa 65 per cent. The most recent national access plan (2015-2019) shows a 52 per cent participation rate in higher education for the 18-20 year old 'school completer' cohort.

15 Clancy, 2015: 30.

16 Clancy 2015: 40. Pat O'Mahony (*The Irish Times*: January 26, 2016) notes that we now have the highest proportion of young people with third level qualifications across the EU.

17 Clancy 2015: 197.

18 In April, 2016 the Minister for Children and Youth Affairs and the Minister for Education and Skills announced a major new higher education programme aimed at providing best practice education and training in the inclusion of children with a disability in pre-school. A consortium led by Mary Immaculate College, Limerick, in partnership with the Froebel Department in Maynooth University and Early Childhood Ireland, were selected to deliver on this commitment.

19 Ireland Country Report for the OECD: Study on Pathways for Disabled Students into Tertiary Education and Employment (National Access Office, 2012). Page 10.

20 Department of Education and Science (website statistics).

21 Some educationalists spoken to expressed a concern that if an extreme 'right wing' government came into power, these *social gains* cited could be rolled backwards. While it's possible, the 'business case' made later in this book would show that policy to be economic suicide.

22 Professor Áine Hyland. In Paul Downes and Ann Louise Gilligan, *Beyond Educational Disadvantage.*

23 The 25 per cent refers to students who complete the Leaving Certificate but get poor results. The lower figure of 10 per cent refers to students who don't complete the Leaving Certificate and are lost to the education system.

24 The 'per capita' model for the funding of the Institutes of Technology was historically different to the Universities. The funding model has changed in recent years with the HEA now being responsible for funding all third level colleges. The funding model for the IOT's is similar but not identical to the universities.

25 Aine O'Keefe makes the important point that the exact same issue applies to access funding in both primary and post-primary schools.

26 The topic of educational disadvantage is not new. In Ireland, a focus on under-represented groups and access to Higher Education can be traced back to the 1971 HEA Act, which identified 'equality of opportunity' in HE as a key function for the Higher Education Authority.

27 It's not a universally held view. One person interviewed decried the 'decline in education standards', citing the Leaving Certificate Applied

as *evidence* of this. He suggested that the letters LCA stood for 'Let's Count Apples'.

28 This poses a communications challenge. To use a driving analogy. Motorways, National Roads and Secondary Roads offer alternative routes to reach the same destination. However, as each new route is developed, choosing the *optimum route* becomes a more complex decision.

29 While there are no absolute middle class versus working class definitions, there are some amusing captures of this on Politics.ie e.g. a middle class person is 'Someone who has fruit in the house when no one is sick'. Another contributor suggested: 'Middle class are just working class people who don't understand socialist terminology'. The generally accepted view of middle class is the broad group of people in contemporary society who fall socio-economically between the working class and the upper class. The common measures of what constitutes middle class vary significantly among cultures. A sizable and healthy middle class can be viewed as a characteristic of a healthy society. The issues around class are explored in some detail in a later chapter.

30 The primary source for much of this data is the brilliantly comprehensive work completed over many years by Patrick Clancy, Emeritus Professor of Sociology in UCD. To use the most up-to-date statistics, I've drawn heavily from his latest book published in 2015.

31 OECD: 2006.

32 Clancy 2015: 62.

33 Kouchy, J.; Bartnusek, A. and Kovarovic, J. *Who Gets A Degree? Access to Tertiary Education in Europe 1950-2009*. Charles University, Prague.

34 Atomism is a philosophical term that captures this tendency to view individuals in isolation from their surroundings. In short, it ignores the cultural and structural factors that impinge on behaviour. An alternative view is that very little happens in isolation and that most events are interconnected. See, for example, Hames, R. (2007) *The Five Literacies of Global Leadership: What Authentic Leaders Know and You Need to Find Out*. John Wiley, Chichester.

35 This encapsulates a common mindset and appears to be the oldest English proverb still in regular use today. It was recorded as early as 1175 in Old English Homilies (*'Hwa is thet mei thet hors wettrien the him self nule drinken'* – 'who can give water to the horse that will not drink of its own accord?').

36 2007: Xiii. Dr. Paul Downes has since suggested that 'socio-economic exclusion' is a better term, but this label retains a *deficit* concept. While it's not easy to find appropriate language here, the broad point

is accepted that we should find language which does not stigmatise this group.

37 Travellers are Ireland's indigenous ethnic community, albeit their official status as an ethnic group is contested. There are an estimated 25,000 Travellers in Ireland, which represents circa 0.5 per cent of the total national population.

38 The anger has gone beyond armchair bickering and spilled over onto the streets. In recent times public protests and 'Days of Action' have increased. There have been objections to 'specific cuts' (e.g. over-70s means tested medical cards) and more general protests which signal people will not just roll over like tabby cats ('we don't accept it just because you say so'). The old trade union mantra 'what we have we hold' is tattooed into the psyche of most workers and there seems to be a growing group of activists from all walks of life believing 'we have to stand up and be counted.' While you could make an argument that all of this is 'good for democracy' – it's hard to see 'access to education' being on any placard in the near future.

39 Orla Christle in the HEA pushed back on this point. Orla acknowledges a policy weakness in the lack of a 'whole of education' response, but made the point that this specific issue is listed in the current National Access Plan (in terms of an overall principle and a specific goal). While it's too early to judge the impact, it is good to see this point being formally noted.

40 Toner, 1996: 4. I've drawn liberally from Bill Toner's paper here (opposite citation). The analysis was so clear, it was easier to *steal* the ideas rather than try to replicate them in a poorer fashion.

41 The notion of *endless debates* might be overstated. Other than a small group of people with specialist interests, no one is even discussing this. Educational disadvantage is the 'greatest story *never* told.'

42 Example: Suppose that a 'College Awareness' programme is developed in a disadvantaged area and 10 pupils from the Leaving Certificate class subsequently go to college. The 'impact measurement' dilemma is to figure what proportion of these would have gone to college anyway, even if the programme had not been run. Perhaps the *positive impact* was really on the teachers who subsequently set higher expectations for the students? In the social science arena, it is difficult to disentangle these types of issues.

43 The concept in sociology where individuals/groups 'learn to become helpless' over time and don't feel they have control over their own life. A sense of powerlessness can sometimes arise from a traumatic event

or persistent failure to succeed. In psychiatry, it is thought to be one of the underlying causes of depression.

44 Downes, P. Maunsell C. and Ivers, J. (2006) 'A Holistic Approach to Early School Leaving and School Retention in Blanchardstown: Current Issues and Future Steps for Services and Schools'. Blanchardstown Area Partnership: Dublin.

45 Ryan, William (1971) *Blaming the Victim.* Pantheon Books, p. 8.

46 The HEA conducted a market survey for college awareness week (www.collegeaware.ie) in 2013 that confirms this broad point.

47 By implication, the parents I've met directly are those who are most interested in the general topic of education. There's a strong likelihood of a 'biased sample' here and the views expressed may not reflect the general views across disadvantaged communities.

48 Charles Douglas Jackson served as Special Assistant to President Dwight D. Eisenhower (1953/1954).

49 Dr. Mary-Liz Trant, formerly head of Access in the Higher Education Authority, is now working in Solas.

50 The *personnel turnover* during each Dáil election is up to 40 per cent. This is a huge churn and it takes time for people to understand the role and to prepare for the 'next election'. The policy-making bit (which happens in between elections) can therefore be quite short. A great insider view of how this system works is provided in Ivan Yates' autobiography *Full On* (2014) which is exceptionally honest.

51 *The Second Curve: Thoughts on Reinventing Society* (2015). Random House Books.

52 A methodology of understanding sub-cultures and their values. Symbols and artifacts are the outward (visible) elements of this; just below the *waterline* are the underpinning values and assumptions.

53 Opposite citation.

54 There are alternative political viewpoints. During the 2012 elections, the 'People Before Profit' posters had 'Clearing out the Establishment' as the rallying call – but these are minority views in terms of the number of votes secured.

55 The *equal participation* argument may be setting the bar height low. It can be argued that the focus shouldn't be on *participation* in education, but *parity* in educational achievement and outcomes. While I understand this point, it makes sense to aim for targets which are achievable in the medium-term.

56 Former Manchester United player who, along with his teammates, died in the Munich Air Disaster.

57 An English translation of a Yiddish proverb: *'Der mentsh trakht un got lakht'.*

58 Up to the mid-1960s, 5 per cent of 18-year olds went to college But, in working class areas the numbers were much lower, less than .5 per cent of semi-skilled and unskilled groups generally (Clancy 2015: 1). This number was lower again in some geographical areas (there's no specific data for Cabra West from that period).

59 In 1979 this was called the College of Industrial Relations and was based in Ranelagh, Dublin 6. Subsequently renamed as the National College of Ireland, it now resides on a modern campus in the IFSC.

60 This examination was called the Intermediate Certificate. The name change occurred in 1992.

61 There's a *hierarchy* of colleges. Colleges have a 'brand image'. Top of the totem pole are the seven universities. The enormous efforts made by Waterford Institute of Technology and Dublin Institute of Technology to achieve university status highlights the perceived importance (and the difficulty) of being allowed into this club. Sitting at the very top is Trinity College, the university in the centre of Dublin city. Trinity boasts '4 centuries of scholarship and a historical campus'. Is there a belief among students or parents that the quality of education is different there? I don't think so. But there is certainly a belief that Trinity attracts the best of the best students (based on the high points required to gain entry), that high-level contacts made there will last a lifetime and that this 'superior' brand is a real asset on a CV.

62 I've changed some details here to 'protect the guilty'.

63 I've also seen the exact opposite – where parents have completely caved in to kids who avoided the discipline of studying. If I was able to write the manual 'How to Handle Difficult Teenagers', the retirement fund would be sorted!

64 Intelligence is no longer understood as a fixed entity that's stable over time, nor is it only defined in narrow logical terms. Fontes, P. and Kellaghan, T. (1983) 'Opinions of the Irish Pubic on Intelligence' *The Irish Journal of Education*, Vol. XVII, No 2. pp. 55-67. The work of Howard Gardner has also been widely disseminated. He codified '8 types' of intelligence – a much wider palette that the single focus on IQ (Intelligence Quotient) that was historically relied upon. See: *Frames of Mind: The Theory of Multiple Intelligences*, 1983.

65 This is a complex and controversial topic. Arguably, in common with a number of other countries, Ireland has adopted a binary system of third level education. This places the universities at the top of the rankings – which are often 'research biased'. The Institutes of Tech-

nology and some other third level providers have a higher focus on *teaching* and somewhat less focus on research. Of course, the actual picture is more complex than this simple explanation.

66 Behaviour Genetics (1994 May) 24(3):207-15. 'Variability and stability in cognitive abilities are largely genetic later in life'. Plomin R, Pedersen NL, Lichtenstein P, McClearn GE.

67 Successive National Skills Strategies suggest otherwise. According to Orla Christle, Ireland will require 50,000 more graduates to meet skills needs to 2030.

68 Building labourer. In conversation with the author. January 2016.

69 To borrow the memorable phrase of Dr. Michael Crow, President, Arizona State College, a person with a lifelong commitment to tackling educational disadvantage.

70 Source: Higher Education Authority figures for 2011-2012.

71 In reality, my job as College President was primarily 'managerial' (Finances and Human Resources) rather than 'educational' (focused on improving the core teaching/learning processes). I got more exposure to the 'Access' question when completing a consulting role for the Higher Education Authority in 2014.

72 The minimum wage as it applied at that time. The numbers have been rounded up/down to make them easier to remember. According to the OECD (2011), third level graduates in Ireland earn on average 64 per cent more than those who have a Leaving Certificate only. Source: Seán Healy, Sara Bourke, Ann Leahy, Eamonn Murphy, Michelle Murphy an Brigid Reynolds (2016) 'Choices for Equity and Sustainability'. *Socio-Economic Review*. Social Justice Ireland. p. 188.

73 The position with Travellers is particularly stark. At the moment 13 per cent complete second level education versus 90 per cent of the general population. We have to ask why so little progress has been made with this group?

74 Lynn, who grew up in Tallaght, became a single mother in her teens. Later she completed her studies at Trinity College Dublin and subsequently became President of the Trinity Students Union. Lynn was a successful candidate for the Senate election in 2016, formally elected on April 28.

Chapter 2

1 Of course, there are 'broader arguments' that a university is a place of learning, artistic endeavor, music, language and so on i.e. everything shouldn't be reduced to economics. The myriad additional benefits of

having a healthy and vibrant third level sector are outside of the scope of this book. These additional support arguments don't in any way detract from the central thesis.

2   This number falls to €34,928 for a similar qualifications in an Institute of Technology. We've used a 4-year (Honours Level) degree in this calculation. For 3-year programmes, the investment costs cited will be 25 per cent lower. Source: Higher Education System Performance: First Report 2014-2016. Higher Education Authority. Dublin. pp 11-19.

3   About 10 years ago, the government issued a long 'Smart Economy' paper (100+ pages) but it was unfocused, more of a 'brainstormed list' of areas that *could* be important in the future. It wasn't a defined strategy in the sense that choices had actually been made.

4   There's no *absolute definition* of the term 'high tech' economy. The general consensus in economics is that societies go through three phases of development – agricultural, manufacturing and services. The skills required at each stage of economic development are different. Ireland has now entered this third phase with a strong requirement for graduates to fill open positions in software development, pharmaceuticals, medical devices and so on.

5   European Commission, 2010. Taken from: Seán Healy, Sara Bourke, Ann Leahy, Eamonn Murphy, Michelle Murphy an Brigid Reynolds (2016) 'Choices for Equity and Sustainability'. *Socio-Economic Review*. Social Justice Ireland. p. 179.

6   The actual numbers are 87 per cent versus 46 per cent. Clancy (2015). op cit, p. 198.

7   This follows a much longer trend in the changing nature of jobs. In 1926, 58 per cent of men in Ireland were employed in agriculture. Today, that figure stands at 9 per cent (Whelan: 1995).

8   Similar arguments were deployed in the USA in the 'pushback' against the 'Common Core' initiative to set baseline standards for teaching Maths and English. Some of the supporters of that initiative were accused of turning America's children into 'Mindless drones for the Corporate Salt Mines' ('Business Gets Schooled'. *Fortune*: January 2016: 27).

9   During the recession, there was an increase in unemployment from 6.4 per cent in 2008 to 14.7 per cent in 2012. Ireland now spends 16.4 per cent of GDP on social protection. This highlights (again) the need for joined-up thinking. It's not just the € level of dole payments, but the entire funding structure which includes medical cards, rent supplements and so on – often making it difficult for people to see the

benefit of taking on low-paid work and thus becoming 'trapped' in the poverty net.

10 The compacting trucks in use today were an innovation from the 1970's onwards.

11 Negotiations Specialist with Dublin City Council. February 2016.

12 Delma Byrne and Emer Smyth (2010) *No Way Back? The Dynamics of Early School Leaving*. ESRI. The Liffey Press: Dublin.

13 Community Leader, Inner City Dublin. January 2016.

14 In reality, even where there is full employment, there will always be a cohort of people who remain out of work for a variety of reasons. Some choose this as a lifestyle – taking government subsidies and working in the black economy where they don't pay tax. There are some people with physical and/or mental health problems which effectively disbar them from employment. There's also a tiny element of criminality – where unemployment is consciously chosen. None of these groups are the target audience for this book.

15 *The Competitive Advantage: Creating and Sustaining Superior Performance*. NY: Free Press, 1985.

16 Patrick Clancy (2015) op. cit, p. 194.

17 Michelle Share and Carmel Carroll (2013) 'Ripples of Hope: The family and community impact of Trinity College Dublin'. Children's Research Centre Trinity College Dublin. p. 10.

18 Statistic from the OECD PIACC (Programme for the International Assessment of Adult Competencies) study conclusively demonstrated that children whose parents have low levels of education, have significant lower proficiency than those whose parents have higher education. In short, the cycle of disadvantage becomes inter-generational.

19 In the interest of avoiding misunderstanding, 'college' includes both further and higher education. Each year, tens of thousands complete further education and training, apprenticeships, PLC or VTOS courses and a variety of traineeships. The National Framework of Qualifications (which we will review later) recognises the value of qualifications at a range of levels, not just those provided within the higher education system.

20 *Education at a Glance: OECD Indicators* (1996) Paris, OECD. Page 9.

Chapter 3

1 The significant provision in community and adult education falls under the 'further education' umbrella.

2 Clancy 2015: 222.

3 GDP may actually be a poor measure of national income as it reflects the outputs from multinationals e.g. it includes transfer pricing which, it can be argued, inflates Irish profits to reduce tax bills because of the relatively benign corporation tax regime in Ireland.

4 Cormac Lucey: Economic Outlook. *The Sunday Times*, 14 February 2015.

5 Because this is already in place, we take the standard curriculum idea for granted. In some countries, the idea of a standard curriculum is hugely controversial e.g. the debate in the USA around 'Common Core' which aims to have a standard blueprint for the teaching of Maths and English to improve the USA's poor (relative) educational performance when matched against other developed countries.

6 STEM subjects (science, technology, engineering and mathematics).

7 Address by Liz O'Donnell TD, then Minister of State with special responsibility for Overseas Development Assistance and Human Rights. ASTI Education Conference (Education for all at Second Level), 2001.

8 It's changed now and NCI accept Foundation Maths for several courses, as do some other colleges.

9 The school leaving age was raised to 15 years in 1972 and increased to 16 in 2000. While it's possible to do home schooling, very few parents choose this option and there's little practical support. Even those who select this route, often move their children back into the system at second level to be part of the exam cycle.

10 The area of Special Needs is governed by the Education for Persons with Special Needs Act 2004. Schooling for these children is addressed in a couple of ways: a. Ordinary Classes: The child attends ordinary classes in mainstream Schools. Special Schools: There are some 'special schools' e.g. St. Patrick's school in Drumcondra runs a programme for children with speech and language disabilities. Children attend for up to two years and then return to the mainstream. c. Learning Support: Learning Support Teachers and Special Needs Assistants (SNAs) are in place (within mainstream schools) to support the teachers. Each child who is identified with special needs should have a Personal Education Plan (to the best of my knowledge, this particular idea has not been implemented).

11 Delma Byrne and Emer Smyth (2010) *No Way Back: The Dynamics of Early School Leaving*. ERSI, Liffey Press: Dublin

12 The introduction of free education in 1967 led to huge increases in participation in post-primary education. In 1965 there were 134,090 students in full-time post-primary education. That number tops

360,000 today, an increase that can't be accounted for by population growth alone (Keane 2013: 7).

13 My understanding is that this applies to all children with the exception of children who have special needs where extra supports may be required: 'Instead of the Government helping people like us, I feel we're being punished. I have a child with a disability and I'm to pay more than a person with a child that doesn't have a disability' Niamh (parent) quoted in Mag Coogan 'Children: Some more equal than others'. In Brian Mooney (Ed). *Education Matters*. 2015. Opposite citation.

14 There are several challenges posed by this system. Many facilities have closed. Aine O'Keefe suggested that the governance issues to be managed by local volunteers are often unreasonable. This is outside of the scope of this book and I didn't spend any time drilling into how this currently works.

15 In addition to the publicly offered places, there are countless 'informal' childcare arrangements, often a mother minding children in her home. Data on the exact numbers of informal arrangements is not available as they operate in the black economy.

16 The general rule in organisation development is as follows: You 'fix' something centrally then decentralise it. Starting with a decentralisation strategy is a recipe for confusion and poor quality.

17 Fergus is a strong and brave advocate for children's rights over many years. The statement, made at a Teachers Union Conference, caused some controversy at the time.

18 Síolta (translates as 'seeds') is the National Quality Framework for Early Childhood Education. Developed by the Centre for Early Childhood Development and Education (St Patrick's College) on behalf of the DES, the Framework was published in 2006, following a 3-year developmental process, which involved extensive consultation (childcare workers, teachers, parents, policy makers etc.). Síolta is designed to define, assess and improve quality across all aspects of early childhood care and education (from birth to six years old). The National Council for Curriculum and Assessment (NCCA) also developed Aistear (Early Childhood Curriculum Framework) in partnership with the early childhood sector. As with Síolta, a number of groups worked together to agree best-practice standards in early childhood settings, based on informed research.

19 The picture is changing. There's an intent to publish Early Years (Pre-School) regulations which will set out the qualifications required for people working in the sector along with the curriculum to be followed. On 15 October 2015, a new association was launched: PLE

(Pedagogy, Learning, Education). Overall, there is some hope that this sector will be professionalised albeit the current situation is quite fluid.

20 On the National Framework of Qualifications. We will explore this idea later.

21 Assistant General Secretary, Department of Children and Youth Affairs. Launch of Preparing for Life Results. Mansion House, Dublin. 17 May 2016.

22 This is an improvement on the historical system where very little time was invested in second-level teacher formation. Students with a degree in a particular subject could become a 'teacher' in that subject by completing a Higher Diploma, a post-graduate programme of study which lasted one academic year.

23 A private provider, Hibernia College, offers on line teaching programmes on a fee-paying basis. Getting into teaching may be a little easier now than it was historically, albeit access students won't be able to take up this route unless they can pay high fees.

24 For a good discussion on this, see Rosenthal, R. and Jacobson, L. (1992). *Pygmalion in the Classroom*, Expanded edition. New York: Irvington.

25 Emer Smyth, Merike Darmody, Frances McGinnity and Delma Byrne (2009) 'Adapting to Diversity: Irish Schools and Newcomer Students'. Economic and Social Research Institute.

26 While some of these children may since have left the education system (moving out of Ireland with their families following the collapse of the 'Celtic Tiger' economy), many schools remain multicultural. Source: Intercultural Education Strategy 2010/2015: DES and the Office of the Minister for Integration (2010).

27 Delma Byrne and Emer Smyth (2010) *No Way Back: The Dynamics of Early School Leaving*. The Liffey Press/Economic and Social Research Institute. Dublin.

28 Students in the Gaelscoileanna acquire the Irish language through language immersion, and study the standard curriculum through it. Unlike English-medium schools, Gaelscoileanna have the reputation of producing competent Irish speakers.

29 For a good example of this, see *The Sunday Times* annual School League Tables. League tables are a sensitive issue for schools. There are huge reservations about using a single criterion (the number of children who go on to college) which doesn't reflect the extraordinary efforts made in some schools to get disadvantaged students 'over the exam line'. Progression rates to college from individual schools are of-

ten sought by parents as a selection device for deciding on a particular school for their child.

30 See 'Who Went to College in 2004?' (HEA, 2006).

31 Comments on this have come from one interesting source e.g. Archbishop Diarmuid Martin has spoken on this topic several times.

32 Vocational Education Act 1930. This legislation built on the earlier work completed by the Report of the Commission of Technical Education which concluded in 1927. What's interesting here is the allocation of responsibility for education to different parts of the political establishment, an ownership confusion which persists to this day. This led to the establishment of VEC committees, part of an 'umbrella of services' offered by local authorities, a structure which also remains in place, albeit the VECs have morphed into Education and Training Boards.

33 This predated the establishment of AnCo in the 1960s (AnCo later became Fás, which has since morphed into Solas). AnCo took over the responsibility for apprenticeship training which was removed from the secondary school system and conducted in specialist education centres.

34 For a brilliant discussion of one period in this history see: 'The Decade of Upheaval: Irish Trade Unions in the 1960s' by Charles McCarthy. Institute of Public Administration.

35 Even to this day, a huge percentage of executives in banking started life working in branches. Many completed their 'managerial education' later, attending college at night. The Leaving Certificate was the passport into banking.

36 European Economic Community (EEC) at that time.

37 Community Schools essentially offer the same educational model - albeit there are some differences in the 'Establishment Deeds' i.e. how these are legally framed.

38 See Gaelport.com. A variety of *Irish Times* articles have also touched on this subject.

39 Mea culpa! I've mislaid this reference. The comment was made in one of the main daily newspapers either the *Independent* or the *Irish Times*.

40 The ASTI represents 18,000 second-level teachers. The TUI has circa 15,000 members.

41 Programme was jointly developed by NCCA, the National Access Office, and a group of HE access officers and post-primary career guidance counsellors.

42 A new scoring system is being introduced but this does not fundamentally alter the arguments made.

43 Clancy, P. 2015: 87.

44 There's an irony here that might be funny, if it wasn't so serious. Students still 'hand write' all of their examinations, even those taking degrees in computing.

45 Since then, my kids have stupidly decided to live their own lives, rather than the great life that we had planned for them. There's another book in that story...

46 With some notable exceptions. For example, Clive Byrne and Professor Brian MacCraith have been outspoken on the deficits of the present system. Ruairí Quinn set in train changes which are resulting in a new points system to lessen the pressure, a review of the predictability of the Leaving Certificate questions and a halt to the escalation in the number of CAO options.

Chapter 4

1 There is an argument to change the designation to Educational Equality Schools, a pushback against the word 'disadvantage' because of the negative connotations of this term.

2 Address by Mary Hanafin T.D. Minister for Education and Science at ASTI Annual Congress 1(8 April, 2006) 'Ensuring a Supportive Climate for Teaching and Learning in All Our Schools.'

3 There are three categories of disadvantage at primary level: urban band 1 schools which receive 'most' support (199 schools): urban band 2 schools (141 schools) and rural schools (333 rural DEIS schools).

4 In 2008, there were 333 rural DEIS and 203 urban DEIS post-primary schools. There have been, and continue to be, differences in the socio-demographic intake of different types of schools. Generally, vocational and community schools have higher proportions of students from lower socio-economic groups when compared with secondary schools.

5 Emer Smyth and Selina McCoy (2011). 'Improving Second Level Education: Using Evidence for Policy Development'. Renewal Series Paper 5. Economic and Social Research Institute. Dublin.

6 Data is the most recent available e.g. 2013/2014

7 Department of Education and Science (2005) 'Guidelines for Second Level Schools on the implications of Section 9 (c) of the Education Act (1998), relating to students' access to appropriate guidance.' The Stationary Office: Dublin. p. 4.

8   Dr Paul Downes mentioned Latvia and Estonia, two international examples that he's familiar with.

9   The two key features of the DEIS system are (a) a reduced Teacher: Pupil ratio in classrooms and (b) providing increased financial assistance to the schools. These were the main 'policy foundations' in both the Breaking the Cycle (1996) and in the more recent Giving Children an Even Break (2001) policy documents. The increased financial support is to provide a range of educational supports as follows: Support Teachers Project: This targets individuals with behavioral difficulties (disruptive, withdrawn, disturbed etc.). Focus is working on their strengths. Disadvantaged Area Scheme: Increased capital grants/finance for equipment. Literacy/Numeracy Schemes: First Steps; Reading Recovery; Maths Recovery.

10 For example, Susan Weir and Sylvia Denner (2012) 'The Evaluation of the School Support Programme Under DEIS: Changes in Pupil Achievement in Urban Primary Schools between 2007 and 2013'. St Patrick's College: Dublin.

11 Susan Weir, Laura McAvinue, Eva Moran, and Adrian O'Flaherty (2014) 'A Report On The Evaluation of DEIS at Second Level'. Educational Research Centre, St Patrick's College. Dublin.

12 In conversation with John Lonergan, former Governor at Mountjoy Prison. March 2009.

13 Coyne, C and Donohoe, J. (2013) *Youth and Youth Work in Ireland.* Gill and Macmillan, Dublin.

14 It's hard to keep up with all of the structural changes. This is now called the Education and Welfare Service and is run by Tusla under the umbrella of the Department of Children and Youth Affairs.

15 Devine, Dympna, Fahie Declan and McGillicuddy, Deirdre (2011) 'What is "good" teaching? Teacher beliefs and practices about their teaching'. *Irish Educational Studies*, 32:1, 83-108, DOI.

16 In 2015, 37 per cent of Leaving Certificate students achieved less than 300 points. Majella Dempsey: 'Gearing up for Skills Development' – A Challenge to Junior Cycle Reform' in Brian Mooney (Ed) *Education Matters*. 2015-2016 Yearbook: Dublin.

17 Byrne and Smyth (2010). Opposite citation.

18 National Economic and Social Forum, 2002.

19 Hourigan, N. and Campbell, M. (2010). The TEACH report: 'Traveller Education and Adults: Crisis, Challenge and Change'. National Association of Travellers' Centres (NATC).

20 A similar argument is often made about the 'Leadership dynamic' in the third level sector where academics 'take turns' as Department Head but don't want to *rock the boat* as they will return to the fold.

21 Dympna Mulkerrins (2007) 'The Transformational Potential of the Home School Community Liaison Scheme'. In Paul Downes and Ann Louise Gilligan (Eds.). *Beyond Educational Disadvantage* (2007) Institute of Public Administration: Dublin.

22 For a useful discussion on causality, see the ESRI report https://www.esri.ie/publications/review-of-the-school-completion-programme.

23 The net effect of this structure is that volunteers can become embroiled in complex tasks like HR and Finance – which should be managed centrally – leaving the local groups to focus on services development.

24 The move from the Department of Education and Science took place in 2010.

25 Fine, M (1990) *Framing Dropouts: Notes on the Politics of Urban High School.* Albany, NY: State University of New York Press.

26 Shakespeare: *Henry IV.*

27 According to Dr. Josephine Bleach, through Forbairt and Misneach leadership support for principals and vice principals has been underway for some years. For example, a Centre for School Leadership was established in April 2015 for an initial three-year period with an outlay of €3 million. With the goal to become a 'hub of excellence for school leaders' this is certainly a positive development.

28 Tom Costello who worked with Atlantic Philanthropies made an interesting point on this. He said: 'We are often obsessed with the inputs, sometimes the outputs, but seldom the outcomes.' In some organisations the process becomes elevated and more important than the product. Some people would be happy if you developed concrete lifejackets, provided that they were all made the same way!

29 In relation to money, Maria O'Neill, a hugely committed former primary school teacher, made the following observation: 'I had a budget of €100 per year to spend. With 28 kids in the class, that was about enough money to buy each of them a lollipop from time to time.'

30 According to Dr Paul Downes in St. Patrick's, circa 5 per cent of children are suspended each year from secondary school i.e. about 15,000 students.

31 The statistics highlight that a disproportionate number of Traveller children are impacted by this.

32 Smyth, Emer and McCoy, Selina (2011) 'Improving Second-Level Education: Using Evidence for Policy Development'. Economic and Social Research Institute: Dublin.

33 Elaine Keane (2011), 'Dependence-Deconstruction: Widening Participation and Traditional-Entry Students Transitioning from School to Higher Education in Ireland'. *Teaching in Higher Education*, 16 (6):707-718.

34 For a wonderful demonstration of this see Ken Robinson's TED talk http://www.ted.com/talks/ken_robinson_how_to_escape_education_s_death_valley.

35 This student's original name had been changed to protect his identity. His comment is so smart, he has a potentially bright future as a copy writer in advertising.

36 Elaine Keane (2011). Opposite citation.

37 Primary schools in Ireland are open for circa 179 days and secondary schools are open for 167 days. Missing 20 days therefore represents a large per cent of the available time. Figures on school attendance are prepared by the National Education Welfare Board. Absenteeism rates during the 2010/2011 school year revealed that almost 110,000 children miss over a month of school every year. More than 31,000 primary pupils and more than 24,600 second-level students are missing from school every day. As a proportion of all days lost in the school year, this is 6.1 per cent at primary and 7.8 per cent at second level. Rates have been falling slightly for the past number of years. There are strong differences in absenteeism between different types of schools.

38 When a SAN is issued, the educational welfare officer begins a formal monitoring process of the child's situation. During this time the parent/guardian is provided with the opportunity to address the underlying issues in liaison with the officer and the school. If there's no progress and the child remains out of school, the board will consider taking a prosecution to the District Court as a 'last resort'.

39 The courses take place in Youthreach Centres managed by Education and Training Boards (ETBs) and SOLAS Community Training Centres. Youthreach centres are open for 35 hours per week (Monday to Friday).

40 For trainees over 18 years old, this payment can increase to €160 per week or their current 'Social Welfare Payment' if this is higher.

41 The proportion of early school leavers (Junior Certificate Education) in 2013 was 6.9 per cent. In disadvantaged schools, this rate can rise as high as 18 per cent. Source: Seán Healy, Sara Bourke, Ann Leahy, Eamonn Murphy, Michelle Murphy an Brigid Reynolds (2016)

'Choices for Equity and Sustainability'. *Socio-Economic Review*. Social Justice Ireland. p. 184.

42 There may not be universal agreement on this point. One commentator made the point that 'teachers' in Youthreach have come from the general teaching pool and are not specially trained to deal with this cohort of learners (and, inadvertently, follow the standard, mainstream curriculum). In contrast, John Walshe argued that Youthreach projects he visited were all very different and didn't mirror mainstream curricula.

43 There are additional initiatives e.g. 'Back to Education' which targets young people and adults who are unemployed (holders of medical cards or dependents of people who hold medical cards). There are also a couple of 'more innovative' programmes in place where children are given the opportunity to work with horses, learn how to fix cars and so on.

44 An educational initiative in Dublin 5 and Dublin 17.

Chapter 5

1 Late intervention is expensive and often ineffective as health, social and behavioural problems become deeply entrenched. Delayed intervention increases the cost of providing a remedy and reduces the likelihood of actually achieving one. Lessons 'not learnt' in the formative period, become harder and harder to learn later in life.

2 Paul Downes and Ann Louise Gilligan (2007) *Beyond Educational Disadvantage*. Op. Cit., p. 478.

3 Students don't have to make all 20 selections but are usually encouraged to fill in as many choices as possible. It's like backing '20 horses' in the same race (one of them is bound to come home).

4 We've seen throughout that the available *choices* are both a *good thing* (there's a wide range of options) and a *bad thing* (the sheer range of choices can leave some students confused). The further development of information resources such as www.QualifaX.ie would go a long way towards this.

5 Some countries, like Ireland, base the entry criteria on performance at end-of-study exams (either audited nationally or 'school-based'). In other countries, standardised scholastic aptitude tests (SATs) are used in addition to the school assessments. In some jurisdictions, interviews, letters of recommendation and personal statements ('why I want to study this topic') are used as part of the entry criteria. The Netherlands use a lottery to allocate scarce college places while Germany places a priority weighting on candidates who've served a 'wait-

ing period' for their chosen programmes. There's no one-best-way to do this.

6   The Central Applications Office (CAO) was established in 1976. This nationally administered system manages the application process for all undergraduate programmes. Immigrant students have to fulfill criteria around residency and citizenship status to be eligible for the 'Free Fees' initiative.

7   Clancy 2015: 88.

8   Regardless of whether these are regulated by Quality and Qualifications Ireland (QQI) or where individual colleges are the awarding institution. QQI is a state agency established by the Quality Assurance and Qualifications (Education and Training) Act 2012. The functions include those previously carried out by the Further Education and Training Awards Council (FETAC); the Higher Education and Training Awards Council (HETAC); the Irish Universities Quality Board (IUQB) and the National Qualifications Authority of Ireland (NQAI). In the area of qualifications, QQI are responsible for maintaining the ten-level NFQ (National Framework of Qualifications), set standards for awards and validate education and training programmes. The universities and institutes of technology largely make their own awards.

9   There's another factor at play here which explains the high points required. In the past 20 years the number of college courses has tripled. But, 85 per cent of the 'choices' admit fewer than 25 students. So the points required for these course is often very high – artificially so, based on the small student numbers accepted into individual programmes. This inflates the points required for individual courses and creates the impression that high points are required 'across the board'. Once they get in those same students may find themselves sitting side by side in shared classes with students from other courses (who have scored lower points) in a large lecture theatre. For a good discussion on this, see Professor Philip Nolan, President, Maynooth University, 'Transitions Reform and the Points Race: What, Why and Where Next?" In Brian Mooney (Ed) (2015) *Education Matters*. Opposite citation.

10 While the seven universities and Dublin Institute of Technology accredit their own awards, these are linked to the NFQ levels. This is also intended to map onto the European Qualification Framework allowing greater educational mobility across the EU. Both FETAC and HETAC were dissolved and their functions passed to Quality and Qualifications Ireland (QQI) in November 2012 on the basis that a single awards and standards body would be more coherent.

11 The educational and training targets for 2012, as set out by the Expert Group on Future Skills Needs (EGFSN), were that 48 per cent of the labour force would be qualified at levels 6-10 on the NFQ, with 45 per cent holding levels of 4 and 5, and 7 per cent of the workforce would be educated at levels 1 to 3.

12 We see this in discussions about the 'Ivy League' universities in the USA, the UK, France etc. The universities generally argue that they *earn this* through a system of international audits that compares them against international peers.

13 In courses that require 'higher points' HEAR students can get a larger discount.

14 Bursaries (essentially the same thing as scholarships, just smaller € amounts) are also available. College Foundations, the fund-raising arm of third level colleges, often collect money in smaller amounts and aggregate this to support students.

15 Published by AHEAD (2009). Dublin.

16 Defined as people 23 years (or older) on January 1st of their year of entry into higher education. It has been national access policy since 2005 to target mature students who have not previously benefited from higher education and who enter college to complete a full-time course. A target of 20 per cent was set for achievement in 2013 for this group. This target has not been achieved and the figures available for 2013 show that progress, while evident for some years, has now fallen back to 2006 levels.

17 'Realising Opportunities: A Vision for Further Education and Training' (2014) National Association of Principals and Deputy Principals. Dublin, p. 32.

18 During the 1970/1980s there was also an element of streaming of men and women. At that time, a lot of women completed secretarial courses in specialised secretarial schools but both men and women now typically study together (the number of secretarial positions massively declined as executives learned to type and manage their own diaries).

19 FETAC = Further Education and Training Awards Council, the awarding body for certification of programmes between level 1 and level 6 of the National Qualification Framework. Set up mid-2001, it 'regularised' the standards awarded by a host of independent bodies e.g. the National Council for Educational Awards and FAS. Programmes between level 6 and level 10 (sub-Degree, Degree and post-graduate awards) were made by HETAC i.e. Higher Education and Training

Awards Council. Both of these bodies have now been amalgamated into QQI.

20 In 2012-2013, the number of 'funded places' on PLC programmes was 32,688 while the actual number of students was 35,524. So, approximately 8 per cent of students were taken in 'over the cap' as unfunded learners to meet learner demand.

21 There are also some 'fee paying' (self-financed students) who elect to do courses during the day or at night. These are often *elective* programmes e.g. learning a language or to play a musical instrument.

22 Some programmes (Justice Workshops) are funded by Department of Justice, Equality and Law Reform. Here again we see 'confusion' in provision, with an overlap of responsibilities assigned to more than a single government department.

23 Certification is available at a range of levels, including Junior Certificate and Leaving Certificate, and Foundation, Level 1 and Level 2 certificates of the National Council for Vocational Awards (NCVA). There are no course fees.

24 HEA (2011) 'Evaluation of Springboard: First Stage Report'. Higher Education Authority, Dublin.

25 HEA (2013) 'Springboard: Second-Stage Report'. Higher Education Authority, Dublin.

26 'Realising Opportunities: A Vision for Further Education and Training' (2014) National Association of Principals and Deputy Principals. Dublin.

27 'Realising Opportunities: A Vision for Further Education and Training' (2014). Opposite citation p. 31.

28 This is currently in a state of flux. A new system of local Education and Training Boards has integrated the former VECs with significant former elements of FAS.

29 Probably derived from 'An institution is the lengthened shadow of one person', Ralph Waldo Emerson. *Self-Reliance*. 1841.

30 The methodology of measuring participation has changed over time which makes an 'apples versus apples' comparison quite difficult. As a broad comparison, Orla Christle in the HEA cited the following numbers: Dublin 17 (Darndale): 1998 = 8 per cent; 2011 = 15 per cent; Dublin 10 (Ballyfermot): 1998 = 7 per cent; 2011 = 16 per cent; Dublin 7 (Cabra): 1998 = 20 per cent; 2011 = 41 per cent; Dublin 11 (Finglas): 1998 = 14 per cent; 2011 = 28 per cent; Dublin 24 (Tallaght): 1998 = 26 per cent; 2011 = 29 per cent.

31 Denny, K. 'What Did Abolishing University Fees in Ireland Do?' UCD Geary Institute. Discussion Paper Series, 20 May 2010.

32 For a good discussion on the abuses of the covenant scheme which was supposed to help families get tax relief for paying for their children's tuition fees, see 'A New Partnership in Education', John Walshe IPA (1999) p. 127.

33 Clancy, Patrick (2015:135).

34 While the National Office of Equity of Access to Higher Education currently coordinates work in this area, efforts to improve access predates the establishment of this office in 2003. In reality, significant work at institutional and community levels has been underway since the 1990s.

35 'Towards the Best Education for All: An Evaluation of Higher Education Access Programmes' (2006). HEA, Dublin.

36 Access to Higher Education 2008-2013: HEA, 2008.

37 http://www.irishtimes.com/news/behaviour-problems-embedded-in-dublin-school-1.1275177.

38 Over €21 million was awarded to support access projects directly through the Strategic Innovation Fund (SIF) Cycles I and II. However, investment in many projects focused on general learning/teaching practices along with student support. In total, 22 projects focused on access or lifelong learning, were funded by SIF (HEA, 2010). This particular funding stream has now been discontinued.

39 Interestingly, the third level colleges don't 'fish in the same pool'; named DEIS schools are aligned with particular colleges which makes sense.

40 All colleges get students who've had access support from elsewhere so this evens out.

41 This integrated approach is a feature of many of the best-run access programmes. I've some familiarity with the models run in Dublin City University and the Dublin Institute of Technology which are equally impressive.

42 The grading systems vary depending on the institution. The passing grade is normally 40 per cent of the maximum mark for a course (third class honour). A second class honour is given at 50-59 per cent (2.2); an upper second class honour (2.1) is provided for a score in the range of 60-69 per cent. A first class honour is given when the score is above 70 per cent.

43 Several people working in the Access area highlighted the strongly positive impact of a defined 'buddy system' i.e. new students having a friend on campus to 'show them around' and someone to confide in.

44 If you stopped 50 people in the street and asked, 'What's the "correct age" at which career guidance should be taught?', my guess is that most people would say about 16. According to Dr Josephine Bleach in NCI, the research evidence suggests that this should be taught in 'third class' i.e. with kids as young as 9.

45 The numbers differ slightly depending on the information source. According to Dr. Niamh Moore-Cherry, every year in Ireland 7,000 students (1-in-6 of the intake) fail to progress to second year in college. 'Why Students Leave: Student Non-Completion in Higher Education in Ireland'. In Brian Mooney (Ed.) *Education Matters* (2015) Opposite Citation.

46 Learning outcomes, continuous vs. terminal assessment, the use of Virtual Learning Environments such as Blackboard and Moodle and so on. The Learning and Teaching centres play a key role in providing support to academics to develop their pedagogical and student support practice.

47 Most students complete their course of study on time with about 15 per cent graduating *late* through postponements. Clancy 2015: 99.

48 There is, perhaps, another factor at play for a small number of students. When working in NCI I met some students who had chosen another college as their first choice but had to accept a place in NCI when they didn't secure enough points for university. So, they came reluctantly, sometimes resentfully. Lacking motivation or being annoyed that they were *denied* their first preference, they underperformed (had to repeat) or dropped out altogether, compounding their initial underperformance in the Leaving Certificate. Aware of this possibility, I specifically included this in the 'commencement' lecture given to all new students but it's impossible to know if this had any impact.

49 There's one financial stumbling block that's often not understood. When a student is faced with a repeat they often believe that the cost is going to be €3,000 i.e. the same as the registration cost. But, such students are faced with the 'fully loaded' cost of the course which can range between €6,000 and €12,000. This *unexpected* financial hurdle causes students to drop out (the solution is to add this amount onto the end of the student loan – see later recommendations).

50 Murphy J, Bowe, C, Keogh. C, McLoughlin, C, Lynch, G, Bent, M., and O'Connor, D. (2013) 'An Exploration of the Impact of Widening

participation Initiatives for Leaving Certificate Students Entering Full Time Undergraduate (Level 8) Programmes in 2007 in Five Irish Universities' in How Equal? Access to Higher Education in Ireland: Research Papers. Higher Education Authority: Dublin.

51 Quinn, J. (2103) 'Drop-out and Completion in Higher Education in Europe'. European Commission DG Education and Culture. Brussels

52 Keane, Elaine (2011) 'Distancing to self-protect: The perpetuation of inequality in higher education through socio-relational dis-engagement'. *British Journal of Sociology of Education*, 32 (3) pp 449-466.

53 Even with the increasing numbers of access students, colleges like UCD are predominantly populated with 'south side students', many from fee-paying schools. According to Dr Kevin O'Higgins SJ, there's a continuing problem of class/cultural bias in the Irish system at third level. This influences both the content of what is taught and the manner in which it is delivered. He argues that 'working class students are obliged to assimilate and become middle class'.

54 Clancy 2015: 120.

55 While it's difficult to generalise on this, bias is alive and well in some quarters. I worked with one large law firm where several of the partners were fixated on sourcing what they termed 'crème de la crème' students, the highest performing students from the *best* universities, essentially recruiting 'mini-me's – people from the exact same background as themselves. Of course, what they couldn't determine is whether this narrow group of recruits actually perform better or worse than a more diverse group, but there was no appetite to discover this. In the UK, just 7 per cent of children attend fee-paying schools, but they make up 40 per cent of the trainees in law firms and a whopping 70 per cent of the trainees in the most successful accounting firms. 'Want to Go to Oxford? Is your Name Eleanor? (CIPD, March 2016: 27).

56 Studenfinance.ie has attracted almost 4 million hits since it was launched in January 2008.

57 For many years administrative inefficiencies in the arrangement of student grants were highlighted. The call was for the grants system to be streamlined and delivered by a single agency like the CAO. The Student Support Act (2011) led to the establishment of a single, unified and efficient grant application process. SUSI, the online grant application portal, was set up and all grant applications are now made online.

58 The reckonable income thresholds were €59,595 and €50,325 respectively.

59 As would be expected, the percentage of students in the Institutes of Technology sector receiving maintenance grants is higher than in the universities, reflecting the 'higher Leaving Certificate points' required by universities and the direct relationship between 'high points/high income' shown earlier.

60 National Access Office, 2012: 8. The full maintenance grant since 2013 is €3,025 per annum for students who live more than 45 kilometers from the college attended and €1,215 for those who live *adjacent* i.e. closer than this. Maintenance grants are widely regarded as inadequate.

61 Details are available at http://www.studentfinance.ie/mp9490/other-finance/index.html.

62 Grants are not given to students who study in fee-paying colleges e.g. Griffith College. In what he termed a 'schizophrenic approach' Dr Diarmuid Hegarty, Griffith College President, questioned the government's logic to this single approach in education, only funding 'free fees' students when they are happy to encourage a two-tier system (public and private) in several other areas e.g. health. The same point applies to students with disabilities who do not receive support if they decide to attend a private (fee-paying) college. Presumably, the counter-argument is that if you can afford to pay for college, you don't need a maintenance grant.

63 Peter McGuire. 'A Plan to haul apprenticeships into the 21st Century'. *The Irish Times*, 26 January 2016.

64 It's a small point in the overall scheme of things, but I'm not sure that calling these new programmes 'Apprenticeships' was a good call. The word is indelibly linked with the traditional form of apprenticeships described elsewhere. Using the same name (to describe something different) is likely to cause confusion.

65 Dr. Mary-Liz Trant and Ray Kelly. 'Ireland Embarks on Major Expansion of Apprenticeship route to education, training and careers'. In Brian Mooney (2015) *Education Matters*. Opposite citation.

66 Solas is the Gaelic word for light. This organisation replaced FAS. A rebranding of FAS was required to overcome the negative PR which followed internal 'Corporate Governance' scandals.

67 2010 HEA Mid-Term Review.

68 Clear Definitions: There's agreement on the point that access can usefully be segmented into five 'categories' e.g. socio/economic disadvantaged students, disabled students, mature students, Travelers and ethnic minorities. However, there's no agreement on how these

groups are *defined* other than in this headline way e.g. what is a migrant and how do we define disability?

69 Many companies operate talent management systems. However, this mostly applies to high potential staff, who are often *outside* the educational disadvantaged categories which we are focusing on.

Chapter 6

1 Wyness M,G. (1996) 'Keeping Tabs on an Uncivil Society: Positive Parental Control' *Sociology*. Vol. 28. No. 1, February, p. 55.

2 'Working class' is actually a poor umbrella term for 3 distinct groups that can be further subdivided. There are the *working class* as traditionally defined e.g. people who occupy low-skills jobs that don't require a professional education. Then there's a *welfare class*, people who don't work and are wholly reliant on state benefits. There is also a smaller *criminal class* who actively choose this as an alternative lifestyle.

3 Should the state intervene in people's lives? The state already intervenes at the moment in two specific areas. With newborn babies, the district nurse comes around and 'checks' to see if new mothers are coping well, offering practical advice on the myriad of issues surrounding a new birth. This contact is normally welcomed and is *light* in terms of the actual time spent with families and the number of visits. The second is where social workers intervene in families, often at the suggestion of someone *outside* the family (the school, police, neighbours) and so on. The contact is normally un-welcome, with a strong perception of middle class social workers coming into an area, doing their job and leaving as quickly as possible.

4 Laura Hanlon (2005) *Early Assessment and Intervention in Educational Disadvantage*. Centre for Social and Educational Research. Dublin Institute of Technology.

5 Department of Education and Science (2006) 'Recommendations for a Traveller Education Strategy 2006-2010'. Joint Working Group on Traveller Education, Dublin. p. 22.

6 Not all middle class kids take this route. Family therapists encounter a phenomenon where some kids *don't compete* with high achieving parents and almost become 'drop-outs'. However, this is the exception, rather than the norm and can sometimes overlap with psychiatric problems experienced by the individual.

7 'Everybody Knows' is a song written by Canadian singer-songwriter Leonard Cohen. Released on the album *I'm Your Man*, February 1988.

8   Sean, a midwife in the Rotunda Maternity Hospital, was one of the people met during the research phase.

9   'The Dilemma of Difference'. In Paul Downes and Ann Louise Gilligan (Eds.). Opposite citation.

10 According to Barnardos, the most recent child poverty figures show the number of children living in consistent poverty jumped by 23,000 (an additional 2 per cent) between 2012 and 2013. Source: Rise Up for Children Report. 2016.

11 See, for example, Kelleghan, T. et al. (1995) 'Educational Disadvantage in Ireland'. Department of Education; Dublin. Nolan, B., Smyth, E. (1999), 'Educational Inequalities among School Leavers in Ireland, 1979-1994'. *Economic and Social Review* Vol. 30, July: 267-284; Smyth, E. and Hannon, D. (2000), 'Education and Inequality' in Nolan, B., O'Connell, P. and Whelan, C., *Bust or Boom*, IPA: Dublin.

12 For a good discussion on this see combatpoverty.ie.

13 Thomas Kellaghan, Susan Weir, Seamus O'hUallachain and Mark Morgan (1995). 'Educational Disadvantage in Ireland'. Educational Research Centre, Department of Education: Dublin.

14 A *favela* is a shantytown or slum within an urban area. The first *favelas* appeared in the late nineteenth century, built by returning soldiers who had nowhere to live.

15 The song was released in 1966, the opening track to the UK version of their 1966 album *Aftermath*.

16 Clancy, P. (1995) 'Access to College: Patterns of Continuity and Change'. Higher Education Authority, Dublin, p. 168.

17 'Working Class Cultures, Can they Adapt?' Jesuit Centre of Faith and Justice: Dublin.

18 'One City, Two Tiers: A Theological Reflection on Life in a Divided City'. Cherry Orchard Faith and Justice Group (1996).

19 This is not a 'new' idea. The National Access Plan (2015) reiterates the importance of this issue and calls for action around the Continuous Professional Development of teachers (i.e. the role of Teaching Council and the development of new framework for CPD).

20 Abrahamson, P., Boje, T.P. and Greve, B. (2005) *Welfare and Families in Europe*. Asgate Publishing: Aldershot: UK. p. 47.

21 The idea in counselling that you have a 'pattern' of ideas written at a very young age and follow that pattern for life.

22 Chevalier, A, Denny, K. and Mc Mahon, D. (2009) 'Intergeneration Mobility and Education Equality'. In P. Dolton, R. Asplund and E.

Barth (Eds.) *Equality in Education and Inequality Across Europe*. Edward Elgar: London.

23 For example, one suggestion in the 2016 programme for government is to withhold children's allowance payments to families who don't send their kids to school. Whatever your views on the particular suggestion, at least it highlights the issue.

24 John Donne, English Poet, 1572–1631.

25 In practice we tend to speak about two classes – working class and middle class. The 'upper class' group is small and we are ignoring this for the purpose of these discussions. For your amusement, check out some of the personal engagements announced on the back page of *The Irish Times*, which can seem more like corporate mergers than marriages.

26 Lareau, A. (1997) 'Social-Class Differences in Family-School Relationships: The Importance of Cultural Capital.' p. 710 in Hasley, A.H, Lauder, H, Brown, P and Well, A.M. (Eds.), *Education: Culture, Economy and Society*. Oxford University Press: Oxford.

27 Howard Gardner (2001) *Leading Minds: An Anatomy of Leadership*. Harper-Collins: USA.

28 There are many ways to 'compare and contrast' social classes. A full discussion of this it outside of our scope here and we can only touch on the key points.

29 Herbert H. Hyman (1967) *The Values Systems of Different Classes: A Social Psychological Contribution to the Analysis of Stratification*. (Reprint Series in Social Sciences). Irvington: USA.

30 Barry Sugarman (1970) *Sociology*. Heinemann Educational Books: London.

31 *Class Subcultures and Education* (1994).

32 Many professionals now work extremely long hours. In 2015, I worked with one law firm partner who'd taken six days annual leave during the year. It was not uncommon for lawyers who worked there to punch in more than 60 hours each week.

33 Teachers represent authority. Parents who've had unhappy experiences at school or with authority figures in the past may be reluctant to meet them. It should be noted that data doesn't always *measure* parental interest in education, but teachers' *perceptions* of their interest. It's possible that teachers perceive middle class parents as more interested than working class parents because of the way they interact or even because they are more 'like us' (i.e. they are from the same *tribe*). Evidence from the National Child Development Study found that 89

per cent of middle class children attended a school where there was a well-established system of parent-school contacts making it *easier* to stay abreast of children's educational progress. But the evidence on this is 'mixed'. In *Parental Involvement in Primary Education* Dr. Josephine Bleach found no difference between middle class and working class areas under this heading.

34 Bill Toner suggested that there are parallel arguments around housing policy. For example, if more ambitious families receive the best education and then get good jobs, they pay 'more rent' than people who are unemployed. Perceiving this as unfair, they move on. Should we be encouraging *permanent residency,* that is, should incentives to leave be replaced by incentives to stay? (Toner 1996: 7).

35 The prosperity of the Celtic Tiger years allowed resources to be poured into this. Arguably, these communities have been disadvantaged disproportionately during the recession over the past seven years.

36 Commenced in 2001. There were a number of forerunners to RAPID (The EU Poverty Programme, The Operational Programme for Local Urban and Rural Development, The EU Urban Programme and the Integrated Services Process). While each programme had a slightly different emphasis, they shared a common mission, that is, to promote the social and economic development of targeted areas classified as 'disadvantaged'.

37 RAPID Programme in Focus: Implementation. *Case Studies of Input into RAPID by Government Departments and Stage Agencies.* Sharon Cosgrove. September 2004.

38 The examples illustrate a general point about expertise and scale. There are lots of excellent 'local' organisations who do outstanding work e.g. Belvedere Youth Club in Buckingham Street, Dublin.

39 The term 'quasi-autonomous non-governmental organisation' was created in 1967 by Alan Pifer (Carnegie Foundation) in an essay on independence and accountability in public-funded bodies incorporated in the private sector. The term was later shortened to 'Quango', essentially an organisation to which a government has devolved power.

40 Kellaghan, T., Weir, S., O'hUallacháin, S, and Morgan, M. (1995) 'Educational Disadvantage in Ireland'. Department of Education, Dublin. p. 8.

41 'Delivering Homes, Sustaining Communities', Department of the Environment, Heritage and Local Government. February.

42 'The Ballad of East and West'. Rudyard Kipling. Published in 1889.

43 There was an interesting recent example in the debate around the construction of 'temporary' housing. While there were myriad argu-

ments around 'type' and 'cost' there was very little argument around the location for these new, low-cost, *temporary* units. They were set up in areas already *disadvantaged*.

44 I've borrowed this phrase from Dr. Leo Casey in the National College of Ireland. Leo is hugely committed to education generally and to developing pedagogy that *works* and is enjoyable.

45 My understanding is that the primary school curriculum was re-cast circa 1999. There's no suggestion here of a fundamental redesign of this.

46 Once again, this is not a *new* idea. Action 1.7 in the national plan is to increase access by students from target groups to initial teacher education. There will be a 'call' for proposals from HEIs and partners later this year for projects to commence in the 2016-17 academic year.

47 *No Way Back*: op cit, p. 94.

48 Some names/places are deliberately vague as I don't want to stigmatize particular schools.

49 Claxton, G. (2008) *What's the Point of School? Rediscovering the Heart of Education*. Oneworld Publications: Oxford.

50 NCCP: Dublin National Council for Curriculum and Assessment (2006) *Key Skills Framework*. p. 1.

51 A Living Curriculum – A.R Ammons.

52 Kelly, D.M. 1995. 'School Dropouts', in Carnoy, M. (Ed), *International Encyclopedia of Education*. Oxford: Elsevier Science, 2nd edition.

53 Joint Committee on Education and Skills First Report (2010) Staying in Education: A New Way Forward. School and Out-of-School Factors Protecting Against Early School Leaving.

54 On a slightly separate but related point, it's difficult not to feel sympathy for those people in religious life who continue to 'fight the good fight' on social justice issues. Sr. Stanislaus Kennedy, Peter McVerry SJ and Brother Kevin Crowley immediately spring to mind because of their high media presence. But there are many more religious people offering education and other social services in the background of Irish society.

55 Some 96 per cent of primary schools are under religious control, that is, the ownership of buildings and land is outside of state control.

56 Central Statistics Office (2007) p. 31.

57 Robert Putnam (2000) *Bowling Alone: The Collapse and Revival of American Community*. Simon and Schuster. New York. p. 118.

58 See Irish Human Rights Commission, 2011.

59 Orla Christle suggested that this argument is somewhat 1-sided and lacks balance. To support this she cited the fact that the decline in vocations, in effect means that the management of catholic schools is by secular boards of teachers and parents. So the level of 'religious interference' is actually very low.

60 Anne Henderson and Nancy Berla (1994) 'A New Generation of Evidence: The Family is Critical to Student Achievement'. National Committee for Citizens in Education. Washington DC. 1.

61 Wyness M.G. (1996) *School, Welfare and Parental Responsibility.* Falmer Press: London.

62 Dr. Josephine Bleach (2010) *Parental Involvement in Primary Education in Ireland.* Liffey Press. Dublin.

63 Robert D. Putnam (2000) *Bowling Alone: The Collapse and Revival of American Community.* Simon and Schuster. New York. p. 118.

64 Principle of Our Lady of the Wayside National School, A DEIS Band One Primary School in Dublin 12. 'DEIS? No Chance – A Case Study of one Principal's Experiences in a DEIS school in 2015'. Taken from Brian Mooney (Ed). *Education Matters* (2015) Opposite Citation.

65 'Living and Learning: The Way Forward: Evaluation of the Dublin Docklands Education Programme'. Professor Áine Hyland and Cynthia Deane, October 2008. There were many more 'community activities' funded by the DDDA outside of the focus on education.

66 Budgeted costs didn't include administration staff costs and overheads, that is, the actual costs were higher than those shown here.

67 This is just less than double the 'Capitation Grant' allocated from the Department of Education and Science which was €173.00 per pupil at that time.

68 The 'cause and effect' issue highlighted earlier is at play here. Side by side with the DDDA investments in education, the schools were also part of national programmes to tackle educational disadvantage. So, it's not possible to disentangle the various projects and clinically 'prove' the exact impact.

69 Under the Student Support Act 2011 each HEI is required to have an access plan. See UCD example: http://www.ucd.ie/t4cms/Opening per cent20Worlds.pdf. Under the Universities Act 1997 and IoT Act 2006, each HEI is required to have a policy to promote access and to implement this. So, the legislative framework is already in place.

70 Neil Thompson (2016). *The Authentic Leader,* p. 9.

71 Department of Education and Science (2011) pp. 15-16.

72 A point that often gets *lost* is that approximately 50 per cent of water losses are due to faulty pipework – something that's completely outside of the control of consumers.

73 Increasing an existing tax (e.g. revenue contributions on payroll) doesn't seem to 'raise the hackles' quite as much, even when the absolute amounts are similar.

74 O'Halloran (2004) 'The Privatisation of Citizenship? Exploring frameworks for membership of the Irish polity'. *Administration*. Volume 52. No. 1, Spring. p. 23.

75 Example: Some of the access initiatives have second level students 'shadowing' a college student to understand 'a day in the life'. These high contact activities are expensive to maintain.

76 Historically, the size of the funding was directly linked to the size of the full-time student cohort in the colleges. Now the fund has a hybrid approach, with 50 per cent of the overall budget allocated in this way and the remaining 50 per cent linked to *performance* on access (socio-economic group targets). Institutions that have a greater proportion of socio-economically disadvantaged new entrants will receive a higher allocation under the current model than was the case previously.

77 I've written about this specific topic elsewhere. *The Irish Times* 'Inside Third Level'. 20 March 2012.

Chapter 7

1 Julie Bernard in DIT pushed back on the issue of developing a 'list' of responses to resolve educational disadvantage on the basis that there's a lot of 'missing data' and additional research still needs to be completed. For example, her research yielded an interesting finding in relation to parental support for further education after school leaving – with an indicator that a tolerance for their children participating in further education, rather than actively encouraging it, was sufficient. Therefore including this aspect of education support in large 'parental 'involvement' programmes, along the lines suggested in this book, could be redundant. On one level, it's impossible to argue against the basic point that 'you need to understand something before you try to change it'. However my overall sense if that we have enough research to 'begin now' to tackle educational disadvantage – which doesn't mean that we can't continue (in parallel) to tease out some of the important questions that remain unanswered.

2 Ben Okri. Extract from *Mental Fight*.

3   For example, the Bridging the Gap project, working with 40 designated disadvantaged schools in Cork. There are many similar 'tried and tested' initiatives.

4   For example, the final report of the statutory Education Disadvantage Committee (Moving Beyond Educational Disadvantage: 2005), identified several strands in a co-coordinated approach to educational disadvantage including: Curriculum Adaptation (a focus on numeracy and literacy); early intervention and prevention rather than remediation; high level of parental involvement in homes and in schools; reform of school organisation (unity of purpose) along with building on strengths of teachers and pupils; adequate financial resources for schools to operate; significant involvement with other community agencies. There's a strong overlap between this list and the recommendations made here.

5   Rise Up for Children Report. Barnardos. (2016) p. 14.

6   In 2014, TUSLA received 43,630 child welfare and protection referrals. That was a 40 per cent increase on the 2011 numbers. These are the cases that come to the attention of the authorities. Focusing on crisis intervention (rather than proactively resourcing families) is a vicious cycle in which children are the biggest losers.

7   Rise Up for Children. Barnardos .(2016) p. 15.

8   Property developers have become a maligned group in recent years. They are generally seen as 'one of the four horsemen' of the Celtic Tiger crash (alongside politicians, bankers and financial regulators). You can make up your own mind on that question. My personal experience with a small number of developers is of incredible personal generosity with their money and time around tackling educational disadvantage. All of this is done in a completely 'low-key' way in which their involvement is downplayed with zero publicity.

9   The locals call them 'The Book People'. Perhaps the most descriptive title would be Parent Educators because that's what they actually do - educate the parents how to teach the children.

10 This is consistent with the estimated costs of providing an effective family support programme through Barnardos (€3K-€5K per annum).

11 The programme has been run in the USA for many years and there's a host of positive data. In Ireland, the programme has been rigorously monitored by Professor Mark Morgan of St. Patrick's and also subject to a full review by Trinity College (Children's Research Centre). There are many similar initiatives elsewhere, for example, Doodle Den which focuses on developing literacy skills through games and fun activities in an after-school setting. Parental involvement is a key

element with parents gaining skills to support their children's literacy needs as well as having the opportunity to engage in a range of activities with their children throughout the year.

12 As I can't improve on this, I'm copying this recommendation from Barnardos, Rise Up for Children Report, 2016, p. 5.

13 It's not just a 'give.' When parents volunteer in a school, it can help to build their own confidence. One teacher related a story about a dad in a tough north Dublin community. Her first impression was certainly less than positive. He came to the school and verbally 'attacked' her about the lack of progress his son was making. Shook by the incident, she thought a lot about the man and (with some trepidation) asked him back in to discuss the issue in a calmer manner. They eventually figured out a 'joint plan' to work with the child and that dad ended up volunteering to supervise children in the yard, which he really enjoyed. He later told her about his aversion to school and teachers, based on past experience.

14 Liz Waters (2007) 'Community Education: A View from the Margins'. In Paul Downes and Ann Louise Gilligan (Eds.). *Beyond Educational Disadvantage* (2007) Institute of Public Administration: Dublin.

15 'Charities for Homeless are not "value for money"'. Philip Ryan. *Sunday Independent*, 10 January 2016.

16 The Boundary Wall: A needs analysis in the North Wall area of Dublin with a particular focus on education and young people. March 2013. In more recent times (18 May 2016) Patricia Quinn launched a website (Benefacts.ie) which is 'designed to transform the accessibility and transparency of all nonprofits in Ireland'. More than 18,849 individual organisations are listed. See www.benefacts.ie.

17 The name Foróige is derived from the Irish words *forbairt na hóige*, meaning development of youth. Foróige is Ireland's leading youth organization and has been working with young people since 1952.

18 For a great overview on Atlantic Philanthropies, read Conor O'Cleary's book *The Billionaire Who Wasn't: How Chuck Feeney Made and Gave Away a Fortune Without Anyone Knowing*. The One Foundation was established by Declan Ryan (son of Tony Ryan) and focused on 'social entrepreneur' programmes including a range of educational projects. In both cases, they brought a professionalization into the not-for-profit sector on par or better than anything which exists in the private sector.

19 Children's Rights Alliance.

20 Wilkinson, R and Picket, K. (2009) *The Spirit Level*. Penguin Books: London.

21 This point is not universally accepted. Dr. Josephine Bleach argued the need for caution here. She believes that there's too much competition and too little collaboration and was concerned that 'public recognition' events might actually worsen this. I understand the point but take a different stance on this.

22 The removal of compulsory Irish this might have an 'unintended consequence' of not allowing people to sit the Bar exams or joining the civil service. We would have to change the rules in those areas too or risk creating additional discrimination.

23 In practice we may already be developing an 'Irish solution to an Irish problem' here. A report in *The Irish Times* 'Growing Number of Students Exempt from Studying Irish due to Disabilities' (Monday, April 25th, 2016) reported an ESRI study that highlighted 32,000 students (2014 figures) were exempted from studying Irish, a 60 per cent increase from 2004. The ERSI report stated that Irish is the 'least popular' subject and was rated as the 'most difficult'.

24 Editorial Comment: Brian Mooney (2015) *Education Matters*. Opposite Citation, p. 111.

25 A Transition Year module was developed in 2008-9 and made available nationally. While there was positive feedback (via NCCA) on the module and this is being used by some schools, no evaluation of the impact of the module was carried out by either HEA or NCCA. The baseline module was used as a basis for further development in a project by DIT called 'Bridges to Higher Education'. Bottom Line: there's a lot of expertise around how this year can be made to work really well.

26 Robert D. Putnam (2000). *Bowling Alone: The Collapse and Revival of American Community*. Simon and Schuster. New York. p. 411.

27 The Binet-Stanford Intelligence Scales began in 1916 when Lewis Terman completed his American revision of the Binet-Simon Scale (1905, 1908). Through various editions, this assessment has become widely known and is acknowledged as the standard for intelligence measurement.

28 *The Irish Times*, 30 January 2016.

29 The research data clearly demonstrates that students are more likely to drop out of college in their first year. One possibility would be to consider a minimum compulsory class attendance (circa 75 per cent) to ensure that the discipline of class attendance becomes ingrained. In academic circles this idea is sometimes frowned upon with the counter argument that students should be treated as adults and awarded grades based on exam results rather than 'inputs' like attendance. While I agree that we should help students *transition* to being treated

as adults, I'm not convinced that this should be the expectation from Day 1 in college.

30 Irish National Teachers' Organisation (INTO) (2000) 'A Fair Start'. Dublin: INTO.

31 For the avoidance of doubt, I spend about 30-40 per cent of my time working in this space.

32 Not a universally popular idea. Here's Dr. Josephine Bleach's reaction to this: 'Check out the Teaching Council and their Féilte – encouraging teachers to use action research to improve their practice – this is the way to go rather than competitions where people are left behind.'

33 In terms of practical classroom management, a couple of teachers suggested a need for more Learning Support Teachers (qualified teachers) and SNAs, special needs assistants, who are invaluable in the classroom. I haven't made this as a formal recommendation as it would be prohibitively expensive. The use of volunteers along the lines suggested earlier would achieve much the same outcome at a fraction of the cost.

34 Lindquist, Bengt. Special Rapporteur. (1994) World Conference on Special Needs Education: Access and Quality. UNESCO. Paris.

35 McCoy, E. Smyth, D. Watson, M Darmody (2014) 'Leaving School in Ireland: A Longitudinal Study of Post School Transitions'. Research Series Number 36, August, ESRI: Dublin.

36 Chaired by Professor Áine Hyland – opposite citation.

37 There are many detailed studies completed on the broader issue of traveller education. Personally, I've very limited exposure to this area. This recommendation addresses a single facet and is not a comprehensive response to this broad question.

38 Numbers are calculated as follows. The cost of providing 'secure care' in Ireland for circa 50 children who are currently incarcerated is €25 million per annum i.e. €500,000 per child.

39 We've seen earlier that not all children who are disadvantaged attend DEIS schools. There can be pockets of disadvantage in wealthy areas. To address this, all school principals should be able to resource 'discretionary' support for pupils who meet particular criteria (exact methodology to be determined).

40 Noreen Flynn (2007) 'Tackling Educational Disadvantage: Home and School'. p. 99. In Paul Downes and Ann Louise Gilligan (Eds.). *Beyond Educational Disadvantage* (2007) Institute of Public Administration: Dublin.

41 'School Matters' (2006) The Report of the Task Force on Student Behaviour in Second Level Schools. Department of Education: Dublin.

42 HSE Performance Assurance Report, July 2015.

43 Obesity is a growing problem in Ireland that's also common in children. Obesity is linked to the lack of healthy and affordable food. The estimated cost of treating obesity is €1.3 billion each year. Safefood Ireland (2012) 'The Cost of Overweight and Obesity on the Island of Ireland'.

44 I'm particularly grateful to Dr Mary-Liz Trant and Orla Christle for their inputs and critique on earlier versions of this idea.

45 Archer, P. (2001) 'Public Spending on Education, Inequality and Poverty'. In: Cantillon, S., Corrigan, C., Kirby, P. and O'Flynn, J. (Eds.) *Rich and Poor: Perspectives on Tackling Inequality in Ireland*. Oak Tree Press, Dublin. p. 226.

46 See Schooldays.ie (2015) About School League Tables and Department of Education and Skills (2015) https://www.education.ie/en/find-a-school.

47 I sent two of my own kids to fee-paying schools, so I'm not 'squeaky-clean' here.

48 Stokes, D. (2003). Early school leaving in Ireland: The matrix of influences explored. Unpublished Doctoral dissertation, NUI Maynooth. p. 178.

49 One of the Jesuit run fee-paying schools raised €14 million from parents and past pupils for a new building, while a new building in a Jesuit run (non fee-paying) school was paid for by the State.

50 The role of Catholic religious orders in fostering an elite educational sector (via exclusive fee-paying schools) is criticised from within the church. Dr Kevin O'Higgins SJ suggests that a possible new role for the Church is to specifically focus on disadvantaged groups like Travellers. This would connect with the social justice orientation of projects like JUST mentioned elsewhere.

51 I asked Robert Ward, the marketing Director in NCI, to estimate how much money is spent on advertising by third level colleges. His analysis showed that circa €2 million was spent in 2015 for full-time courses across a variety of media. Picture the following billboard advertisement: 'Broken Leg? Come to St. James Hospital. Expert surgical team. We'll set you right'. I'm guessing that there would be outrage that a publicly funded institution was spending taxpayers' money trying to lure patients with 'broken legs' to a particular hospital. Doesn't the exact same point apply to colleges? For sure, colleges need to spend money on promotion – to articulate their offerings in a prospectus,

keep websites up-to-date and so on. But when this baseline market-ing spills over into 'luring' a student from College A to attend College B the taxpayer is being stung. Some colleges argue that they are not publicly funded (only a percentage of their income comes from the public purse) and they want to retain the autonomy to spend money as they see fit. But many are 100 per cent funded. Overall, this is a waste of taxpayers' money.

52 At the risk of repeating the same point, these are not 'brand new' ideas, for example, a College Awareness Week initiative has been sup-ported by HEA since 2013. www.collegeaware.ie.

53 Bleiklie, I. and Kogan, J. (2007): 'Organization and Governance of Universities'. *Higher Education Policy,* 20: 477-493.

54 One project called the Roadmap for Employer-Academic Partnership (REAP), focused on identifying learning needs in workplaces. Led by Cork Institute of Technology, with a number of other Higher Educa-tion Institutions on board, this was funded under the Strategic Inno-vation Fund. The goal: develop a partnership between Higher Educa-tion and employers so that these needs could be addressed. People who've been working for many years soak up a huge amount of tacit information. By 'recognising' that learning, mature students are given a 'head-start' in terms of getting back into education. Orla Christle made the point that work on this is being progressed as part of the implementation of the National Access Plan 2015-2019.

55 The HEA have gathered this information periodically from HEIs. Orla Christle argued strongly that how funding is allocated internally for any activity is a matter that is managed by each HEI in line with their functions and responsibilities under the universities act. The HEA does not micro-manage senior managers or management functions in each institution and they are accountable separately to CandAG.

56 This specific point is disputed. In 2010 and 2013 HEA have sought and received reports of progress on access from each HEI. In 2015 each HEI reported on progress on their access objectives as part of *compacts* agreed in 2013.

57 Example: The 'DIT Access Foundation Programme', aimed at sup-porting individuals in the community to reach their full educational and life potential.

58 Under the heading Campus Engage, the issue of service learning is already on the agenda. My understanding is that the Irish Universities Association are actively engaged in how this might work. Great!

59 The 'sheep dip' analogy assumes that all of the *sheep* are run through the mix in the interests of efficiency. It's like being told that your

doctor's appointment is for 10.00 am. When you show up, 14 other people are in the queue who've arrived for an appointment at exactly the same time. The doctor can't be inconvenienced. But, it's okay to disrupt the patient's diaries because their time is deemed *less important*. In college, the 'system' expectation is normally that the student will fit into the mould, rather than vice versa.

60 Service Learning is often driven by the leadership of particular academic staff. I've seen Service Learning embraced by some faculties/departments but completely ignored by others – within the same college.

61 As part of the National Access Plan, a review of this fund was recently completed but was not published at the time of writing up this section.

62 In recent times, the National Advisory Group on Access has been disbanded and the responsibility for this area has shifted directly to the Department of Education and Skills. From a distance, I can't quite figure out the logic of this. In fairness, the running of this system has been assigned to a senior Department of Education official. We will await developments.

63 Including AMA, DAWN, MSI (mature students Ireland), pre-entry support network and post-entry support network, the IUA (Irish University Association and IOTI (Institute of Technology Ireland Access).

64 This touches on a slightly wider point around the resources available to pursue the access agenda. For example, Massive Open Online Courses (MOOC) run by internationally reputable higher education institutions, for example, Open University, Coursera (Princeton, Standford, Michigan and Pennsylvania Universities) offer a wide variety of free educational programmes. This could have a significant time-saving impact on the way we 'design' courses in Ireland. By saving time/money on course design, more time could be made available to work with access students. The area of third level productivity is a huge (but separate) agenda.

65 Speaking at a conference on Access run by the HEA. Dublin, 2014.

66 Seán Healy, Sara Bourke, Ann Leahy, Eamonn Murphy, Michelle Murphy an Brigid Reynolds (2016) 'Choices for Equity and Sustainability'. *Socio-Economic Review*. Social Justice Ireland. p. 192.

Chapter 8

1 Paul Mooney (2010) *Accidental Leadership*. The Liffey Press: Dublin.

2   I had some fairly 'strong' pushback from John Walshe on this point. John suggested that I might have to revise the contention that there's little political interest in educational disadvantage (in the light of the document which Fine Gael circulated to the independent TDs as part of a new government formation in April 2016). While not directly involved at the time, John made the additional point that the Labour Party was very strong on education in the 2011 election based on the manifesto produced (he touches on this in his book on the Irish education system). I have to respectfully disagree with John on this. Pre-election policy formation is one thing; on-the-ground changes to the education system is something entirely different. We are in agreement that there's a strong 'political leaning' in favour of many of the arguments made in this book. But, unfortunately, there's clear blue water between the expressed philosophy and the level of changes actually delivered.

3   It's not that nothing's in place at the moment. The ABC Programme, for which ELI is the lead agency in the Docklands and East Inner City, is part of an integrated plan to eliminate educational disadvantage. There is also the Better Outcomes Brigher Futures document, a national children's strategy. While a lot of the 'thinking' is already in place, we don't have a joined up mechanism to ensure that this gets executed professionally and cost-effectively.

4   This operates under the Education (Welfare) Act, 2000, the legislation that governs school attendance, participation and retention.

5   Áine Hyland (Chairperson). Moving Beyond Educational Disadvantage (2002-2005). Report of the Educational Disadvantage Committee.

6   Later work completed on this showed this number to be slightly overstated and the actual costs were circa €85 million.

7   Some really good work was completed by the 'Hands Up for Children Campaign' where lots of organisations worked together to ensure that children were part of the next Programme for Government. Overall, there's tons of good material which we could draw from.

8   Some recommendations should be cost reducing e.g. a single model of community development and a smaller number of key players delivering services. This rationalisation of the community sector should save substantial resources, albeit it's impossible to cost this in advance.

9   The argument wasn't specifically made about educational disadvantage – but the point holds regardless of what the money is spent on.

10 Paul Downes and Ann Louise Gilligan: 'Some Conclusions': In *Beyond Educational Disadvantage* (2007). Opposite citation.

11 The good news here, as shown earlier, is that investment in this area offers a positive a return to Irish society, far greater than the financial investment made. There's a win:win outcome here (higher equality which is also highly cost effective).

12 The Sinn Féin election manifesto (2016) suggested the elimination of Registration Fees for all students. While all parties practice populist politics, to the best of my knowledge, Sinn Fein were the only party that suggested this specific policy. Of course, any Government could simply decide to make a bigger investment in education, avoiding the college fees debate. But, the money will have to come from somewhere.

13 Some courses of study that require a lot of laboratory work, fieldwork etc. can be enormously expensive. There's a need to devise some 'rule of thumb' formula, which broadly allocates costs in a simple way without requiring a huge amount of additional effort to collate the numbers. It's likely that programmes would be categorized within a number of 'cost bands' to avoid creating an *industry* of cost measurement.

14 At the moment there's a difference between daytime and part-time students in this regard. My experience: daytime students see a cancelled lecture as a reason for celebration. Part-time students (who pay fees) are much more demanding and will not accept poor service. Perhaps some of this difference can be explained by 'age' (as part-time students are generally older/more mature). Dr Dermot Hegarty (Griffith College) suggested something similar. His belief was that undergraduate fee-paying students were generally more committed and more demanding than undergraduate students who were 'free fees'. He further argued that overseas Non-EU students (who pay even higher fees) were the most demanding on a college.

15 Arguments against this are that it will act as a disincentive for graduates thinking about returning to Ireland after an overseas stint and the likely default rate (how the monies would be recouped and so on). These arguments, while legitimate, don't overturn the central rationale. The loan system could be administered by the Revenue Commissioners, arguably the most efficient 'tax collection' mechanism in the state (demonstrated most recently in the introduction of the property tax).

16 It's easier for the self-employed to manipulate income rather than wealth. This is a 'fairer' system to determine actual means.

17 To cite one final example: St Joseph's in Rush, now linked with Trinity's Access Programme, has seen its third-level progression rate rise from 15 per cent to 85 per cent over the past decade.

18 John P. Kotter, 'Leading Change. Why transformation efforts fail', *Harvard Business Review*, January 2007, pp. 92-107.

19 Seán Healy, Sara Bourke, Ann Leahy, Eamonn Murphy, Michelle Murphy an Brigid Reynolds (2016) 'Choices for Equity and Sustainability'. *Socio-Economic Review*. Social Justice Ireland. p. 178.

20 Source: Department of Public Expenditure and Reform (2015) Capital Investment Plan 2016-2021.

21 Rise Up for Children Report. Barnardos (2016) p. 5.

22 In an address made to the Joint Houses of the US Congress, 15 November 1989.

Appendices

1 I am hugely grateful to Dr. Brian O'Kelly for pulling this section together.

2 This is the suggested checklist offering 'best-practice' ideas for third level. The exact same idea would be applied at every level of the education system and within communities.

3 Ireland may be ahead in this regard. Launched in February 2013, the European Commission's U-Multirank proposes to rate universities in five separate areas: reputation for research, quality of teaching and learning, international orientation, success in knowledge transfer and start-up contribution to regional growth. According to Dr Paul Downes, a glaring omission is a focus on access and community engagement. He suggested that this is indicative of the low priority level given at European Commission level to educational access for marginalised groups.

Dr. Paul Mooney: Summary Profile

For over 20 years, Paul Mooney has been helping leaders to address personal and professional challenges along with supporting organisations to resolve problems and develop capability. Widely recognised as an expert on organisation and individual change, Paul holds a Ph.D. and a Post-Graduate Diploma in Industrial Sociology (Trinity College) along with an MSc. and Post-Graduate Diploma in Executive and Business Coaching (University College Dublin). He also has a National Diploma in Industrial Relations (National College of Ireland) and is a Fellow of the Chartered Institute of Personnel and Development.

Paul began his working life as a butcher in Dublin. After completing an apprenticeship, he moved into production management. He subsequently joined General Electric and held a number of human resource roles. After G.E, Paul worked with Sterling Drug in Ireland and the Pacific Rim, with responsibility for all HR activity across Asia.

In 1993, he established a consulting company specialising in Organisation and Management Development. Between 2007 and 2010, Paul held the position of President, National College of Ireland. He currently leads Tandem Consulting, a team of senior OD/Change specialists. Tandem's client list reads like a 'Who's Who' of Irish and Multinational Organisations with consulting assignments across 20+ countries – for both public and private sector clients.

Paul is the author of 12 books covering a wide span of topics around organisation performance and personal change. Areas of expertise include:

- Organisational Development/Change and Conflict Resolution
- Leadership Development/Executive Coaching
- Human Resource Management/Employee Engagement

He writes a bi-weekly blog 'Confessions of a Consultant' which can be sourced at http://tandemconsulting.wordpress.com.

Mobile: 353-87-2439019 Email: paul@tandemconsulting.ie Web: www.tandemconsulting.ie

Books by Paul Mooney

- *Amie: The True Story of Adoption in Asia*

- *Developing High Performance Organisations*

- *The Effective Consultant*

- *Keeping Your Best Staff*

- *Turbocharging the HR Function*

- *The Badger Ruse (crime novel)*

- *Union Free: Creating a Committed and Competent Workforce*

- *Desperate Executives: Coaching, Change and Personal Growth*

- *Accidental Leadership: A Personal Journey*

- *The Transformation Roadmap: Accelerating Organisation Change*

- *Fog Clearance: Mapping the Boundary between Coaching and Counselling*

- *The Million Euro Decision: How Education Changes Lives*